ONTOLOGICAL TERROR

Continue to think
and Challege

Calvin
Warren

Publication of this open monograph was the result of
Emory University's participation in TOME (Toward
an Open Monograph Ecosystem), a collaboration
of the Association of American Universities, the
Association of University Presses, and the Association
of Research Libraries. TOME aims to expand the reach
of long-form humanities and social science scholarship
including digital scholarship. Additionally, the program
looks to ensure the sustainability of university press
monograph publishing by supporting the highest
quality scholarship and promoting a new ecology of
scholarly publishing in which authors' institutions bear
the publication costs.

Funding from Emory University and the Andrew W.
Mellon Foundation made it possible to open this
publication to the world.

WWW.OPENMONOGRAPHS.ORG

ONTOLOGICAL

BLACKNESS, NIHILISM, AND EMANCIPATION

TERROR

Calvin L. Warren

DUKE UNIVERSITY PRESS | DURHAM AND LONDON | 2018

Designed by Matthew Tauch
Typeset in Warnock Pro by Copperline Book Services

Library of Congress Cataloging-in-Publication Data
Names: Warren, Calvin L., [date–] author.
Title: Ontological terror : Blackness, nihilism, and
emancipation / Calvin L. Warren.
Description: Durham : Duke University Press, 2018. |
Includes bibliographical references and index.
Identifiers: LCCN 2017045250 (print) |
LCCN 2017051441 (ebook)
ISBN 9780822371847 (ebook)
ISBN 9780822370727 (hardcover : alk. paper)
ISBN 9780822370871 (pbk. : alk. paper)
Subjects: LCSH: Race—Political aspects. | Racism. | Race
awareness. | Blacks—Race identity. | Nihilism (Philosophy) |
Ontology.
Classification: LCC HT1523 (ebook) | LCC HT1523 .W375 2018
(print) | DDC 305.8—dc23
LC record available at https://lccn.loc.gov/2017045250

Cover art: Sondra Perry, still from *Black/Cloud*, 2010.
Courtesy Bridget Donahue Gallery, NYC.

Fannie Warren, Lurene Brunson, and Jane Elven

(my three mothers)

For their love, patience, and unending support

CONTENTS

ACKNOWLEDGMENTS

This book is born out of numerous conversations, spirited debates, noetic experiments, and silent reflections. My intention is to reinvigorate and expand a philosophical field, one often neglected and ignored: black nihilism. The thinking here represents my attempt to center the ontological crisis blackness presents to an antiblack world. This is a difficult task, and many have provided intellectual and emotional support to accomplish it. I am grateful for those who have endured my negativity, unconventional thinking, and exasperation. It takes an exceptional constitution to support a nihilistic thinker, especially when the very ground upon which the support is extended is also called into question. Words are inadequate to express my deep gratitude for those willing to travel to the depths with me, the "valley of the shadow of death," and think what seems ineffable.

Identifying origins is always difficult, since innumerable factors influence the emergence of thought, but Yale University has been formative in my thinking. I would like to thank Dr. Robert Stepto and Dr. Glenda Gilmore for supporting my graduate work. Dr. Diane Rubenstein's rigorous postmodern/psychoanalytic engagement and intellectual generosity have cultivated my thinking since I was an undergraduate, and I continue to learn from her work. I am exceptionally grateful for her continued support. Dr. Hortense Spillers has left an indelible imprint on my thinking and has provided me with a model of intellectual courage, excellence, and generosity. We all need intellectual aspirations, and she constitutes such an aspiration in my life. I hope that this project reflects my deep indebtedness and admiration for her philosophical contributions.

Darien Parker, Carlos Miranda, Suzette Spencer, Uri McMillan, Shana Redmond, Nicole Ivy, Sarah Haley, Kimberly Brown, Erin Chapman, Libby Anker, Jennifer Nash, Melvin Rogers, Gregory Childs, Jared Sexton, Chelsey Faloona, Christina Sharpe, and Zakiyyah Jackson have greatly enriched my thinking through intense dialogue, humor, and friendship. I am especially grateful to Melani McAlister, Gayle Wald, Floyd Hayes, Shannon Sullivan, and Marshall Alcorn for supporting my work and encouraging me through uncertainty. Tommy Curry and Rinaldo Walcott are not only tremendous interlocutors, but also extraordinary mentors and friends—their presence is invaluable. The Ford Foundation, Mellon Mayes Fellowship, and the Woodrow Wilson Career Enhancement Fellowship provided necessary institutional support for this project.

Colleagues at Emory University have helped me expand my thinking and given me an intellectual home. I would like to thank Elizabeth Wilson, Lynne Huffer, Kadji Amin, Irene Brown, Rachel Dudley, Carla Freeman, Michael Moon, Beth Reingold, Pamela Scully, and Deboleena Roy for making the Department of Women's, Gender, and Sexuality Studies a rigorous place in which to think. I am especially grateful to Falguni Sheth for friendship, intellectual rigor, and mentorship.

I am fortunate to have friends and family who have made this journey bearable: Fred Willis, Kelnesha Smalls, Christopher Shaw, Cynthia Beaver, Dwayne Britt, Chrystal and Michael Emery, Nkosi Brown, Jeff Brown, Chris Roberson, Bob Carter, Duvalier Malone, Dr. Timothy Hatchett, Aaron Davis, Kenzio Howard, Demetrius White, Damas Djagli, Trevor Reaves, Jaccob Miller, Donnie Wynn, Cody Hugley. Without the love and support of Peter Flegel, Brandi Hughes, Lisa Head, Candace Kenyatta, Michaelangelo Wright, Mariah Morrison, Carolle Hepburn, and Helen Bjerum, Tina, Tonya, Jess, and Greg Robbie, this project would never have seen the light of day. They keep me looking beyond the dark clouds into the sun. This book is dedicated to Fannie Warren, Lurene Brunson, and Jane Elven for sustaining my spirit.

Duke University Press provided wonderful editorial support. Elizabeth Ault believed in the project from the very beginning, and I could not ask for a better editor. Her keen eye, patience, and support are truly remarkable. I am grateful for all her hard work. Susan Albury provided invaluable suggestions, editing, and helped me refine my ideas. I would also like to thank my two anonymous readers, who helped expand my thinking and clarify my ideas.

I would like to thank the journals *Nineteenth Century Contexts* and CR: *The New Centennial Review* for publishing earlier iterations of chapter 3 and a section of my current introduction.

Kevin Lamonte Jones, Esq., has been with this project since the beginning. He has not only given encouragement, support, and advice, but also enabled me to endure the heaviness of antiblackness. I am eternally grateful for his presence and perseverance.

I thank my Creator and the ancestors for courage, power, and revelation.

INTRODUCTION

THE FREE BLACK ~~IS~~ NOTHING

> When we got about half way to St. Michael's, while the constables having us in charge were looking ahead, Henry inquired of me what he should do with his pass. I told him to eat it with his biscuit, and own nothing; and we passed the word around, *"Own nothing"* and *"Own nothing!"* said we all.
>
> **FREDERICK DOUGLASS**, *The Narrative of the Life of Frederick Douglass*

OWNING NOTHING

A deep abyss, or a *terrifying question*, engenders the declaration "Black Lives Matter." The declaration, in fact, conceals this question even as it purports to have answered it resolutely. "Black Lives Matter," then, carries a certain terror in its dissemination, a terror we dare to approach with uncertainty, urgency, and exhaustion. This question pertains to the "metaphysical infrastructure," as Nahum Chandler might call it, that conditions our world and our thinking about the world. "Black Lives Matter" is an important declaration, not just because it foregrounds the question of unbearable brutality, but also because it performs philosophical labor—it *compels* us to face the terrifying question, despite our desire to look away. The declaration presents a difficult syntax or an accretion of tensions and ambiguities within its organization: can blacks have life? What would such life *mean* within an antiblack world? What axiological measurement determines the mattering of the life in question? Does the assembly of these terms shatter philosophical coherence or what metaphysical infrastructure provides stability, coherence, and intelligibility for the declaration? These questions of value, meaning, stability, and intelligibility lead us to the terror of the declaration, the question it conceals but engages: what *ontological* ground provides the occasion for the declaration? Can such ground be assumed, and if not, is the declaration even possible without it? "Black Lives Matter" *assumes* ontological ground, which propels the deployment of its terms and sustains them throughout the treacheries of antiblack epistemologies. Put differently, the human *being* provides an anchor for the declaration, and since the *being* of the human is invaluable, then black life *must* also matter, if the black is a human (the declaration anchors mattering in the human's *Being*). But we reach a point of terror with this syllogistic reasoning. One must take a step backward and ask the fundamental question: is the black, in fact, a human *being*? Or can black(ness) ground itself in the *being* of the human? If it cannot, then on what bases can we assert the mattering of black existence? If it can, then why would the phrase need to be repeated and recited incessantly? Do the affirmative declaration and its insistence undermine this very ontological ground? The statement declares, then, *too soon*—a declaration that is really an unanswered (or unanswerable) question. We must trace this question and declaration back to its philosophical roots: the Negro Question.[1]

This question reemerges within a world of antiblack brutality, a world in which black torture, dismemberment, fatality, and fracturing are routinized and ritualized—a *global*, sadistic pleasure principle. I was invited to meditate on this globalized sadism in the context of Michael Brown's murder and the police state. The invitation filled me with dread as I anticipated a festival of humanism in which presenters would share solutions to the problem of antiblackness (if they even acknowledged antiblackness) and inundate the audience with "yes we can!" rhetoric and unbounded optimism. I decided to participate, despite this dread, once students began asking me deep questions, questions that also filled them with dread and confusion. I, of course, was correct about my misgivings. I listened to one speaker after the next describe a bright future, where black life is valued and blacks are respected as humans—if we *just* keep fighting, they said, "we're almost there!" A political scientist introduced statistics and graphs laying out voting patterns and districts; he argued that blacks just did not realize how much power they had (an unfortunate ignorance, I guess). If they just collectively voted they could change antiblack police practices and make this world a better place. The audience clapped enthusiastically; I remained silent. Next, a professor of law implored the audience to keep fighting for legal change because the law is a powerful weapon for ending discrimination and restoring justice. We just needed to return to the universal principles that founded our Constitution, "liberty, equality, and justice!" (I thought about the exception clause in the Thirteenth Amendment, the Three-Fifths Compromise, and the way the sharecropping system exploited the Fourteenth Amendment in order to reenslave through contract. I continued to sit in silence.) The audience shouted and applauded. I felt a pit in my stomach because I knew what I had to do; it was my time to step up to the podium—it was my *nihilistic responsibility*. I told the audience there was no solution to the problem of antiblackness; it will continue without end, as long as the world exists. Furthermore, all the solutions presented rely on antiblack instruments to address antiblackness, a vicious and tortuous cycle that will only produce more pain and disappointment. I also said that humanist *affect* (the good feeling we get from hopeful solutions) will not translate into freedom, justice, recognition, or resolution. It merely provides temporary reprieve from the fact that blacks are not safe in an antiblack world, a fact that can become overwhelming. The form of antiblackness might alter, but antiblackness itself will remain a constant—despite the power of our imagination and political yearnings. I continued this nihilistic analysis of the situation until I heard complete silence.

A woman stood up after my presentation and shouted, "How dare you tell this to our youth! That is so very negative! Of course we can change things; we have power, and we are free." Her voice began to increase in intensity. I waited for her to finish and asked her, "Then tell us how to end police brutality and the slaughter of the youth you want to protect from my nihilism." "If these solutions are so credible, why have they consistently failed? Are we awaiting for some novel, extraordinary solution— one no one had ever imagined—to end antiblack violence and misery?" Silence. "In what manner will this 'power' deliver us from antiblackness?" How long must we *insist* on a humanity that is not recognized—an insistence that humiliates in its inefficacy? "If we are progressing, why are black youth being slaughtered at staggering rates in the twenty-first century— if we are, indeed, humans just like everyone else?" People began to respond that things are getting better, despite the increasing death toll, the unchecked power of the police state, the lack of conviction rates for police murdering blacks, the prison industrial complex and the modern reenslavement of an entire generation, the unbelievable black infant mortality rate, the lack of jobs for black youth and debilitating poverty. "This is *better*?" I asked. "At least we are not slaves!" someone shouted. I asked them to read the Thirteenth Amendment closely. But the intensity of the dialogic exchange taught me that *affect* runs both ways: it is not just that solutions make us feel good because we feel powerful/hopeful, but that pressing the ontological question presents *terror*—the terror that ontological security is gone, the terror that ethical claims no longer have an anchor, and the terror of inhabiting existence outside the precincts of humanity and its humanism. *Ontological Terror* engages this question and the forms of terror it produces.[2]

The event also put the metaphysical infrastructure into perspective for me. Two philosophical forces were colluding (and at times conflicting) to orient the solutions proposed and the audiences' responses, and both presented "free black" as a concept with meaning: black humanism and postmetaphysics. I use these two terms to docket a certain posture toward metaphysics—and the ontological ground metaphysics offers. Black humanism enters into romance with metaphysics. It appropriates schematization, calculation, technology, probability, and universality—all the instruments of metaphysical thinking—to make epistemological, ethical, and ontological claims concerning blackness and freedom. Freedom is possible, then, because metaphysics provides it with ontology; from there, all sorts of solutions, policies, and practices emerge to address antiblackness. Scientific reasoning, technological innovation, and legality are tools black humanists use to quantify suffering, measure progress, proffer universal narratives of humanity, and reason with antiblack institutions. All problems have solutions for black humanists, and their task is to uncover the solution the problem conceals, as this uncovering equates to an eradication of the problem. Black humanism relies on an eclectic approach to antiblackness—Hegelian synthesis, Kantian rationalism, Platonic universals/idealism, Cartesian representation, and empiricism. In short, black humanists lay claim to the *being* of the human (and the human's freedom) through metaphysical thinking and instruments.

Postmetaphysics, in contrast, attempts the surmounting or twisting [*verwunden*] of the ground and logic of metaphysics.[3] It insists that metaphysics reproduces pain and misery and restricts human freedom. Representing the human as an object of scientific thinking (e.g., biology, economics, law) destroys the spontaneity and uniqueness of the human—things that make the human special. The *ground*, then, upon which metaphysics relies is problematic, and this ground must be destroyed (i.e., twisted) and deconstructed (i.e., displaced) to free the human. Postmetaphysics would advocate for a self-consumption of this ground through hermeneutical strategies, unending deconstructions, and forms of plurality (such as hermeneutic nihilism). The *post* is rather a misnomer, if we think of *post* as an overcoming [*überwunden*]; the postmetaphysician will never overcome metaphysics. A residue will *always* remain, but the postmetaphysician hopes to reduce this metaphysical residue to render it inoperative. The postmetaphysician understands antiblackness as a problem of metaphysics, especially the way scientific thinking has classified being along racial difference and biology. The task of the postmetaphysical project is to free blacks from the misery metaphysics produces by undermining its ground. Hermeneutical strategies, which contest ultimate foundations, would question the ground of race (racial metaphysics) and its claim to universal truth.

Black humanism and postmetaphysics, however, leave the question of being unattended as it concerns black(ness). Both assume being is applicable and operative—black humanism relies on metaphysical being and postmetaphysics relies on multiple interpretations or manifestations of being. In other words, the human's *being* grounds both philosophical perspectives. Although postmetaphysics allows for a capacious understanding of the human and Being, it still posits being *universally* as it concerns freedom; no entity is without it, even if it manifests differently, or *as* difference, if we follow Deleuze. This is to suggest that both discourses proceed as if the *question* of being has been settled and that we no longer need to return to it—the question, indeed, has been elided in critical discourses concerning blackness. *Ontological Terror* seeks to put the question back in its proper place: at the *center* of any discourse about Being.

Ontological Terror meditates on this (non)relation between blackness and Being by arguing that black ~~being~~ incarnates metaphysical nothing, the terror of metaphysics, in an antiblack world. Blacks, then, have function but not Being—the function of black(ness) is to give form to a terrifying formlessness (nothing). Being claims function as its property (all functions rely on Being, according to this logic, for philosophical presentation), but the aim of black nihilism is to expose the unbridgeable rift between Being and function for blackness. The puzzle of blackness, then, is that it functions in an antiblack world without being—much like "nothing" functions philosophically without our metaphysical understanding of being, an extraordinary mystery. Put differently, metaphysics is obsessed with both blackness and nothing, and the two become synonyms for that which ruptures metaphysical organization and form. The Negro is black because the Negro must assume the function of nothing in a metaphysical world. The world needs this labor. This obsession, however, also transforms into hatred, since nothing is incorrigible—it shatters ontological ground and security. Nothing terrifies metaphysics, and metaphysics attempts to dominate it by turning nothing into an object of knowledge, something it can dominate, analyze, calculate, and schematize. When I speak of function, I mean the projection of nothing's terror onto black(ness) as a strategy of metaphysics' will to power. How, then, does metaphysics dominate nothing? By objectifying nothing through the black Negro.

In this analysis, metaphysics can *never* provide freedom or humanity for blacks, since it is the objectification, domination, and extermination of blacks that keep the metaphysical world intact. Metaphysics uses blacks to maintain a sense of security and to sustain the fantasy of triumph—the triumph over the nothing that limits human freedom. Without blacks, I argue, nothing's terror debilitates metaphysical procedures, epistemologies, boundaries, and institutions. Black freedom, then, would constitute a form of *world destruction*, and this is precisely why humanism has failed to accomplish its romantic goals of equality, justice, and recognition. In short, black humanism has neglected the relationship between black(ness) and nothing in its yearning for belonging, acceptance, and freedom. The Negro was *invented* to fulfill this function for metaphysics, and the humanist dream of transforming invention into human *being* is continually deferred (because it is impossible). *Ontological Terror* challenges the claim that blacks are human and can ground existence in the same being of the human. I argue that blacks are introduced into the metaphysical world as available equipment in human form.

Black thinking, then, must return to the question of Being and the relation between this question and the antiblack violence sustaining the world. It is my contention that black thinking is given a tremendous task: to approach the ontological abyss and the metaphysical violence sustaining the world. *Ontological Terror* suggests that black thinking cannot be overcome— we will never reach the end of black thinking or its culmination, unlike the end of philosophy describing postmetaphysical enterprises.[4] In other words, postmetaphysics has broached the question of being and has commenced the destruction [*Destruktion*] of the metaphysical infrastructure, which systemically forgets being. Postmetaphysics, then, is a project of remnants, as Santiago Zabala suggests. After we have used hermeneutics, deconstruction, rhizomes, and mathematical sets to devastate metaphysics, we are left with ontological rubble—a trace of metaphysics and a reconstructed being. Postmetaphysics, then, must ask, "How is it going with Being?" Or what is the state of Being in this contemporary moment, and how does the world remain open to Being's unfolding and happening (as well as its withdrawal and abandoning of *Dasein*)? "How is it going with Being?" is *the fundamental* question of our era, according to postmetaphysics; only the twisting and severe rearranging [verwunden] of metaphysics can usher this question into the world.

Both metaphysics and postmetaphysics, however, have forgotten the Negro, just as they have forgotten Being—*to remember Being one must also remember the Negro.* The Negro Question and the Question of Being are intertwined. Postmetaphysical enterprises reach a limit in destruction, since it is the Negro that sustains metaphysics and enables the forgetting of Being (i.e., metaphysics can forget Being because it *uses* the Negro to project nothing's terror and forget Being). In a sense, the global use of the Negro fulfills the ontological function of forgetting Being's terror, majesty, and incorrigibility. The consequence of this is that as long as postmetaphysical enterprises leave the Negro unattended in their thinking, it inadvertently sustains metaphysical pain and violence. *This,* I argue, is why we will *never* overcome [überwunden] metaphysics because the world cannot overcome the Negro—the world needs the Negro, even as the world despises it.

This is, of course, a Heideggerian approach to the thinking of Being and Nothing. More than any other philosopher, Heidegger pursued metaphysical violence and the question of Being relentlessly, and for this reason I find his philosophy indispensable and necessary. *Ontological Terror* thinks with and against Heidegger, since I believe Heidegger's destruction of metaphysics can assist black studies in the tremendous task of *thinking* Being and blackness, as Grant Farred has suggested.[5] Heidegger's *Destruktion* covers a wide range of philosophical issues, and it is not my objective to address all of these complexities; my interest is the relation between Heidegger's critique of metaphysical violence, available equipment, and the task of remembering as it concerns blackness. What I hope to broach in this book, with all the aporias such as broaching encounters, is that the Negro is the missing element in Heidegger's thinking (as well as in that of those postmetaphysicians indebted to Heidegger, such as Jean-Luc Nancy, Giorgio Agamben, Alain Badiou, and Gianni Vattimo). If, as we learn in *Being and Time*, Dasein uses tools to experience its thrownness in the world (establishing its facticity) and to develop its unique project oriented toward the future (projectionality), the Negro—as commodity, object, slave, putative backdrop, prisoner, refugee, and corpse—is the *quintessential* tool Dasein uses. The *use* of the Negro metaphysically and ontologically, as a tool, is what *black* thinking is tasked with pursuing. Thus, black thinking (and postmetaphysics) must ask the unasked question "How is it going with black ~~being~~?" Without broaching this question, all forms of destruction are just reconstitutions, since the world continues to use the Negro (as black and nothing) to forget Being and the sadistic pleasure of this forgetfulness.

I shared this argument with a good friend at a conference, and he politely whispered to me, "You know Heidegger was sympathetic to Nazism, don't you?" I immediately whispered back, "Even more reason for black studies to read and engage him!" Heidegger might well be the most influential philosopher of the twentieth century, since the question of Being resides at the crux of every philosophical enterprise, and he raised this question relentlessly. For me, this means that we cannot escape Heidegger; his *Destruktion* of Being has left its trace on all our thinking—whether we admit it or not. We cannot escape Heidegger because we cannot escape the question of Being. If the trace of Heidegger has left an indelible impression, despite the attempts to purge him/his thought, contemporary thinking still bears the abhorrent, the unforgivable, the disaster, the devastation. The *question*, then, is not just whether Heidegger was a Nazi (or antiblack for my purposes), but what his critique of metaphysics can teach us about systemic violence and devastation.[6] Turning a blind eye to Heidegger will not resolve anything, although *affect* might make us feel ethically enlightened. Confronting/engaging Heidegger, I argue, helps us understand the relation between black suffering and metaphysics, slavery and objectification, antiblackness and forgetfulness, thinking and remembering. (*Heidegger's philosophy, in many ways, can be read as an allegory of antiblackness and black suffering—the metaphysical violence of the transatlantic slave trade.*)[7] To broach the insatiable question "Why are blacks continually injured, degraded, pulverized, and killed?" would require, then, an understanding of metaphysical violence and pain—since black suffering is metaphysical violence, the violence of schematization, objectification, and calculative thinking Heidegger spent his entire professional career exposing. Perhaps Heidegger was *really* talking about black(ness) and black suffering all along.

BLACK NIHILISM AND ANTIBLACKNESS

A mentor once asked me a terrifying question: why are blacks *hated* all over the world? Stunned, I remained silent, but the question remained with me. This book, in many ways, is a return to my mentor's question, a question that might lack any sufficient answer, but a question that must be presented nonetheless. We can call this hatred *antiblackness*: an accretion of practices, knowledge systems, and institutions designed to impose nothing onto blackness and the unending domination/eradication of black presence *as* nothing incarnated. Put differently, antiblackness *is* anti-nothing. What is hated about blacks is this nothing, the ontological terror, they must embody for the metaphysical world. Every lynching, castration, rape, shooting, and murder of blacks is an engagement with this nothing and the fantasy that nothing can be dominated once and for all. Therefore, unlike Heidegger, nothing is not a cause for celebration in my analysis; it is the *source* of terror, violence, and domination for blacks. Heideggerian anxiety transforms into antiblack violence when Dasein flees the anxiety nothing stimulates and projects it as terror onto blacks. The unfolding of Being for Dasein, through the aperture of nothing, is predicated on the imposition of nothing's terror onto blacks. This is why,

I argue, the world *needs* blacks, even as it tries to eliminate them (this is the tension between necessity and hatred).

Ontological Terror insists, then, that Heidegger's *Introduction to Metaphysics*, for example, be read to understand the antiblack strategies the world employs to avoid nothing (as Heidegger says, "The world wants to know nothing of nothing") and its terror—how Dasein deals with its "own oppression by its own nothingness," as Oren Ben-Dor might call it.[8] Dasein's freedom is contingent on avoiding this nothing metaphysically— even though Heidegger would insist that nothing provides the opening for a new thinking about Being. Thus, calculative thinking, as I will argue in chapter 3, is a strategy for imposing nothing onto blacks. In understanding the particular way metaphysics oppresses, we get a better understanding of antiblackness *as* metaphysics. Antiblackness provides the instruments and framework for binary thinking, the thinking of being as presence (e.g., the obsession with physicality and skin complexion), the objectification of Being (one only needs to think of slave ledgers as the extremity of Heidegger's metaphysical nightmare, for example), and technocratic oppression (e.g., racial surveillance, police warfare equipment). The aim of postmetaphysicians, then, is to *weaken* metaphysics; this is the nihilistic strategy of the enterprise—to first weaken philosophy and its rigid foundations. Nihilism is important because it undermines the metaphysics, which sustains extreme forms of violence and destruction. But it reaches its limit when antiblackness is left unchecked.

The Italian nihilist Gianni Vattimo has revived and developed the philosophical tradition of nihilism in gravid ways that speak to contemporary threats of annihilation and destruction. His project is important because it permutes the thought of Nietzsche and Heidegger, and in doing so, it not only offers an important critique of modernity but also puts this critique in the service of a politico-philosophical imagination—an imagination that conceives of the weakening of metaphysical Being (nihilism) as the solution to the rationalization and fracturing of humanity (the source of modern suffering or pain). In short, this project attempts to restore dignity, individuality, and freedom to society by remembering Being (proper Being, not metaphysical Being) and allowing for the necessary contextualization and historicization of Being as event.

In *The End of Modernity* (1988) and *Nihilism and Emancipation* (2004), Vattimo reads Heidegger's destruction of ontology as a philosophical complement to Nietzsche's declaration of the death of God. Both Nietzsche and Heidegger offer trenchant critiques of metaphysics, and by reading them together, he fills in certain gaps—in particular, the relationship between metaphysics and social rationalization, foundations and ontology, and sociological philosophy and thinking itself. We can understand both Vattimo's and Heidegger's projects as the attempt to capture the relationship between what we might call *metaphysical Being* (fraudulent Being as object) and *Being* (in its proper contextualized sense). This relationship, indeed, has been particularly violent and has produced various forms of suffering. This suffering is the essence of metaphysics, or what Vattimo would call "pain," and it is sustained through the will to power, violence (e.g., physical, psychic, spiritual, and philosophical), and the destruction of liberty. The metaphysical tradition has reduced Being (an event that structures historical reality and possibility itself) to an object, and this objectification of Being is accomplished through the instruments of science and schematization. The result of this process is that Being is forgotten; the grand aperture that has provided the condition for relationality for many epochs is now reified as a static presence, a presence to be possessed and analyzed. In this sense, we lose the grandeur of Being and confuse it for being, the particularity of a certain epoch. The nihilist, then, must overcome the oblivion of Being through the weakening of metaphysical Being (what Vattimo will call "weak thought"). Vattimo recovers Heidegger's term *Verwundung* (distorting acceptance, resignation, or twisting) as a strategy to weaken metaphysical Being, since the nihilist can never truly destroy metaphysics or completely overcome it (überwunden). This strategy of twisting and distorting metaphysics helps us to remember and re-collect [*andenken*] the grandeur of Being (*Ge-Schick* as the ultimate gathering of the various epochal presentations of being)[9] and to place metaphysical Being back in its proper place as a particular manifestation of this great historical process. Only by inserting our present signification of Being into the grand gathering of Being (*Ge-Shick*) can we properly contextualize our own epoch—the epoch of social rationalization, technocracy, metaphysical domination.[10]

For the black nihilist, however, the question is this: will the dissolution of metaphysical Being that Vattimo and Heidegger advance eliminate antiblack violence and redress black suffering? What would freedom entail for black objects (as distinct from the human that grounds Vattimo's project)? Antiblackness becomes somewhat of an unacknowledged inter-locutor for Vattimo: "Philosophy follows paths that are not insulated or cut off from the social and political transformations of the West (*since the end of metaphysics is unthinkable without the end of colonialism and Eurocentrism*) and 'discovers' that the meaning of the history of modernity is not progress toward a final perfection characterized by fullness, total transparency, and the presence finally realized of the essence of man and the world."[11]

Vattimo adumbrates a relationship between metaphysics and colonialism/ Eurocentrism that renders them coterminous. If, as Vattimo argues, "the end of metaphysics is unthinkable without the end of colonialism and Eurocentrism"—which I will suggest are varieties of antiblack violence—then traditional nihilism must advance an escape from antiblackness to accomplish its agenda. Furthermore, if philosophy follows paths created by sociopolitical realities, then we must talk about antiblackness not just as a violent political formation but also as a *philosophical orientation*. The social rationalization, loss of individuality, economic expansionism, and technocratic domination that both Vattimo and Heidegger analyze actually depend on antiblackness.

Ontological Terror opens a path of black nihilistic inquiries. The objective, here, is to trouble the ontological foundations of both postmetaphysical and black humanist discourses. In chapter 1, I argue that the question of black ~~being~~ constitutes a proper metaphysical question, and this questioning leads us into the abyss of ontology: blackness lacks Being (which is why we write being under erasure in relation to black). Unlike humanists and postmetaphysicians, I argue that Being is not universal or applicable to blacks. Now, some might offer the rejoinder that everything has Being—even an object.[12] It is here that I will introduce a distinction between ontology and existence, one that Fanon insisted in *Black Skin, White Masks*. Blacks have an existence in an antiblack world, but ontology does not explain this existence, as Fanon argued. Furthermore, we might also gain clarity from Heidegger's rereading of Greek philosophy. He suggests:

For the Greeks "Being" says *constancy* in a twofold sense:
    1. Standing-in-itself as arising and standing forth (*phusis*)
    2. But, as such, "constantly" that is, enduringly, abiding (*ousia*)
Not-to-be accordingly, means to step out of constancy that has stood-

forth in itself; *existasthai*—"existence," "to exist," means, for the Greeks, precisely not-to-be. The thoughtlessness and vapidity with which one uses the words "existence" and "to exist" as designators for Being offer fresh evidence of our alienation from being and from an originally powerful and definitive interpretation of it.[13]

My presentation of black existence, then, reworks this Greek understanding of existence *as* non-being (or more precisely "not-to-be"), according to Heidegger (since this Greek presentation of the human's being, I will argue, has already excluded the Hottentot, the black thing). To allow Being's unfolding, or *to be*, is the melding of standing-forth and abiding, or enduring, such standing. In an antiblack world, such standing forth, or emerging/becoming, is obliterated, and this is what we will call the "metaphysical holocaust"—the systematic concealment, descent, and withholding of blackness through technologies of terror, violence, and abjection. To exist, as black, is to inhabit a world through permanent "falling" (in the Greek *ptosis* and *enklisis*). David Marriott might describe this as an interminable fall, in which

> there is neither event nor becoming; indeed the falling figures [black ~~being~~] do not come to their end, nor is there any possibility of destination . . . these falls are unending, and precisely because they fall into nothing . . . these falls inaugurate nothing but waiting, a sort of non-event, an event of nothing which both calls for and annuls repetition.[14]

To be, according to Heidegger, is to become, to emerge and move within Being-as-event. But what happens when such becoming does not occur? When the event of Being does not stimulate a productive anxiety of actualization, but gets caught in a repetition of event-less demise and nothingness? To inhabit such a condition is to exist as perpetual falling, without standing-forth, without Being. This, then, is the devastation of the metaphysical holocaust: black ~~being~~ never becomes, or stands forth, but exists in concealment, falling, and inconsistency. When I say, then, that blacks lack being but have existence, I mean that they inhabit the world in concealment and non-movement (this is the condition of objects, despite the work of object-oriented ontologists who project humanism onto objects). Thus, the task of black thinking is to limn the devastating distinction between "existence" (inhabitation) and "being."

What is black existence without Being? This is the question black thought orbits—the question that emerges through urgency, devastation, or the declaration "black lives matter."[15] It is a question that, perhaps, cannot be answered adequately—or any answer resides outside the world, in an unimaginable time/space horizon. My objective, then, is to build a way into an abyss—without recourse to the metaphysical finality-teleology of an answer. (Even the term *existence* is inadequate to describe what is black ~~being~~, as it still retains metaphysical resonance.) The lack of language and grammar to describe what preconditions Being makes the enterprise a difficult one—inevitably encountering explanatory impasse. We, however, attempt to undermine metaphysics as we deploy it.

The concept "nothing" provides a paradigmatic frame for describing this black thing without ontology. For nothing constitutes a mystery or ontological exception. We cannot reduce it to Being completely, but it is something outside metaphysical ontology (and at its very core), and, at the same time, it is what enables Being (humans experience Beings unfolding through the anxiety nothing presents in death or the breakdown of symbolic functions/meaning). What is nothing? This metaphysical question undermines itself from its very deployment, since it debilitates every copula formulation. Heidegger argued that the metaphysical copula formulation (what is) provided the frame for our metaphysical domination of Being, but nothing is precisely what lacks isness, by providing it with its condition of possibility. To claim, as I do throughout this book, that black ~~being~~ is nothing is to read the ontological puzzle of blackness (the unanswerable copula query) through the puzzle of nothing. There is no coincidence, then, when philosopher David Alain or Afro-pessimist scholars argue that black is nothing. Blacks are the nothing of ontology and do not have being like those beings for whom the ontological question is an issue (i.e., human being). In chapter 1, I read Hortense Spillers, Frantz Fanon, Sylvia Wynter, Ronald Judy, and Nahum Chandler through and against Heidegger to present this ontological puzzle. Even though it can never be answered apodictically, since this would mean the death of the world, my presentation will lead to more questions, complications, impasses, and silences; this is unavoidable when broaching the question of black ~~being~~. Philosophy lacks a grammar and a tradition to explain accurately the Negro Question. Thus, *Ontological Terror* wrestles or tarries with critical traditions designed to exclude black(ness), including, most of all, Being and ontology.

PARADIGM, HISTORY, AND THE FREE BLACK

The term *free black* carries tension within its structure; it brings two disparate grammars into collusion and produces an ontological catastrophe. The term *black* is precisely the puzzle, the great abyss, of something outside the precincts of ontology. It is a metaphysical invention, void of Being, for the purpose of securing Being for the human. It has something like existence but no recourse to the unfolding of Being or the revelation of its withdrawal. It is *nothing*—the nonhuman, equipment, and the mysterious. Freedom, however, is the site of this unfolding for the human; it is the *condition* of caring for Being and embracing its withdrawal and unfolding.[16] Freedom, in other words, is a (non)relation to Being for Dasein—it propels its project (projectionality) into the world. Freedom is ontological. As Heidegger insisted in his critique of Kantian freedom (metaphysical causality), "The question concerning the essence of human freedom is the fundamental question of philosophy, in which is rooted even the question of being . . . freedom is the condition of the possibility of the manifestness of the being of beings, of understanding of being."[17] Humanism often conflates freedom with liberty, rights, and emancipation, but this conflation undermines the ontological ground, which makes any claim to freedom possible. In other words, reducing freedom to political, social, or legal conceptions leaves the question of being unattended. Freedom exists *for* Being—it enables the manifestation of Being through Dasein. Our metaphysical notions of freedom also reduce antiblackness to social, political, and legal understandings, and we miss the ontological *function* of antiblackness—to deny the ontological ground of freedom by severing the (non)relation between blackness and Being. What I am suggesting is that our metaphysical conceptions of freedom neglect the ontological horrors of antiblackness by assuming freedom can be attained through political, social, or legal action. This is a humanist fantasy, one that masks subjection in emancipatory rhetoric.[18]

"Free black," then, stages an impossible encounter: between the ontological (non)relation and the mysterious abyss of nothing. Put differently, it expresses a Hegelian desire of synthesis between "two warring ideas," as Dubois might call it. We might, then, envision the encounter as a form of war, an ontological disaster from which various forms of antiblack violence emerge. "Free Black" is a grammatical and syntactical battlefield upon which dead bodies—Trayvon Martin, Renisha McBride, Michael Brown, among countless others—are displayed. We can also call this disaster the "metaphysical holocaust," as Frantz Fanon describes it. It is the systemic and relentless wiping out of black cosmologies, histories, and frames of reference/orientation. The metaphysical holocaust is violence without end, violence constitutive of a metaphysical world. It is a "violence that continuously repositions the Black as a void of historical movement," as Frank Wilderson describes it.[19] This void and stasis of temporal linearity is precisely the nothing blacks incarnate. The term *free black*, then, is the syntactical reflection of the metaphysical holocaust, the violence between the terms *free* and *black* that is unresolvable.

Throughout this book, I use the term *free black* in two ways: (1) as a philosophical concept capturing the continuous metaphysical violence between black ~~being~~ and human being/ontometaphysics and (2) as a particular historical figure that allegorizes metaphysical violence. Thus, the free black here is both philosophical allegory and historical figure. But, the problematic that the latter presents (i.e., the free black as historical figure) is that such a figure does not exist. It is impossible for any black to be free in an antiblack world.

The term *free black* is a misnomer for describing a historical condition, or particularity, of blackness, since the ontological relation is severed. It is precisely this misnomer, a taxonomic necessity of sorts for historiography and legal studies, that is of interest to me. The struggles and challenges that free blacks experienced in antebellum society were really ontological problems. The free black presents or forces confrontation with the Negro Question. It is through the free black that the Negro Question emerges with ferocity. Can black "things" become free? What is the status of such ~~beings~~? These questions are not merely legal questions or questions of legal status, but primarily ontological questions, I argue. The debates concerning free black citizenship were deceptive in that antebellum society mobilized them to answer the ontological question, "How is it going with black ~~being~~?" Has the metaphysical world evolved such that blacks can ground existence, indisputably, in the being of the human? Thus, it made little difference whether one was born free, received the "gift" of freedom from a master, purchased freedom, resided in the North or South; the ontological question, the Negro Question, remained. The intransigence of the question and its continuity across diverse space and temporalities is what concerns me. For we might look to the historical figure of the free black to understand the birth of the proper metaphysical question, since society could not resolve the tension between human freedom and black objects. As Maurice S. Lee suggests, philosophical perspectives on blackness and metaphysics were articulated in many ways before the Civil War (in particular the literary form for him).[20] My objective here is to read the Negro Question as a philosophical site of anxiety, terror, and metaphysical sensibilities.

Although engaging the historiographical figure "free black" (the invention of the historiographer), this book is not intended to contribute to historiography; rather, my objective is to question the ontological ground or metaphysical infrastructure upon which such historiographies proceed.[21] Antebellum free-black historiography is rich with archival discoveries, and to this my research is indebted. But we reach a problem with historical narration, or what the historiographer does with the archival material retrieved. Historiographical narration is not a philosophically neutral enterprise; it is loaded with philosophical presumptions, primarily metaphysical humanism. As Possenti asserts, "it is precisely metaphysics that keeps watch over history; not because it engulfs or digests history as irrelevant, but because it can direct history toward its goal."[22] It often proceeds without broaching the ontological question—or taking the historian Ira Berlin's phrase slaves without masters seriously.[23] When historian Dr. John Hope Franklin remarks, "The free negro as a subject for historical treatment abounds in elusive and difficult problems," I understand these problems not just as archival but also as an inherent problem of narrating within a humanist framework.[24] The research acknowledges tension between blackness and freedom (freedom often described as a set of liberties and rights, not an ontological position) but resolves this tension into a synthesis of metaphysical humanism—that is, blacks are still human, even though they experience captivity and systemic discrimination. What ground enables the historiographer to make such a claim or presume apodictically this black humanity? The research carries a philosophy of universal humanism into its reading and narration practices. Historiography reinforces philosophical humanism. It is precisely these presumptions that *Ontological Terror* intends to unravel. I bring the Negro Question to historiography to suggest that the metaphysical holocaust destabilizes such humanism.[25] We need to imagine an antimetaphysical historiography (a thinking against metaphysics), one that proceeds from the puzzle of black ~~being~~ and confronts the ontometaphysical question.

Thus, my objective in this book is to introduce an ontological complication that exceeds, but also engenders discriminatory law (mandatory emigration laws in Southern states, for example), surveillance, and physical brutality (the free black whipped just like the slave) of free blacks. These antiblack tactics have been well documented, as it concerns the disciplining and subordination of free blacks. What has been neglected, however, is an analysis of what exactly happens to blacks once emancipated, or free—the transubstantiation between property and something else. Did the black become a human once free? If we answer in the affirmative, does the freedom paper undermine the being of the human, given that without it, such claim to humanity cannot be sustained? Are "masterless slaves," as free blacks have been called, still property—property of whom? What determines the distinction between human masters and masterless slaves? Is emancipation ontological creation, and what enables the malleability of black ~~being~~? These questions, questions still remaining, build a path into a discussion of ontological complications the free black presents. *Ontological Terror* broaches these questions to illumine something more sinister about the condition of black ~~being~~, a condition that impacts all blacks in an antiblack world, not just the antebellum free black. The historical singularity of free blacks knots together a deep philosophical conflict between Being, blackness, and freedom—it is an extraordinary paradigm for black thinking. My hope is that historians, philosophers, and theorists will consider the free black, much more than an anomalous population, a speculative frame within which the foundations of humanism and metaphysics in general are challenged.

Furthermore, my concern is not to fetishize agency or will. It is certainly the case that those ~~beings~~ we call "free blacks" experienced the world through bonds, courage, despair, friendship, and hope. These cannot be denied, but I do not think these render these beings human or answer the metaphysical question in the affirmative. No matter the bond, the act of courage, the indefatigable fortitude, or the institutions established, the metaphysical holocaust remains consistent. No political action has or ever will end it—it is necessary for the world. Thus, if we bundle certain capacities into something we call "agency," this bundle does not undermine metaphysical violence or the exclusion of blackness from Being. The existence that provides the condition for something we might call "agency" is not human ontology and not freedom. Our desperation to incorporate blacks into a narrative of humanistic heroism often results in a disavowal of the problem of ontology, which engenders the condition against which the courageous fight in the first place. Black thinking, then, must explore what existence without Being entails. Free blacks do not inhabit the world in the way the human does—historiography proceeds as if the problem of existence has been resolved. It has not.[26] My focus, here, will be on the condition of the metaphysical holocaust or its manifestations and not on individual narratives of free blacks. That work is certainly important, too, but in this project I want to read the archive to understand an ontological condition of execration.

Ontological Terror confronts both the ontological puzzle (metaphysical holocaust) and the historical figure we call "free black" through a paradigmatic approach. In *The Signature of All Things*, Agamben describes the paradigm as not obeying

> the logic of the metaphorical transfer of meaning but the analogical logic of the example. Here we are not dealing with a signifier that is extended to designate heterogeneous phenomena by virtue of the same semantic structure; more akin to allegory than to metaphor, the paradigm is a singular case that is isolated from its context only insofar as, by exhibiting its own singularity, it makes intelligible a new ensemble, whose homogeneity it itself constitutes. That is to say, to give an example is a complex act which supposes that the term functioning as a paradigm is deactivated from its normal use, not in order to be moved into another context, but on the contrary, to present the canon—the rule—of that use, which can not be shown in any other way.[27]

A paradigmatic approach uses the structure of allegory—juxtaposing two singularities—for the purpose of illumining a new ensemble of relations, or what we can call "paradigm." The singularity must be *deactivated*, meaning it must be momentarily extracted from its usual context and conceptualized in another way. The deactivation is necessary because we can only understand or illumine the paradigm by extracting, deactivating, and juxtaposing the singularity, or example. It is a paradoxical figure: both example and other than example. *Ontological Terror* approaches the problem of *black* as *nothing* through a paradigmatic juxtaposing of the free black and the critique of metaphysical violence Heidegger and others (including Agamben and Jean-Luc Nancy) present. Since nothing is also a paradox, both *outside* Being and as an opening for Being, one could *only approach it through a set of allegories.* In other words, we can never fully understand nothing with our metaphysical instruments, even with the most rigorous destructive or deconstructive procedure—something of nothing always escapes. *Ontological Terror* deactivates the antebellum free black (and the general concept *free black*) to set it alongside metaphysical violence to illumine the paradigm of black nothingness or ontological terror. The free black, then, serves as a historical allegory for metaphysical violence, and metaphysical violence serves as an allegory for the tension between free and black that the historical figure *free black* experiences. My objective is not to rob or neglect the singularity of the free black—although the category itself is under suspicion—but to demonstrate how this singularity is much more than traditionally thought by historians.

Given this, my objective in *Ontological Terror* is also to address what I consider a form of philosophical antiblackness: the neglect of black archives. Rarely, if ever, do nihilistic or postmetaphysical philosophers engage black archives. A philosophy of history or a philosophical anthropology very often proceeds with an archive (i.e., Homo sacer, Nazi concentration camp, Greek polis) to illumine a paradigm. The choice of archive is also a philosophical statement; it reflects what body of knowledge is worthy of philosophical examination and what experiences contribute more to thinking than *just* singularity. Black archives are often reduced to mere singularity, perhaps an interesting singularity, but never taken up paradigmatically. Or as Alexander Weheliye cogently states the problem, there is "a broader tendency in which theoretical formulations by white European thinkers are granted conceptual carte blanche, while those uttered from the view point of minority discourse that speak to the same questions are almost exclusively relegated to the jurisdiction of ethnographic locality."[28] As distinguished philosopher Tommy Curry has argued, "Traditionally, in philosophy, the only limitation of philosophical concepts is the extent to which the conceptualize-er imagines; however, when the task placed before whites entails a philosophical encounter with the realities of Blacks, philosophy is suddenly limited—incarcerated by the white imagination's inability to confront its corporeal reflection."[29] *Ontological Terror* confronts philosophy's vapidity when confronted with blackness. Furthermore, the fact that post-metaphysics claims to destroy metaphysics, but leaves the *triumph* of metaphysics unattended (antiblack violence) is disturbing and befuddling (especially when Vattimo claims that destroying metaphysics is unthinkable without addressing Euro-centrism). What this reveals to me is that antiblackness is a juggernaut that must be fought on *many* battlefields—including philosophical formations.

Thus, I read postmetaphysics alongside the free black archives (such as *The African Repository*, freedom papers, and *The Census of 1840*) in order to illumine the philosophical richness of the black experience in an antiblack world.

ITINERARY

The book builds upon the arguments that blacks incarnate nothing in a metaphysical world and that the world is both fascinated with this nothing and terrified of it. Antiblack violence is violence against nothing, the nothing that unsettles the human because it can never be captured and dominated. Blacks, then, allow the human to engage in a fantasy—the domination of nothing. By projecting this nothing as terror onto blacks, the human seeks to dominate nothing by dominating black ~~being~~, to eradicate nothing by eradicating black ~~being~~. The free black, as the conceptual/ embodied intersection between nothing and blackness, is absolutely essential to a metaphysical world desperate to avoid the terror of nothing. The book proceeds by engaging the projection and terror of this nothing. As I have mentioned before, the field of free black historiography is capacious, and there are numerous issues to investigate. I proceed, here, by choosing four fields of inquiry, in which the free black presents ontometaphysical problems: philosophy, law, science/math, and visuality. I chose these fields to demonstrate what Foucault might call a polymorphous relation.[30] By this, I mean that philosophy, law, science/math, and visuality constitute intersecting vectors of terror for black ~~being~~—each producing and sustaining the destruction of black ~~being~~ in its own way, but accomplishing the same objective (i.e., severing of the flesh or the metaphysical holocaust). I hope to demonstrate that ontological terror unites these diverse fields, and the proper metaphysical question (i.e., "What is black ~~being~~?/How is it going with black ~~being~~?") constitutes the vehicle of movement between the fields. Ultimately, I suggest that these fields expose a deep problem: given the failure of postmetaphysics to twist [verwunden] antiblackness severely and black humanism's romance with metaphysical schemas of humanity and freedom, black thinking can only ask a metaphysical question, the question that remains after destruction.

In chapter 1, "The Question of Black ~~Being~~," I present the Negro Question as what Heidegger would call a "proper metaphysical question." The aim is to understand how the problem of metaphysical blackness and the concept of nothing converge on the Negro as a way of resolving the tension. I read Hortense Spillers, in particular, as an ontometaphysician who describes metaphysical violence as the "severing of the flesh." In reading Spillers through and against Heidegger, I intend to show how the transatlantic slave trade realized the horror Heidegger dreaded and sought to destroy in *Introduction to Metaphysics*, *Being and Time*, and *The Question Concerning Technology*, among others. But Spillers also questions the process of *Destruktion*, I argue, because no such twisting, or reconfiguring, of metaphysics is possible for blackness—the ontological relation is severed permanently—no recourse to Being is possible.

In chapter 2, "Outlawing," I present two notions of law: the Law of Being (the law of abandonment determining the relation between the human and Being) and the being of law (the metaphysical instantiation of law as rights, amendments, judicial opinions, legislations). Building off postmetaphysical work, I argue that the being of law is subordinate or subject to the Law of Being—ontic distortion conceals this fact. Turning to *Dred Scott*, freedom papers, and emancipation, I suggest that the legal problems free blacks presented to antebellum society were not merely problems for the being of law (the restriction of rights, liberties) but a deeper problem with the Law of Being (the nonrelation between blackness and Being). In other words, the reification of black ~~being~~ in materiality (freedom papers), the terroristic space of emancipation, the uncertainty of what *free black* constituted legally were all symptoms of ungrounded black ~~being~~. The being of law merely reflects the exclusion of blacks from Being and into a space of ontological terror.

In chapter 3, "Scientific Horror," I think through the way scientific and mathematical thinking relies on blacks to explore nothing. It is both a horror and a fascination and perhaps the only way science can contend with nothing. The chapter reads the writing of Samuel Cartwright, Benjamin Rush, and the Census of 1840 as philosophical discourses hiding behind epidemiology, vital statistics, and neurology. The aim is to strip through scientific presentations to expose the metaphysical obsession with blackness as nothing.

In chapter 4, "Catachrestic Fantasies," I argue that nothing is visualized through fantasies and catachresis (the lack of a proper referent), thus enabling boundless fantasizing about blacks. I turn to illustrated journalism and the artwork of Edward Clay as visualizations of black as nothing. The question "What is black ~~being~~?" is answered in different ways through different illustrations. I suggest that philosophy relies on fantasy to make philosophical statements when it reaches its limits of rationality and proofs. Because the free black ~~is~~ nothing, one can only approach this philosophical puzzle with fantasies. I turn to Lacanian psychoanalysis because it provides a frame for understanding fantasy, nothing, and projection in a way I think is productive. The aim is to think of psychoanalytic theory allegorically as it relates to black ~~being~~. I also find it productive in thinking about the unconscious fantasies of humans and the way that black-as-nothing centers these fantasies. In short, the chapter is about human fantasizing of a catachrestic entity through illustrated journalism.

The coda, "Adieu to the Human," argues that the metaphysical holocaust and its question are still with us. Police shootings, routinized humiliation, and disenfranchisement are symptoms of this unending war. Part of the aim, then, is to dethrone the human from its metaphysical pedestal, reject the human, and explore different ways of existing that are not predicated on Being and its humanism. This is the *only* way black thinking can grapple with existence without Being.

This book begins and ends with a question: "How is it going with black ~~Being~~?" This structure reminds us that temporal linearity and narratives of progress are deceptive ontologically. Time rebounds upon itself in a space of ontological terror—there is only temporal circularity or black time, an abyss of time. I challenge linearity (the invention of metaphysics and historiography) throughout this book by defying chronology (I, indeed, have an irreverence for it). Thus, I begin in one period and move to another and then back again, or I begin with the antebellum period and move to the Civil War and back again. This strategy, I hope, will demonstrate that no matter the time period, the metaphysical question remains. Our obsession with chronology and linearity is no more than a humanist fantasy of resolution and movement, which I hope to unravel. I also reject the humanist fantasy (or narcissism) that anything humans have created can be changed. Some creations are no longer in the hands of humans, for they constitute a horizon, or field, upon which human existence itself depends. Antiblackness is such a creation. Thus, chronology provides no relief with its obsession with change concerning antiblackness. What many proponents of the agency thesis (i.e., we have power to change anything we create) are actually doing is comparing different forms of antiblackness and neglecting the terror that antiblackness remains as a consistent variable, despite variations in form. Variations in antiblackness do not signal progress; rather, they are ontic distortions of the underlying ontological problem—blacks lack Being.

We can begin our paradigmatic investigation and end our introduction with a literary allegory, one demonstrative of ontological terror. In Edward P. Jones's Pulitzer Prize–winning novel *The Known World*, we encounter ontological terror.

The scene begins with Augustus, a free black man, returning home from a business transaction by wagon. Patroller Harvey Travis, the symbol of the law, stops Augustus in a routine inspection of the wagon. Travis has stopped Augustus many times before and knows that Augustus is a free black and, as such, has the right to travel and the freedom of movement. Travis demands Augustus's freedom papers, although he's read them many times and basically has them memorized. When Augustus insists that it is his prerogative to travel as a free person, Travis sardonically replies, "You ain't free less me and the law say you free." Travis expresses animus about Augustus's refusal to act obsequiously before white people, to assert a right he does not indeed possess. As Augustus continued to assert his freedom, Travis began to eat the freedom papers. Starting at the bottom right corners, he chewed and swallowed them. After eating the freedom papers, Travis mockingly retorted, "Thas what I think of your right to do anything you got a right to do." Travis licked his fingers in satisfaction and wiped his mouth. "Right ain't got nothing to do with it," he said. "Best meal I've had in many Sundays."

Oden, one of Travis's companions, laughed at him and said, "I wouldn't want to be you in the morning when you have to shit that out." Travis responded, "I don't know. It might make for a smooth run off. Couldn't be no worse than what collard greens do to me." Darcey, a kidnapper of free blacks, purchases free blacks from Travis and sells them as captives for a handsome profit. Travis explains to Darcey that his timing is fortuitous because he has "a nigger who didn't know what to do with his freedom. Thought it meant he was free." Travis sells Augustus to Darcey. Unable to prove his freedom, Augustus becomes the property of Darcey, instantly losing the very rights he was so certain freedom ensured.

Augustus thought that his freedom paper meant he was free, but as Travis demonstrates, this freedom was not freedom at all. What exactly does Travis consume when he eats the freedom papers? Consumption allegorizes the metaphysical holocaust—reducing the free black to a reified object (freedom paper) and it can be eaten (e.g., put between a biscuit and swallowed, as Frederick Douglass instructed) or destroyed at any time or place. Consumption is both a form of domination and sadistic pleasure, as Vincent Woodard would describe it.[31] We, then, must investigate the manner of consuming black flesh and *not* just the body, consuming the flesh *as* consuming the primordial relation itself. *Ontological Terror* exposes the insatiable appetite of antiblackness.

ONE

===

THE QUESTION OF BLACK ~~BEING~~

This essent, through questioning, is held out into the possibility of nonbeing.
Thereby the why takes on a different penetration.
HEIDEGGER, *Introduction to Metaphysics*

A question whose necessity is so fundamental that it must be unasked—the
question of the meaning of black being, the question of the meaning of (black)
things. We study in the sound of an unasked question. Our study is the sound
of an unasked question. We study the sound of an unasked question.
FRED MOTEN, "Blackness and Nothingness (Mysticism in the Flesh)"

BUILDING A WAY

One must ask a certain question of black ~~being~~,[1] a question that opens us
onto a horizon of representational and conceptual crisis. This question
emerges within a context of urgency: the intensity of black suffering, spiritual and physical deprivation, political demoralization, and the prolifera-
tion and permanency of necropolitical agendas. The question, its urgency,
and the crisis that it engenders recycle historically in various guises, and
in each (re)incarnation, it demands an address—an address that seems
impossible, since the discursive material we use to formulate an answer
is also called into question. Hortense Spillers meditates on certain facets
of this redoubling problematic when she suggests that in any investigation
of black ~~being~~, "we are confronted by divergent temporal frames, or beats,
that pose the problem of adequacy—how to reclaim an abandoned site of

inquiry in the critical discourse when the very question that it articulates is carried along as part of the methodological structure [or metaphysical structure], as a feature of the paradigm that is itself under suspicion, while the question itself foregrounds a thematic that cannot be approached in any other way."[2] The "unasked question," as Fred Moten would call it, is this "abandoned site of inquiry." My objective in this chapter is to return us to the abandoned, arid ontometaphysical space—the space and place of the question in ontometaphysics.[3] I use the unasked and unanswerable question to "build a way," as Heidegger would describe it, through the treacherous terrain of ontometaphysics and antiblackness.[4]

What follows is a tracing of this question through the discourses of ontometaphysics and the paradigm of the free black. My propositions attend to the important function of the Negro, or black ~~being~~, in ontometaphysics: (1) The Negro is the incarnation of nothing that a metaphysical world tries tirelessly to eradicate. Black ~~being~~ is invented precisely for this function ontologically; this is the ontological labor that the Negro must perform in an antiblack world. (2) The Negro is invented, or born into modernity, through an ontometaphysical holocaust that destroys the coordinates of African existence. The Negro is not a human, since ~~being~~ in not an issue for it, and instead becomes "available equipment," as Heidegger would call it, for the purpose of supporting the existential journey of the human being. Black ~~being~~ is the evidence of an ontological murder, or onticide, that is irrecoverable and irremediable. The condition of this permanent severing between black ~~being~~ and Being is what I call the "execration of Being." In this sense, Being does not withdraw from the Negro, as it does from the human, for what withdraws can reemerge. Instead, Being curses black ~~being~~ by creating an entity unintelligible within the field of ontology. (3) The Negro Question that becomes the obsession of antebellum culture ("What do we do about our free blacks?") masks the ontological stakes involved in answering the question, since what the question is really about, as I propose, is what we do about the nothing that terrorizes us, that destabilizes our metaphysical structure and ground of existence. The terms *free* and *black* do not just present political problems of citizenship, rights, and inclusion, but also present serious ontological problems, since the boundaries of ontology— between human and property and freedom and unfreedom—are thrown into crisis with the presence of the free black. Ultimately, I propose that the Negro Question is a proper metaphysical question, since the Negro is black and black(ness) has always been a terror for metaphysics. These propositions unfold through an engagement with different ontometaphysical discourses in the black radical tradition alongside and against Heidegger, since Heidegger's critique of metaphysics, as the disavowal, forgetting, and contempt of Nothing assists us in understanding how metaphysics engages the nothing that it despises but needs (the tension between hatred and necessity). I, however, depart from Heidegger, since black ~~being~~ is not human being (or Dasein) but available equipment, equipment in human form, that Heidegger does not consider because of his Eurocentric perspective.

BLACK, NOTHING, AND THE NEGRO

We can consider the Negro Question a proper metaphysical question. Heidegger reminds us that every metaphysical question always grasps the whole of the problematic of metaphysics. A proper question emerges within a context of urgency, but the investigation of the context and the question itself destabilizes the entire edifice within which the investigatory procedure is carried out, since the answer becomes a symptom of a larger problem. It is this larger problem (the "whole of the problematic of metaphysics," as Heidegger calls it) that the proper question is designed to address through a series of questions that, as they unfold, open the horizon of an empowered thinking. The proper question exposes an abyss, a black hole within the ontometaphysical tradition and its attendant discourses or, as Nahum Chandler aptly describes it, "the black in the whiteness of being, in the being of whiteness."[5] The philosophical conditions that enable the tradition are themselves brought forward, questioned, and thrown into relief. To present a proper metaphysical question of black ~~being~~, however, our question, and procedure, must align with the philosophical instruction of Hortense Spillers to "strip down through layers of attenuated meanings, made an excess in time; over time, assigned a particular historical order, and there await whatever marvels of [our] own inventiveness."[6] The objective of this question and our questioning is precisely to strip through layers of metaphysical baggage and attenuated meaning as they violently encrust over deep time and history. We can describe the whole problematic of black ~~being~~, then, as the aggregate, or collection, of these burdensome layers, which are traumatically imposed during the initiation of the transatlantic slave trade. But since "a genuine question is not done away with by finding an answer to it," according to Heidegger, the question remains as a feature of our own inventiveness. In other words, the question remains at the heart of black ~~being~~. And we must ask this question, since there is no getting rid of it, despite the marvelous power of our inventiveness. We can think, then, of Spillers's protocol of stripping through layers of *attenuated meaning* as the correction to Heidegger's Eurocentric *Destruktion*, or the "destructuring of the history of ontology," as he describes it in *Being and Time*. This is to say the destructuring of metaphysics must address the concealment of the Negro—buried deeply beneath layers of metaphysical violence. Our questions bring us to this concealment, within the history of ontology, as that kernel of antiblackness sustaining both metaphysics *and* ontology.[7]

The question has been with black ~~being~~, as a constitutive feature of it, since black ~~being~~ was invented—since modernity gave birth to it through dispossession and abjection. We have grappled with this fundamental question for centuries, in various forms. Dubois asked a variation of this question: "What does it mean to be a problem?"[8] This is, indeed, a proper metaphysical question, since it requires us to strip through layers of pulverizing meaning to arrive at a kernel of (non)meaning, or meaninglessness, as the answer to the question of black ~~being~~. The question that Dubois presents, "What does it mean to be a problem?," is both a metaphysical riddle and a formulation of black ~~being~~—black ~~being~~ is this riddle. The question of black ~~being~~ must, then, start with the *ontology of the problem*. To *be* a problem is the being-ness of blackness. It is this problem that will preoccupy our concern here—the question of black ~~being~~ *as* the problem of ontometaphysics (put differently, we can rewrite Dubois's question as "what does it mean to be the problem of ontometaphysics?" What is the *condition*, or inhabitation, of this problem?). It is impossible to uncouple black ~~being~~ from this problem. Exactly *how* does one *be* a problem? Or "inhabit" a problem, as Nahum Chandler might suggest is the riddle of blackness in modernity. When Hortense Spillers suggests that the black body is "reduced to a thing, to being for the captor,"[9] we can understand this being as the problem itself. Black being embodies an ontometaphysical problem for the captor. Black ~~being~~ becomes a site of projection and absorption of the problem of metaphysics—a problem that the captor would wish to ignore or neglect by imposing it onto black ~~being~~. Thus, black ~~being~~ is not only necessary for involuntary labor and pornotroping, but also necessary ontologically; it inhabits the problem of metaphysics.[10] This inhabitation is the ~~space~~ and ~~place~~ of the Negro Question—our proper metaphysical question.

Thinkers from the antebellum period presented this problem as the "Negro Question." The question of the Negro is precisely the question of this problem. For Sylvia Wynter, the Negro Question cannot be a proper object of knowledge, given that the ruling episteme does not accommodate this strange being.[11] Thus, the question itself and the metaphysical problem that it carries are positioned outside the frames of epistemology and its attendant discourses. For Wynter, the Negro is that ~~being~~, or more accurately entity, that is excluded from the discourse of man and its over-representation of being otherwise. The problem that the Negro Question opens up is this position outside of man. We can present a reformulation of this proper metaphysical question, following Wynter: why does this outside position constitute a problem for the whole of metaphysics (and its paradoxical answer)? This problem is spatialized as the outside, which preconditions the metaphysical architecture of man, the privileged inside. But given that this outside position is actually an intimate aspect of the inside, since it provides the inside's condition of possibility, the problem is at the heart of the ontometaphysics of man. Black ~~being~~ is the absent center of the whole of metaphysics, and it, cartographically, constitutes the paradoxical inside/outside position of metaphysics. This begins to provide a path of investigation toward this proper metaphysical question. Why is black ~~being~~ a problem? Why is this problem constitutive of an inside/outside paradox? Answering these questions, however, inevitably leads to more questions, or what I will call a fundamental question: How is it going with black ~~being~~?

In his *Introduction to Metaphysics*, Heidegger presents the question "How is it going with Being" [*Wie steht es um das Sein?*] to indicate that this question is *the* fundamental question, even more fundamental than "why are there beings at all instead of nothing?"[12] The importance of this question resides in the philosophy of the remains of Being, as Santiago Zabala has persuasively argued.[13] Since being has become "just the sound of a word, a used-up term," Heidegger argued that we must destroy, or dismantle, the structure of metaphysics to renew a forgotten relation to Being, not as presence or object, but as the opening of existence itself—what Heidegger will later call "appropriation."[14] Thus, the *proper* metaphysical question "How is it going with Being?" emerges after the destruction, or dismantling, of metaphysics; and after we have worn out the term, we must re-member Being by recollecting the fragments—the ontological pieces left after the destruction. "How is it going with Being?" is a way of inquiring about the status of Being after it has been thoroughly dismantled—what is left? Ontological investigations must now start with this fundamental question, according to Heidegger, to contend with the being abuse that has plagued the philosophical tradition from Plato onward. Reading Heidegger through Spillers, then, we could suggest that the task of *Destruktion* is to strip through layers of attenuated meaning, made in excess through the procedures and practices of metaphysics. The Heideggerian enterprise here is postmetaphysical to the extent that it urges us to twist metaphysics and instigate its self-consumption. This postmetaphysical movement marks the end of philosophy as we know it and inaugurates a thinking otherwise [Andenken] to arrive at a more fruitful understanding of the relation between Being and Dasein. "How is it going with Being?" dockets an uncovered or re-membered relationship between Dasein and Being, and it is the task of philosophy to illumine it.

If the aim of this postmetaphysical enterprise is to urge us to twist metaphysics to ask a more appropriate ontological question (i.e., the move from what *is* being to *How* is Being, as event and happening), it assumes that the metaphysics of being, its ontic science, has been settled and we can now get over metaphysics (even though we are still entrapped). Black ~~being~~, however, does not easily afford this postmetaphysical movement, since the metaphysical question of black ~~being~~—what is it?—has not been resolved, and thus, the ontological question, if one can be truly posed, what is the relationship between black ~~being~~ and Being (or How is it going with black ~~being~~?) is an unanswerable one (which, again, is why we must continually write black ~~being~~ under erasure). Put differently, the *problem* with the Negro Question is that we can never truly arrive at an appropriate *ontological question*, since black ~~being~~ is *not* ontological, but something other, something that lies outside of epistemology and ontology. This makes the Negro Question unanswerable on the register that Heidegger proposed for Dasein. The Negro Question is situated on a plane within/without metaphysics, but also outside the precincts of ontology. The *space* and *place* of the Negro Question are a *problem* for the whole of metaphysics, but a *problem* that provides the condition of possibility for human being to ask its fundamental question, "How is it going with Being?" The unpresentability of the Negro Question is the necessary ground for Dasein's ontological presentation.

To suggest that black ~~being~~ constitutes the *problem* at the center of ontometaphysics, in the form of an unanswerable question, is to suggest that Heidegger's *Destruktion* relies on the *indestructibility* of antiblackness in modernity. Metaphysics can only be dismantled for Dasein because a primordial relationship between it and Being exists that metaphysics cannot pulverize, even though it tries with science, schematization, and technology, according to Heidegger.[15] Thus, the dismantling or destruction of metaphysics is really the opening of a primordial relationality between Dasein and Being. But even though we can destroy metaphysics, in terms of twisting it and instigating its self-consumption [verwunden], we can never completely destroy it; a remainder or remnant will always persist within the very heart of the destructive enterprise. This remainder, this intransigent entity, is indestructible and, in fact, *structures* the project of destruction. It is indeed a paradoxical formulation that destruction depends on the kernel of *indestructability* at its core, but when we consider that something must remain for the philosophical enterprise to continue, then we understand that this remainder keeps the destructive movement going—it is its metaphysical fuel. I would also present another audacious claim and suggest that black ~~being~~ is the *name* of this indestructible element *because black ~~being~~'s function within metaphysics is to inhabit the void of relationality—relationality between it and Being and relationality between it and human-being-ness and the world itself.*[16] Thus, we must reconceptualize black ~~being~~ ontometaphysically as *pure function* and not relation (put differently, black ~~being~~ emerges in modernity primarily to inhabit this treacherous position as *function*, which enables human beingness to engage in its projectionality into the world and to restore its forgotten relationship with Being. In a word, black ~~being~~ helps the human being re-member its relation to Being through its lack of relationality. The essence of black ~~being~~, like the essence of technology, is to open up an understanding for Dasein, it is always ~~being~~ for another. Black ~~being~~, then, is precisely the metaphysical entity that must remain for the postmetaphysical enterprise of freedom (the loosening up of metaphysical strictures) to occur for human beingness (or Dasein). This indestructible remainder is a problem for metaphysics, since it retains the trace of objectification that restricts complete freedom for Dasein, but it is also the answer to metaphysics, given that it serves as the catalyst for the self-consumption that engenders greater freedom, if not complete freedom, for Dasein. But this formulation presents more questions, proper metaphysical questions, that chart the course to the abyss of metaphysics, which is black ~~being~~: why is black ~~being~~ indestructible? Why has metaphysics been unable or unwilling to dismantle its remainder? How do we articulate the problem of black ~~being~~, which is the problem for the whole of metaphysics?

Alain David provides a guide through these difficult questions in his philosophical meditation "On Negroes." David poses a proper metaphysical question of his own: why are Negroes black? I describe this as a proper metaphysical question because the juxtaposition of black and Negro in his inquiry (Negroes are black, as a copula proposition) opens us onto a paradox of black ~~being~~ understood through the Negro. I would formulate this paradox as this, following David: the Negro is the excess of form in an antiblack world, but also the interruption of form, the formless, given that the Negro is blackness within metaphysics. What could this mean? For David, metaphysics encounters a crisis. On the one hand, it attempts to move beyond form, the specificity of beings into the realm of Being (the formless); on the other hand metaphysics cannot seem to free itself completely from anthropologizing metaphysics, of a metaphysics that organizes ontological imagining around differences of race and skin complexion; thus, the purported formless, indifferent field of ontometaphysics is predicated upon anthropological differences, and this interplay between formlessness and form is what David would call "race." For him, "race is that hyperbole of form affirming itself over against that which would prevent form. Race is like a transcendental condition of the ontological argument."[17] When it concerns the Negro (as black ~~being~~), then, the distinction between the indifferent metaphysician and the anthropologist obsessed with difference collapses. But the collapse, I would argue, is necessary given the function of black ~~being~~, of the Negro. The question "Why are Negroes black?" can be approached through the metaphysical question "Why is there something rather than nothing?" for David. It is the status of this nothing that preoccupies the metaphysician, since, according to David, it is this nothing that interrupts form for metaphysics. Nothing occupies the paradoxical position (as Heidegger also argued in his *Introduction to Metaphysics*) of indexing formlessness, the breaking of metaphysics, at the same time conceptualized through metaphysical form (as a something). This leads David to appropriate a childhood riddle for philosophical purposes and ask: what is nothing while being something? The answer to this riddle is black for David:

> Black means nothing, nothing means black. Or, rather, nothing does not exactly mean black, since in nothing positivity is erased. Why is there something rather than black? According to this formulation, "black" is something, and yet, as I've said it is nothing. Nothing other than dazzlement. Light itself. And this black that is nothing, without this nothing being nothing, is the something that prevents any something from belonging to the whole. One must, then, wonder what this positivity is that, inscribed in the nothing—an inscription of the nothing— converts the nothing into its enigmatic nuance of black.[18]

Black, here, is not the color black, but is the index of formlessness, since color would assume a sensible form within metaphysics.[19] Despite indexing this formlessness, black assumes form as a something: positivity. The *function* of this something that is also a nothing is designed to "prevent any something from belonging to the whole," as David argues. In other words, this something serves as the precondition for the whole itself, as its inclusive exclusion (or excluded inclusion); its function is to fracture the whole through its exclusion, which constitutes the center—the absent center. Black is the something that is also nothing, a nothing that cannot be adequately captured within the precinct of metaphysics, but a something upon which metaphysics depends. But David also wonders "what [is] this positivity that, inscribed in the nothing—an inscription of the nothing—converts the nothing into its enigmatic nuance of black?" How, then, is nothing converted into black? How does that which interrupts metaphysical form (its grammar and conceptualization) *appear* as form, as a translation from the ineffable to the conceptual or worldly?

These inquiries return us to David's proper metaphysical question: why are Negroes black? He suggests that this question could be reformulated as "How does the interruption of form appear as form?" Although

David reaches a limit with this metaphysical question, since the philosophical exercise reaches a limit—of both meaning and knowledge (and he begins a discourse of what he calls "imaginary Negroes" to make sense of the senseless)—I would propose a response to David's inquiry: the Negro is black precisely because, within an antiblack world, the Negro is forced (through forms of terror and violence) to inhabit the position of black within metaphysics and to provide form for the formlessness of the interruption (which is why we can call the Negro "black ~~being~~"). If, as Heidegger insists, metaphysics attempts to transform everything into an object so that it can dominate and control it, nothing would become another object that metaphysics desires to dominate—an ultimate object. How does metaphysics transform nothing into something, so it can dominate this nothing? Through the Negro—it gives a form for the formless, but a form that perplexes and threatens. Perhaps this is why Negroes, historically and philosophically, have served as the "intermediaries between animal and man," as David describes it. The Negro is the interstice of metaphysics, the formless form between man and animal, property and human, whose purpose is to embody formlessness as a corporeal sign. As an intermediary, its position within metaphysics is paradoxical, as an excluded inclusion, an untranslatable entity without a proper referent (a catachresis within metaphysics). As Ronald Judy argues, "The Negro cannot enable the representation of meaning, [since] it has no referent."[20]

The Negro, then, is pure function; this function is to be black, but a ~~being~~ that is not (or Fanon's *n'est pas*).[21] And this is why the invention of the Negro is so essential to metaphysics. When, for instance, Afro-pessimists assert that black(ness) is unbearable or that black suffering is illegible, it is a way of articulating blackness as function—black ~~being~~ as pure function, metaphysical utility, nothing more. It is the function of bearing the nothing of metaphysics, black as formless form, that is unbearable and also the crux of black suffering. The world is antiblack because it despises this nothing, this nothing that interrupts its organization of existence, its ground of intelligibility and certainty (which is why antiblack violence is a global problematic). Returning to Wynter, we can understand why the Negro Question can never serve as a proper object of knowledge, since the Negro, as black ~~being~~, constitutes a nothing, a formless form, that epistemology cannot accommodate—nor can ontometaphysics.

How does metaphysics provide form for this formlessness, form as *knowledge*? This has been the task of postmetaphysical thinking (from Heidegger onward) to encourage a thinking outside of metaphysics in order to open up a horizon of the unknowable—unknowable within the grammar and logic of metaphysics (a philosophy *against* the dominance of form). But (post)metaphysical thinking has *forgotten* the Negro, much like man has forgotten Being. This forgetfulness is necessary, since to re-member or integrate the Negro would require a contention with this dreaded nothing. Vattimo suggests that "the end of metaphysics is unthinkable without the end of colonialism and Eurocentrism."[22] I would argue that colonialism and Eurocentricism are antiblack strategies for attempting to obliterate, and to forget, dreaded nothing—since black bodies, cultures, and existence are assigned this unbearable formlessness within modernity. Put differently, the human cannot re-member Being (or its primordial relationship with Being as Dasein) *without* re-membering the Negro. The Negro is invented precisely to absorb the terror of this nothing, of the interruption of time and space, within modernity. This is why it is *unthinkable* to end metaphysics without ending the various systems of antiblackness within the world. Antiblackness and its technologies of destruction are designed to obliterate nothing: nothing as formlessness, nothing as interruption, nothing as black, and, ultimately, nothing as the Negro.

But our original, proper metaphysical question, "How is it going with black being?," opens up the dread of this nothing in an antiblack world. The world and its institutions must mute this question, rendering it absurd and irrational, to sustain the whole of metaphysics (or the world itself, as black nihilism would assert). This question is the fundamental formulation of proper inquiries that have guided our thinking: "Why is the Negro black?" "Why is there something rather than nothing?" "What does it mean to be a problem?" The question "How is it going with black being" exposes the problem of metaphysics, the problem with "black" and "nothing" because it compels thinking about the function, status, utility, and necessity of black within an antiblack world. It forces us to entertain the strange juxtaposition between being and black(ness), between formlessness and form colliding on the existence of the Negro. The disruptive question that Dubois posed, then, "What does it mean to be a problem?," invites us to consider the unbearable suffering of inhabiting this problem for metaphysics— what metaphysics despises, what it hates. What it means to be a problem is to exist as an intermediary between form and formlessness, animal and man, property and human, and nothing and something—to "straddle Nothingness and Infinity," as Fanon would say. What it means to be a problem is that this being (being as a problem) renders both "meaning" and "being" impossible and inadequate. The Negro is the limit of both meaning and being and embodies ontological terror (the terror of the nothing within an antiblack world). Moreover, it means that one must embody a nothing that the world works tirelessly to obliterate—which means that the violence directed toward the Negro, black ~~being~~, is gratuitous and will never end as long as metaphysics remains (and postmetaphysics admits that it is impossible to destroy metaphysics. We can only twist it, but there will always be a remainder). It means, to rephrase the perspicacious insight of Hortense Spillers, "The [world] needs [the Negro], and if [the Negro] were not here, ['it'] would have to be invented."

THE INVENTION OF THE NEGRO
AND THE NECESSITY OF BLACK ~~BEING~~

What is this Negro? Negro as black ~~being~~; Negro as nothing. We return endlessly to this metaphysical question and the tension of the copula (the "is-ness" of a [non]~~being~~) that sets the metaphysical inquiry into motion. Perhaps this question cannot be answered with apodictic certainty, since the Negro is neither a proper object of knowledge nor a proper referent (catachresis). What we can propose, however, is that function, or utility, requires an instrument, and instruments are invented for the purpose of fulfilling the agenda of utility. I have suggested thus far that the Negro serves the function of embodying metaphysical nothing(ness) for modernity—a weighty, burdensome, and dangerous function. The world needed a ~~being~~ that would bear the unbearable and live the unlivable; a ~~being~~ that would exist within the interstice of death and life and straddle Nothing and Infinity. The ~~being~~ invented to embody black as nothing is the Negro. An antiblack world desires to obliterate black as nothing—nothing as the limitation of its dominance—so that its schematization, calculation, and scientific practices are met unchecked by this terrifying hole, nothing. With the Negro, metaphysics can triumph over this nothing by imposing black(ness) onto the Negro and destroying the Negro. The Negro is invented precisely to be destroyed—the delusion of metaphysics is that it will overcome nothing through its destruction and hatred of the Negro. The Negro, then, is both necessary and despised.

But it is important to remember that this Negro, the cipher of metaphysics, is the invention of a desperate world. The Negro is not a human being that is simply mistreated, but is, instead, an invention designed to embody a certain terror for the world. I say this because thinking in this way will require us first to discard naturalism and the conflation of human being with black ~~being~~. This is a difficult task because of the ruse of resemblance (the Negro looks human, so must be one). But as Lindon Barrett taught us, modernity produces "anthropomorphic uncertainty" by which "racial blackness overwhelmingly disappoints the modern resemblance of the human, signaling instead the unleashing of the inhuman that specifies the 'human' population of the modern state."[23] Biological and visual resemblance does not render the Negro a human being—these are nothing more than ontic illusions. Ontologically and metaphysically, the Negro is anything but human. Hortense Spillers might call this an "altered human factor." In describing the transport of Africans to Europe, she suggests that they embodied a radical otherness and alterity for the European self. "Once the 'faithless,' indiscriminate of the three stops of Portuguese skin color, are transported to Europe, they become an altered human factor. . . . The altered human factor renders an alterity to European Ego, an invention, or 'discovery' as decisive in the full range of its social implications as the birth of a newborn."[24] Once on European soil (and in the hold of the ship), the African ceases to exist and instead becomes "other," an alteration of humanity. Something new emerges with the transport of the African. The African becomes black ~~being~~ and secures the boundaries of the European self—its existential and ontological constitution—by embodying utter alterity (metaphysical nothing). Metaphysics gives birth to black ~~being~~ through various forms of antiblack violence, and this birth is tantamount to death or worldlessness. The invention, emergence, and birth of black ~~being~~ are not causes for celebration, however, since this invention is pure instrumentality and function (not the existential freedom, self-actualization, or sacred natality of Hannah Arendt and Jean-Luc Nancy, for example).[25] Black ~~being~~ follows a different trajectory than the celebrated human being of metaphysics and ontology.

Its birth is death—death as nothing, death as the Negro, death as blackness, death as the abyss of metaphysics.

It is also important to reiterate that black ~~being~~ and African existence are not synonymous, although we might argue that African existence is transformed into black ~~being~~ through violence, transport, and rituals of humiliation and terror. Bryan Wagner clarifies the distinction:

> Perhaps the most important thing we have to remember about the black tradition is that Africa and its diaspora are older than blackness. Blackness does not come from Africa. Rather, Africa and its diaspora become black during a particular stage in their history . . . blackness is an adjunct to racial slavery . . . blackness is an indelibly modern condition that cannot be conceptualized apart from the epochal changes in travel, trade, labor, consumption, industry, technology, taxation, warfare, finance, insurance, government, bureaucracy, communication, science, religion and philosophy that were together made possible by the European system of colonial slavery. . . . To be black is to exist in exchange without standing in the modern world system.[26]

To "exist in exchange without standing" is pure instrumentality, a ~~being~~ that is not human being, but something other, something unlike what modernity had known before. The disjuncture between being and black ~~being~~ is the gulf of metaphysical and ontological violence. Black ~~being~~, then, does not originate from Africa but is invented in a (non)temporality that we might call the transatlantic slave trade. Put differently, African existence is an identity, whereas black ~~being~~ is a structural position or instrumentality.[27] Identities circulate within the symbolic of humanity; they are discourses of the human (or genres of man, if we follow Sylvia Wynters). Identities provide symbolic covering for the human and differentiate his/her existence, or mode of being, from other human beings. A structural position, on the other hand, ruptures the logics of symbolic identity and constitutes function or instrumentality. Black ~~being~~ is a structural position and not an identity because it exists, or is invented, precisely as an anchor for human identity (human self adequation); the anchor is an inclusive exclusion and subtends human identity but is not incorporated into it. To be positioned structurally and not symbolically means that structural existence is a preconditioned instrument for the maintenance of the symbolic—the symbolic here meaning the signs, symbols, and relationalities of the world itself. A structural position is pure use value (or function), and it lacks value outside its utility and the antiblack symbolic that determines the matrix of value (axiology). This, of course, is in contradistinction to human being, whose ultimate value resides outside the matrix of symbolism and into the esoteric or the horizon of Being-as-event. Black ~~being~~ is the zero-degree position of nonvalue but, paradoxically, is all too valuable because it enables the very system that excludes it (it is valued because of its utter valuelessness). Thus, black ~~being~~ is not birthed into presence through the generosity of Being, contrary to the genealogy of human being articulated by Heidegger and Jean-Luc Nancy, for example; black ~~being~~ is introduced as the execration of Being; its ultimate withholding of generosity, freedom, and care.

Moreover, the distinction between African existence and black ~~being~~ is the site of onticide, or a murderous ontology. What I am suggesting is that black ~~being~~ is the execration of Being because it emerges through a death sentence, through the death of African existence ("existence" is the best we can do grammatically because of the double bind of the copula formulation inherent in language). Black ~~being~~ is the evidence of an onticidal enterprise. Ronald Judy describes this as "thanatology." In describing the coming-into-being of Equiano (an African captive transformed into black ~~being~~, or the Negro), Judy suggests that the death of African materiality and the African symbolic body (or existence) provides the condition of possibility for the transformation. In short, black ~~being~~ emerges through the murder of African existence and not its generosity:

> The death that is emancipating is the negation of the materiality of Africa. Writing the slave narrative is thus a *thanatology,* a writing of annihilation that applies the taxonomies of death in Reason (natural law) to enable the emergence of the self-reflexive consciousness of the Negro . . . writing the death of the African body is an enforced abstraction. It is an interdiction of the African, a censorship to be inarticulate, to not compel, to have no capacity to move, to be without effect, without agency, without thought. The muted African body is overwritten by the Negro, and the Negro that emerges in the ink flow of Equiano's pen is that which has overwritten itself and so become the representation of the very body it sits on.[28]

Judy's argument here is that the Negro is thought to gain a sense of subjectivity by displaying Reason through writing, since writing is prefigured as the ultimate sign of Reason, and Humanity, within an antiblack symbolic order. But to gain this subjectivity, this Negro-ness, he must first kill the African body (African existence). But, I would argue, if reason and humanity are the purported payoffs for a murder, then the Negro has indeed been defrauded. For displaying reason through writing (slave narratives and otherwise) has not folded the Negro into the family of the human [*Mitsein*] or rendered him a subject—there is nothing the Negro can do to change its structural position. Writing, reading, philosophizing, and intellectualizing have all failed as strategies to gain inclusion into human beingness (despite the hopeful insistence of black humanists). Instead, the Negro remains the nothing that metaphysics depends on to maintain its coherence. With the death of African existence, the Negro, or black ~~being~~, is indeed nothing or no-thing that translates into any recognizable ontology. To say that the Negro is nothing is also to say that the Negro lacks ontological ground. The human being grounds its ontology in the beautiful relation between Being and Dasein (or the "space of existence," as Heidegger would call it). Black ~~being~~, however, lacks any legitimate ground, outside the oppressive logics of use value, for its ~~being~~. Since it emerges through the execration of Being and not the gift of Being, it can lay recourse neither to Being nor to a primordial relation (since this primordial relation has been annihilated or murdered as the condition of its existence).

I would also suggest that the Negro is not responsible for this murder. Metaphysics (or the world and its symbolics) systemically murders this relationality, so that to be born black within modernity is to have always already been the material effect of an ontological murder. In other words, antiblackness is the systematic and global death of this primordial relation, and whether the Negro attempts to write him/herself into existence or not, this death has already occurred. When it comes to the Negro, subjectivity is a fraudulent hoax or ruse.

What do I mean by the "execration of Being"? I simply mean the death or obliteration of African existence. This obliteration provides the necessary condition for the invention of the Negro, or black ~~being~~—black as metaphysical nothing or groundless existence. One anchors one's existence in this primordial relation, but the Negro is precisely the absence of such relationality, a novelty for modernity (or a "new ontology," as Frank Wilderson would describe it). The Negro is born into absence and not presence. We can also describe this death of a primordial relation as a "metaphysical holocaust," following Franz Fanon and Frank Wilderson. For Fanon, "Ontology—once it is finally admitted as leaving existence by the wayside—does not permit us to understand the being of the black man . . . the black man has no ontological resistance in the eyes of the white man . . . his metaphysics, or less pretentiously, his customs and the sources on which they are based, were wiped out because they were in conflict with a civilization that he did not know and that imposed itself on him."[29]

Ontology provides intelligibility and understanding for the human being because she is embedded in a primordial relation with Being (as freedom and care). We can describe the entire field of ontology as the history, evolution, and maintenance of the various customs and resources that the human being needs to secure this relation. But "ontology . . . does not permit us to understand the being of the black man" because ontology is intended to preserve the customs and resources of human beingness and not black being. We will always experience tensions, contradictions, and impasses if we attempt to gain intelligibility for black being from a field that excludes it by necessity—because blackness is outside ontology as this nothing but most intimately situated within ontology as its condition of possibility (its inclusive exclusion). Ontology, then, does not provide the resources to understand this paradoxical thing—blackness is the abyss of ontology.[30] But what is worse is that the customs and resources that once served as grounding for African existence were wiped out. This wiping out of the ontological resources to ground this primordial relation is the thanatology or onticide of African being.[31] This metaphysical holocaust is the execration of Being—it is a particular process of producing black being through the murder of African existence.[32]

The execration of Being also conveys Being's curse and denouncement of the Negro as black (I would also suggest that the pseudo-theological term *Hamitic curse* is a variation of this execration in a different register). Rather than thinking of Being as having abandoned us and that this abandonment can be addressed through temporality, thinking anew, and a renewed relation (as is the position of Heidegger and neo-Heideggerians), the execration of Being is beyond abandonment. It indexes the obliteration of the relation to Being and the absolute irreconcilability between the Negro as black and Being. Thus, the nothing that black ~~being~~ incarnates is not a celebratory portal or opening up onto Being for blacks—as if rejecting metaphysical thinking will reunite us, as it were, with Being as nothing.[33] This only works for the human (and the "black is not a man" within an antiblack metaphysics, as Fanon insists).[34] The essence of black suffering, then, is this very execration, to inhabit permanently the "zone of nonbeing," as Fanon might call it. This zone is a spatiotemporality without a recognizable name or grammar within the philosophical tradition. The problem of black ~~being~~ is precisely the inhabitation of an execrated condition. This is the new ontology that modernity brings into the world—a being that is not one (available equipment in the guise of human form). Black ~~being~~ is paradoxical—it is a metaphysical entity that is invented to illumine something beyond metaphysics, a nothing that metaphysics hates and needs. Within the Negro, metaphysics wages its war against the nothing that terrorizes its power and hegemony.

This, again, explains why the Negro is black, to return to Alain David's proper metaphysical question. The Negro is black because *the Negro is the physical manifestation of an ontological puzzle*: *black as nothing*. The field of ontometaphysics does not have the resources to explain nothing; in fact, it works earnestly to forget and avoid it. This is because the field of ontometaphysics is really the imposition of metaphysical prerogatives and investments. Given this arrangement of resources, nothing is not a proper object of knowledge within ontology as metaphysics because it cannot be explained through its episteme (put differently, the incorporation of nothing would destabilize the metaphysical episteme). Or, to echo Fred Moten, "Blackness and ontology are unavailable for one another."[35] This is to suggest that the problems of nothing are transposed onto the Negro, since it is *embodied nothing* within an antiblack world.

When Fanon suggests that the civilization "imposed itself" on the Negro, I interpret this to mean that the imposition is an ontometaphysical imposition; the Negro does not have ontological resistance because of the metaphysical imposition of black and nothing. Furthermore, we can describe the "two frames of reference," as Fanon would call it, within which the Negro has had to place himself as "nothing" and "black" in an antiblack world. This imposition is the execration of Being or the metaphysical holocaust that produces black ~~being~~. For nothing and the terror that it brings to metaphysics can only manifest itself through this holocaust; and this wiping out is not an event of the past, but is a condition of the world. The world needs it to continue. Antiblackness is the name for the continuous destruction of this primordial relation and the structural position of the Negro as black and nothing.

Hortense Spillers also proffers a phenomenological iteration of this metaphysical violence that is very useful to think alongside Fanon's metaphysical holocaust and the imposition of black and *nothing*:

> But I would make a distinction in this case between "body" and "flesh" and impose that distinction as the central one between captive and liberated positions. In that sense, before the "Body" there is the "flesh," that zero degree of social conceptualization that does not escape concealment under the brush of discourse or the reflexes of iconography. Even though the European hegemonies stole bodies—some of them female—out of West African communities in concert with the African "middleman," we regard this human and social irreparability as high crimes against the *flesh*, as the person of African females and males registered the wounding. If we think of the "flesh" as a primary narrative, then we mean its seared, divided ripped-apartness, riveted to the ship's hole, fallen, or "escaped" overboard."[36]

Although Spillers borrows the concepts of "flesh" and "body" from the traditions of phenomenology, psychoanalysis, and theology, she repurposes them to understand the modern invention of black ~~being~~. I would suggest that "flesh" and "body," read through this register, are philosophical allegories, or metaphors, for the execration of Being. The flesh, here, is the primordial relation that antiblackness works tirelessly to destroy. For Spillers, the flesh is a "primary narrative." This primary narrative is the grounding of African existence, the various customs and resources that provide the proper understanding of this existence—what is wiped out during the metaphysical holocaust that we can call the "transatlantic slave trade." The body, however, emerges from the ashes of this holocaust. It is not strictly corporeality (or physicality), but the signification of nothing that the black body comes to mark in an antiblack symbolic (or, as Spillers describes it, "a category of otherness"). Thus, high crimes against the flesh are the murderous operations that set modernity into motion and produce the black body (or black ~~being~~); these crimes are murders that the discourses of crime and punishment can only approach, but remain unintelligible within its precincts. These crimes are ongoing, and since the guilty party is the world itself, redress or justice is impossible. The flesh, the primary narrative, is the ground of an African existence that is irrecoverable within an antiblack world—it is "seared, divided ripped-apartness, riveted to the ship's hole," or "escaped overboard." This, in essence, is the execration of Being. It is the primordial relation between the African and Being that is ripped apart, seared, and severed; this obliterated relation is the high crime against the flesh. We come to another understanding of black ~~being~~: it is the offspring of an obliterated primary narrative that we can call the flesh. Spillers's "flesh" and Judy's "African body" are thus synonymous articulations of this primordial relation.

In this schematic, the body is a metaphor for instrumentality or abject use value. Spillers suggests that this body "is reduced to a thing, to being for the captor." With the death of African existence (the flesh) an oppressive mode of existence is imposed on the Negro. This existence is unlike human being. The human being's mode of existence is to be for itself, and this being for itself is the structure of care between Dasein and Being. Black ~~being~~ is invented, however, precisely to secure the human's mode of existence. Reading Spillers's metaphysical schema through Heidegger's, we could suggest that the black body or this "thing, being for the captor," is invented to serve as the premier tool or equipment for human being's existential project (and I would argue that this equipment is not equivalent in form to the human, even if the structure of tool-being, as Graham Harman would call it, provides a general explanatory frame).[37] In other words, the mode of existence for black ~~being~~ is what Heidegger would call "availableness." Availableness is "the way of being of those entities which are defined by their use in the whole."[38] To exist as "a thing, being for the captor" is to inhabit a mode of existence dominated by internecine use and function. Black ~~being~~, then, is invented not just to serve the needs of economic interest and cupidity, but also to fulfill the ontological needs of the human. This thing is something like Heidegger's equipment—an object that when used with such regularity becomes almost invisible, or transparent, to the user (blackness is often unthought because the world uses it with such regularity; antiblackness is the systemization of both the use of blackness and the forgetting/concealment of black ~~being~~). Utility eclipses the thing itself. We must, then, understand antiblackness as a global, systemic dealing with black bodies, as available equipment. Heidegger considers dealings the way the Being of entities, or equipment, is revealed phenomenologically through the use of this equipment. Antiblack dealings with black bodies do not expose the essential unfolding, or essence, of the equipment; rather, the purpose of antiblack dealings is to systemically obliterate the flesh, and to impose nothing onto that obliterated space—care and value are obsolete in this encounter.[39] Therefore, equipment structure is predicated on the premier use of blacks within the network of equipment. In other words, black use cuts across every equipmental assignment, making it the ultimate equipment. Why does black equipment cut across all assignments, and why is it the tool Dasein relies on to commence its existential journey? We might say the answer to these difficult questions is that the essence of black equipment is nothing—being is not there. If Heidegger assumes that equipment will reveal its being through its usage, then he did not anticipate the invention of the Negro—equipment in human form, embodied nothingness. Using black equipment reveals existence but not being (existence as non-being for Greek philosophers, according to Heidegger in *Introduction to Metaphysics*). This puzzle is what black philosophy must investigate, must think through, to understand the continuity of antiblackness.

Spillers describes black ~~being~~ as a "living laboratory," and we can conceptualize this laboratory as the source of availableness for modernity. A living laboratory is a collection of instruments for carrying out ontological experimentation, or the construction of the human self. Black ~~beings~~ constitute this irresistible source of availableness for the world. Saidiya Hartman meditates on the ontological utility of black ~~being~~ for the human when she states:

> The relation between pleasure and the possession of slave property, in both the figurative and literal senses, can be explained in part by the fungability of the slave—that is, the joy made possible by virtue of the replaceability and interchangeability endemic to the commodity—and by the extensive capacities of property—that is, the augmentation of the master subject through his embodiment in external objects and persons. Put differently, the fungability of the commodity makes the captive body an abstract and empty vessel vulnerable to the projection of others' feelings, ideas, desires, and values; and, as property, the dis-

possessed body of the enslaved is the surrogate for the master's body since it guarantees his disembodied universality and acts as the sign of his power and dominion.[40]

Instruments, tools, and equipment are interchangeable/replaceable; this is starkly different from human being, whose existential journey in the world renders it incalculable and unique. When I suggest that black ~~being~~ is pure function or utility, I mean precisely the way this ~~being~~ is used as a site of projection for the human's desires, fantasies, and ontological narcissism. The body that Spillers presents is a necessary invention because it is through the human's engagement with instruments (tools and equipment) that the human comes to understand the self. To be for the human is to serve as the empty vessel for the human's reflection on the world and self. In short, what I am suggesting is that black ~~being~~ is invented as an instrument to serve the needs of the human's ontological project. This use, or function, exceeds involuntary labor and economic interest. It is this particular antiblack use that philosophical discourse has neglected. The Negro, as invention, is the dirty secret of ontometaphysics.

If we follow Heidegger's understanding of the human being as Dasein (being there) and thrown into the world, then black ~~being~~ emerges as a different entity: the Negro is precisely the permanence of not being there [*Nicht Da Sein*], an absence from ontology, an existence that is not just gone away (as if it has the potential to return to being there) but an existence that is barred from ever arriving as an ontological entity, since it is stripped of the flesh.[41] To assert that black ~~being~~ is not of the world is to suggest, then, that black ~~being~~ lives not just outside of itself, but outside of any structure of meaning that makes such existence valuable. Black ~~being~~ is situated in a spatiotemporality for which we lack a grammar to capture fully. Spillers's body, then, is the symbolic and material signification of absence from Being. To be black and nothing is not to serve as an aperture of Being for the Negro; rather, it is to constitute something inassimilable and radically other, straddling nothing and infinity. The Negro is the execration of Being for the human; it is with the Negro that the terror of ontology, its emptiness, is projected and materialized. This is the Negro's function.

Inventing the Negro is essential to an ontometaphysical order that wants to eradicate and obliterate such ontological terror (the terror of the nothing); and since ontometaphysics is obsessed with schematization and control, it needs the Negro to bear this unbearable burden, the execration of Being. To return to our proper metaphysical question "How is it going with black ~~being~~?," we can say that neither progressive legislation nor political movements have been able to transform black ~~being~~ into human being, from fleshless bodies to recognized ontologies. Spillers also seems to preempt the question when she states, "Even though the captive flesh/body has been 'liberated,' and no one need pretend that even the quotation marks do not matter . . . it is as if neither time nor history, nor historiography and its topics, show movement, as [the flesh] is 'murdered' over and over again by the passions of a bloodless and anonymous archaism, showing itself in endless disguise."[42] This onticide, the death of the flesh/African existence, continues impervious to legal, historical, and political change. This is to say that the problem of black ~~being~~, as both a form of ontological terror for the human and a site of vicious strategies of obliteration, remains. To ask the (un)asked question "How is it going with black ~~being~~?" is to inquire about the resolution of the problem of black and nothing, ontometaphysically, as it imposes itself onto the Negro. The answer to the Negro Question, then, is that the ritualistic and repetitive murder of the flesh, the primordial relation, is absolutely necessary and indispensable in an antiblack world. And as long as the world exists, this murder must continue.

THE FREE BLACK AS A PARADIGM
OF ONTOLOGICAL TERROR

If the essence (the essential unfolding) of politics is nothing political, as Miguel de Beistegui has argued, then we must look elsewhere for this essence, this center of politics that engenders various organizations of existence.[43] The essence of the political (and the law, as I will argue) brings us back to the question of ontometaphysics; for if we follow the thinking of postmetaphysical thought, then politics is an ontic articulation of Being itself—perhaps a structure through which the human inhabits a particular relation with Being through care. This is to suggest that the question of Being is at the very heart of politics; rather than thinking of politics as disinterested in ontology, it is necessary for us to resituate politics as a premier ontological enterprise—although politics will disavow and suppress such interests. Antebellum politics is no exception. The various debates about black citizenship, freedom, and slavery in the nineteenth century are deceptively philosophical—deceptive precisely because a surface reading of these issues can present them as merely part of the evolution of politics, its bloody and contentious process. But to suggest that the question of Being is at the very heart of these debates is to suggest the essence of these debates must return us to the question of Being itself. Furthermore, the question of black ~~being~~, the problem at the center of ontometaphysics, is the essence of antebellum politics in the nineteenth century. Antebellum politics circulates around the problem of black ~~being~~, the ontological terror that black ~~being~~ is forced to bear in an antiblack world. Antebellum politics is a structure of antiblackness, designed to discipline and obliterate black ~~being~~. Although we can correctly identify certain legislation, writing, and political maneuvers as unjust and inhumane—one only needs to think of the Dred Scott decision, Thomas Jefferson's *Notes on the State of Virginia*, or the Fugitive Slave Act of 1850—I want to understand this injustice as absolutely necessary; necessary because black ~~being~~ is the target of gratuitous violence within an antiblack world, a violence that is essential to the world itself. Thus, the violence that we register as unjust or inhumane—the laceration of the whip, the canine patrol, exclusionary procedures, disenfranchisement, anti-literacy laws, and routinized humiliation and invasion, for example—are ways a metaphysical organization of existence (antebellum politics) contends with black as nothing.

Nahum Chandler, in his beautiful philosophical meditation *X: The Problem of the Negro as a Problem for Thought*, would describe antebellum politics, law, and culture as resting on a certain "metaphysical infrastructural organization" that is often "not so recognized and is far less often thought."[44] Any discussion of a historical subject, white subject, and especially the Negro is enabled by this infrastructure, which bears the weight of the culture in question and its devastating violence. In other words, this metaphysical infrastructure already presumes certain pure ontological positions, and these positions enable the unjust and inhumane. Chandler would argue that the Negro brings into relief the problem of purity—since its ontological constitution presents a problem for thought. Purity, then, constitutes a metaphysical fiction (and a racial privilege), and we could argue that ontological terror is precisely the threat the Negro poses, as always undoing ontological purity with contamination. But the project of purity, I would argue, is a response to the problem of black as nothing—where purity becomes a discourse of this nothing, its symptom or materialization. Antebellum culture deploys the discourse of purity (and its anxiety concerning amalgamation and integration) as a cover for the ontological terror at the heart of the metaphysical infrastructure. Put differently, this infrastructure is precarious and always at risk by its own invention, black ~~being~~, stripped of its primary narrative (the flesh). This, then, is the double bind of the metaphysical infrastructure (or the "whole of metaphysics," as Heidegger would call it): black ~~being~~ is a necessary invention because it bears the nothing, which is uncontrollable with metaphysical instruments, but black ~~being~~ is also hated because its presence is a reminder that the human being itself is a metaphysical fiction—the very ground of humanity is precarious and unreliable (or, as Fanon avers, "Man is nothing, absolutely nothing"). It is at this tension (between necessity and hatred) that ontological terror turns into forms of physical, emotional, and psychic devastation. But we must also take very seriously Chandler's statement that this metaphysical structure is "not so recognized and is far less often thought." This structure is often not recognized and unthought because we think politics, law, and culture on its surface and not its depth (its essence), the structure upon which it rests—thus, we rarely understand that politics is the symptom of this tense metaphysical structure. *Ontological Terror* is an attempt to expose this infrastructure and its presumptions. But to do this, we must think otherwise, or, as Miguel de Beistegui argues, we must look elsewhere for the essence of politics, law, and culture.[45]

It is with this strategy of thinking otherwise, of being mindful of the metaphysical structure that goes undetected, that I understand the antebellum free black as a paradigm of ontological terror. For at least syntactically, the term *free black* holds the tension of this metaphysical infrastructure: to be free is much more than a legal status (although it is often reduced to this); it is an onto-existential condition in which the human can engage in its primordial relation (between self, Being, and its unique project of care). Freedom, then, is the condition of the free, and it indicates a certain ontological orientation in an antiblack world. "Black," however, is the ~~being~~ stripped of this primary narrative, a ~~being~~

that is the target of antiblack violence, since black and nothing become synonymous. In an antiblack world, black ~~being~~ can never be free but can be emancipated—but emancipation fails to resolve the metaphysical problem of black as nothing, which is necessary for anything like black freedom to exist. As long as a metaphysical world exists, a world that obliterates nothing, blacks will never be free. The free black presents syntactical devastation in that it knots human being with black ~~being~~ and freedom with unfreedom. If we read this syntactical chaos as a symptom of the tension at the heart of the metaphysical infrastructure (necessity and hatred), then we understand that the concept of the free black is a problem for thought. One cannot think the free black within an antiblack world without resorting to the fantastical and the absurd.

The free black threatens metaphysical purity by releasing this nothing into the realm of the human—which, of course, is exactly what an *antiblack* world is designed to prevent. This signifier terrorizes, and the beings inhabiting the position "free black" also terrorize, as they become the materialization of this threat to human being. When I suggest that the free black is a paradigm of ontological terror, I do this as an attempt to think otherwise, to think the metaphysical infrastructure that often goes undetected. Thinking through paradigms provides a strategy for this type of thinking. The strategy of the paradigm, according to Agamben, is to juxtapose two entities until at a point of concentration, or intensity, so that they reveal aspects of each other. Entities within a paradigmatic analysis become allegories of each other. One example, or instance, is used to provide insight into another.[46] I think about the free black as an allegory of the problem of metaphysics and the problem of metaphysics as an allegory of the free black. Thus, although the free black marks a particular phenomenological and historical instance (as distinct from other forms of black existence), we can read the free black allegorically to provide insight into the metaphysical infrastructure that goes unnoticed.

Free blacks were situated in diverse geographical locations—the upper South, the deep South, the North, the Midwest; despite these diverse geographical locations and the different forms of antiblack violence each location deployed, the problem of antiblackness and the problem of black ~~being~~ remained a constant.[47] The discourse and debates concerning antebellum free blacks orbit around a tension, an unanswered question, that irrupts in forms of paradox and impasse. The Negro Question, then, presents itself as a political discourse, one obsessed with black citizenship, political inclusion, and rights. But the Negro Question is rooted in a metaphysical infrastructure that attempts to police the boundaries between the white human and its black equipment. This infrastructure is threatened, however, with the presence of the free black, and it is the free black that becomes the obsession of this question. Since the free black knots freedom with unfreedom and human with nonhuman, the boundary between the ontological entities (white human and black slave) unravels. What I am suggesting is that the political discourse about free black citizenship is the articulation of a metaphysical anxiety, one that threatens antebellum culture. Moreover, the Negro Question is, as I have suggested, a proper metaphysical question, since at its core it inquires whether black ~~being~~ can transform into human being. The free black brings this question to the fore in a way that the slave does not. The condition of the slave is one of property, the condition of invention and perverse utility. This, of course, is what modernity intended for black ~~being~~—that it would serve the world as pure function, property, and use. But the word *free* in the term *free black* is more than a legal designation; it is an inquiry into the metaphysical structure itself. For if black being is brought into the world as utility (as Justice Roger Taney would argue in the Dred Scott decision), then a free black would index a different mode of black ~~being~~. Is such a different mode of ~~being~~ possible in an antiblack world? The word *free* absorbs all these metaphysical inquiries and anxieties.

This is precisely why the free black is such an important paradigm of ontological terror: because the free black resituates politics and exposes the metaphysical infrastructure. Thus, when Humen Humphrey, the second president of Amherst College, writes in *The African Repository* that free blacks "are not looked upon as men, in the true and proper sense of the term," he is responding to the proper metaphysical question: can black ~~being~~ transform into human being?[48] Following Humphrey, freedom indexes the "true and proper" sense of man; the truth of man can be located in his primordial relation to Being. But black ~~being~~ lacks this properness, as it marks the execration of Being, and the metaphysical transformation that the word *free* is designed to indicate utterly fails. The free black is a problem for an antiblack world in that his challenge to the metaphysical structure leaves him without a proper place or any metaphysical position that is intelligible.

This lack of properness and metaphysical truth is a symptom of the nothing, for nothing lacks any proper place in metaphysics and cannot be understood through its episteme. Black ~~being~~ as nothing, then, will always be out of place and improper in an antiblack world. It is the terror of the metaphysical infrastructure, and one can never be a true or proper man when one bears the weight of nothing. Through this analysis, we can understand the anxiety concerning black ~~being~~, placement, and nothing in antebellum culture.

In August 1842, for example, the free black population of Philadelphia held a parade commemorating the abolition of slavery in the West Indies. An angry mob of white citizens disrupted the parade, attacked participants, and commenced to destroy black homes and property. Seeking redress through the courts for loss of property and injury, the free black population realized that justice within such a context was impossible, as the grand jury acquitted the rioters and blamed free blacks for inciting this violence. Robert Purvis, a leader in the free black population of Philadelphia, responded to the grand jury's decision with dismay:[49] "The measure of our suffering is full. . . . From the most painful and minute investigation, in the feelings, views and acts of this community—in regard to us—*I am convinced of our utter and complete nothingness* in public estimation [emphasis mine]."[50]

What sparked the riot, this devastating expression of antiblackness? We can locate this eruption of violence at the metaphysical fault line between necessity and hatred. Black ~~being~~ is both a necessary instrument for the human's self-constitution and an object of ferocious hatred, since it bears the nothing of a metaphysical order. In other words, the riot is the symptom of a metaphysical problem: the public celebration of black freedom sparks a terror in that ontological boundaries are challenged and the transformation from black ~~being~~, as invention/instrument, to human being, as free, is not only considered but celebrated. It is also no surprise that the grand jury blamed the victims for the riot, since black freedom is a form of violence for the human, a violence that must be met with extreme force. The riot is a response to ontological terror. "Free," when paired with "black," is recast as a weapon against the human and the metaphysical structure that sustains the human. We are dealing with two registers of violence—one is an ontological violence and another is a physical form of antiblack destruction.

But Purvis's response to the violence is perspicuous. He is "convinced of our utter and complete nothingness in public estimation." If we read this statement as a mere political lamentation, that blacks constitute a political cypher (nothingness) within the law and political processes, then we limit our understanding of the riot as event. The riot, within this reading, is just a form of cruelty or irrational intolerance or a political-economic strategy of subjection. With political readings of antiblack violence, violence is not gratuitous but must be linked to some type of recognizable transgression; when antiblack violence cannot be linked to recognizable transgression, it is considered cruel or irrational—a form of individual pathology and not systemic necessity. If, however, the essence of politics is nothing political, then we might read Purvis's political commentary as a response to the proper metaphysical question. His answer is that black being is nothingness in public estimation. We can understand nothingness as the condition (-ness) of bearing nothing in an antiblack world. Antiblack violence, then, constitutes the structure of this nothing. Black being is always already under attack; peace, within an antiblack world, is a fallacy (much like freedom). The metaphysical infrastructure that supports the fiction of the white human is sustained by antiblack violence. The riot is an ontological necessity, not just political cruelty. We can understand the grand jury's decision philosophically: Being black is both the cause and effect of violence, and when this being claims freedom, extreme violence is always justified and necessary.

After the egregious *Dred Scott* ruling, free blacks protested the decision. But one response to the decision in the *Liberator* intimates the lack of proper place within both politics and law: "[It is] already [a] well known fact that under the Constitution and Government of the United States, *the colored people are nothing, and can be nothing but an alien, disfranchised and degraded class* [emphasis mine]."[51]

The nothing that black being constitutes here is what Jared Sexton would call a "null status."[52] The alien is precisely this improper position, as out of place and, in essence, inhabiting no place within the world at all. This, perhaps, is what it means for black being to ek-sist, not just outside of one's self but outside of the world. Degradation and unfreedom are the manifestations of this nothing, a status within law and politics that is empty—void of the flesh and any substance of biofuturity. Again, on one register we could identify this nothing that the "colored people" constitute as the political cypher, a pariah class within an (un)democratic arrangement of power; but what undergirds this political reading is an ontological reading—since the political reading takes the metaphysical infrastructure for granted and builds upon it. In other words, the null status that translates into political forms of disenfranchisement and degradation depends on the exclusion of black ~~being~~ from the realm of humanity. The "colored people" are nothing precisely because they are not viewed as men in the "true and proper sense," as Humphrey argued (indeed, nothing could never be a proper man within science and philosophy—only a hologram of sorts). The response in the *Liberator* provides an answer to the metaphysical question: the transmogrification between property and human, what we would call "freedom" politically, is deceptive; it is merely a political procedure that is unable to resolve an ontological problem. The problem of black ~~being~~ remains, despite the nominal status "free black." Political oppression is a symptom of the metaphysical dilemma of knotting black ~~being~~ with human freedom. This conceptualization is so threatening and catachrestic that it can only be described as "nothing." But this nothing is not synonymous with nonexistence—once we have put existence by the wayside, as Fanon would suggest—but it is an index of a lack of ontological resistance. *Free* in the term *free black* does not restore ontological resistance (the flesh); it relegates black ~~being~~ to the abyss of the metaphysical infrastructure, the nothing that preconditions politics and law.

The response, then, could also be read as juxtaposing two grammars—the political/juridical and the ontological—to articulate the dilemma of black ~~being~~ within these two registers of existence. The "alien, disfranchised and degraded class" is an index of political violence, but the nothing interposes the ontological register. Neither register provides safe haven or existential (biofuturistic) possibility for black ~~being~~. If the human can at least make recourse to the ontological, the primordial relation, to ground being against political violence, black ~~being~~ is unable to find any resolution in the ontological, as the ontological does not provide an explanation for its ~~being~~—if we follow Fanon. The free black is the sign of a double violence, an onticide, on two registers of existence that would provide value and meaning for being. This fundamental lack of value and meaning is the crisis, or urgency, that the Negro Question is designed to invoke. We get a sense of this in another submission to *The African Repository*:

"Introduced among us by violence, notoriously ignorant, degraded and miserable, mentally diseased, broken spirited, acted upon by no motive to honorable exertions, scarcely reached in their debasement by heavenly light the [free blacks] wander unsettled and unbefriended through our land, or sit indolent, abject and sorrowful, by the streams which witness their captivity."[53]

This wandering assumes a metaphorical and literal instantiation, since black ~~being~~, lacking grounding in both ontology and politics/law, moves and floats throughout the world, without a proper place or any geography that could be identified as home. The free black, unbefriended, indolent, "abject," and "sorrowful," lacks political constituency that is recognized by politics and law (as Justice Roger Taney argued) and is situated in an abyss that is "scarcely reached . . . by heavenly light" (i.e., the Negro as black metaphysically).

Another author, keen to this movement, describes it this way in *The African Repository*: "They [free blacks] remain as a *floating body* in our midst, drifting, as the census table shows, hither and thither, as the effects of climate at the North, or foreign emigration at the East, or prejudices at the South, repel it from the points. It is an interesting subject of investigating to watch the movements of the colored population, and ascertain where they are tending and *whither they will find a resting place* [emphasis mine]."[54]

The "floating body" is an allegorical sign of the nothing that lacks form or placement within a political/ontological landscape (a sign of formlessness). It floats "hither and thither" in the interstitial crevices of existence, without a resting place. A certain liquidity marks the existence of the free black, and the Census attempts to capture something that is difficult—the problem of black ~~being~~. The conjoining of the words *free* and *black*, the domain of the human and the domain of the ontological instrument, opens up this problem discursively and presents it as an incessant movement between established properties (or the "in-between" as Nahum Chandler would call it). The North, South, East, and West are not only geographical regions in the United States, regions that have either barred free blacks from entry or made their residence miserable, but also allegories of livability and the world itself. To ek-sist outside oneself and the world means that one lacks a space of life, meaning, and futurity. Black

~~being~~ is barred from cartographies of livability in much the same way the free black is excluded from states and localities.[55]

We must also remember that this floating body is also a form of terror, ontological terror. For nothing terrorizes the human by rendering the metaphysical infrastructure fallible; its claim to truth is secured only though tremendous violence— antiblack violence. We can read the danger that the free black presents to antebellum culture as particular terror for the human. A contributor to *The African Repository* urges readers to contend with this danger:

> In order to estimate correctly the magnitude of the evil, which will come upon us, unless we take steps in time to arrest the danger, we need only consider the paid increase of the black population in the United States since 1800 . . . the free blacks are also increasing with fearful rapidity, especially in the Southern states. We should not shut our eyes to the danger until it comes upon us in all its fearfulness, but with a wise foresight and manly resolution we should now take the necessary steps to avoid it. It is our duty, then, to commence an early and energetic and systematic movement to prevent the danger . . . it is evident that we must devise some scheme to get clear of the free black population, which is becoming an incubus upon all the states. . . . Tennessee at this time, has not a very large free black population, and we can, if we will commence in time, get rid of them at but little expense, but if we defer the matter much longer the evil will grow upon us in a fearful manner.[56]

This danger assumes a theological and ethical dimension, an evil of tremendous magnitude. For the contributor, the increase in the free black population is a danger to the nation—black presence and danger assume a pernicious interchangeability in this calculus. The objective is for the nation to get rid of them before the danger grows. Part of the contributor's thinking is embedded in the strategy of relocation—in particular, the colonization scheme. Removing the free black presence from U.S. soil becomes an ethical and theological imperative, since this presence threatens to destroy the nation, a political eschatology in which blackness is refigured as the end of days, the end of the order of things. But what about the black presence is so threatening? It seems that freedom and blackness are incompatible concepts for many antebellum thinkers; in particular, blacks are incapable of bearing the burden of freedom. This incompatibility unravels society and produces blacks that are "notoriously ignorant, degraded and miserable, mentally diseased, broken spirited, and acted upon by no motive to honorable exertions." What the contributor is intimating is that the transmogrification between ontological instrument (or equipment) and the human is a destructive enterprise, since it defies the function of black ~~being~~ in modernity. Reading the contributor, it is almost as if emancipation creates monsters from within the laboratory of culture (or what Hortense Spillers would call the "cultural vestibular-ity"). And the ethical and theological implication of this monstrosity can only be captured through the sign of evil. Sylvia Wynter remarks that the Negro must stand in for "all that is evil" to provide the axiological and theological grounding for the human, along skin difference.[57] As available instrument, without flesh or ontological resistance, the Negro stands at the threshold between heaven and hell, a position without any ethical or moral equivalent—a nothing within the symbolic of ethics, morality, or theology. It is this position, as the wretched threshold, that constitutes the evil the contributor imagines. The nation, then, must excise the danger to restore itself. What the author describes as an evil is the ontological function of black ~~being~~: to absorb the anxieties, the violation of sacred boundaries, and the execration of Being.

In other words, we might formulate a link between the discourse of evil and that of the nothing. For nothing is pure execration itself—cursed by Being and by God. Having been cursed, the wretched (non)thing of metaphysics, stained by blackness, terrorizes moral and ethical boundaries of properness. Because the Negro violates sacred boundaries between freedom and humanity, righteousness and whiteness, and blackness and abjection, it is evil. Or the Negro is out of place (and without a place) and collapses metaphysical meaning, as Julia Kristeva would understand abjection.[58] And according to Wynters, this evil cannot serve as a proper object of knowledge or, might I add, a proper object of politics and law.

The condition of the antebellum free black, one in which the technologies of antiblackness render it an object of hatred, mimes or allegorizes the condition of the nothing in an antiblack world as the hated thing that must be destroyed at all cost.[59] The paradigm between the antebellum free black and the (non)metaphysical nothing reaches a point of intense intersection and saturation in which the antebellum free black must *embody* the nothing of this metaphysics. Antebellum culture is an *instance* of an antiblack organization of existence, a microcosm of an *antiblack world*; and the anxiety and hatred that it directs against the free black is its attempt to contend with nothing in its historical instantiation. The free black and antebellum cultures constitute two aspects of a *war without end*. The war is much more pernicious than antebellum society's desire to maintain white supremacy and dominance; it is but one global example of the obsession with destroying this nothing, manifested as the black Negro.

Citizens of Illinois also expressed similar sentiment in that the situation with free blacks was so dire that "[they] would take the matter into [their] own hands, and commence a war of extermination."[60] A participant at an Indiana convention was explicit about the necessity of the violence against the free black: "It would be better to kill them off at once, if there is no other way to get rid of them. After all, we know how the Puritans did with the Indians, who were infinitely more magnanimous and less impudent than the colored race."[61] Extermination and brute force are the responses to the terror that is the free black. The terror that interrupts and fractures the metaphysical infrastructure—the formless nothing that disturbs the form of the human's existential meaning and grounding—must be removed or eliminated. If we rely on a mere political reading of this desire for extermination, we end up in the terrain of the irrational and the cruel. But this reading misses the crucial point that violence against black ~~being~~ is gratuitous precisely because an antiblack world will continuously and relentlessly attempt to eliminate the nothing that is the evil, black Negro (i.e., there isn't a solution or analysis of the violence that aligns with political reasoning or calculus). The gratuity of violence—in all its manifestations—is an ontological problem.

CODA: THE NEGRO QUESTION

What I have attempted to do in this chapter is to nestle into the philosophical crevices of an "unasked question," as Fred Moten describes it in the opening epigraph. Perhaps the question of the meaning of black ~~being~~ is unanswerable because we've lacked a philosophical tradition that would provide refuge and clarity—this is the ultimate meaning of ontometaphysical homelessness. Given that ontology does not provide the resources to understand the ~~being~~ of the black (Fanon) and epistemology is unable to present this ~~being~~ as a proper object of knowledge (Wynters), the question is a profound conundrum, one that we must continue to sing or orbit around. What I have proposed is merely a path toward an exploration of this great abyss. The Negro Question, as I have argued, is an ontometaphysical question, or as Heidegger has called it, a "proper metaphysical question." For the Negro Question gets at the bottom of the ontometaphysical infrastructure, since it is the Negro that, paradoxically, both enables and disables such a structure. But if an answer to a proper metaphysical question does not do away with the question, then the path that I have laid out will produce more questions, more discomforts, and more anxieties. This is unavoidable, given the position of black(ness). My proposition is this: to approach this abyss, the Negro Question, we must first understand the ontological dimensions of terror—for it is this terror that sustains the ontometaphysical infrastructure. In an antiblack, metaphysical world, the object of this terror is nothing. But since nothing itself is impossible to target, given that it fractures the ontic sciences and its instruments (and is not an apprehensible object through these discourses), this nothing must be imposed onto bodies (ontological instruments). Black ~~being~~ is the embodiment of this nothing, and it is black ~~being~~ that is targeted with an unending violence (gratuitous violence). Antiblackness is essentially anti-nothing. Ontological terror, then, is antiblack technologies, tactics, and practices of nothing eradication. But this enterprise attempts an impossible task, and because it is impossible, it will continue obsessively after its impossible object (like the Lacanian drive).[62] Violence against black ~~being~~ will continue until metaphysics itself is destroyed.

Approaching an ontometaphysical form of terror is a difficult enterprise, but I have chosen a paradigmatic approach (following the example of Agamben) to lead me in this direction. The antebellum free black is important, since (1) the Negro Question has often *centered* the free black as the problem, a problem that must be resolved with forms of violence (any analysis of the free black [historical or philosophical] will carry this question with it as part of the investigation); and (2) the free black both *allegorizes* ontological terror and itself is an *instance* of ontological terror. Paradigms allegorize an example by taking the example out of its context, but it also brings the allegorical parallel structure to an intense point of saturation and intersection, thus rendering the decontextualized example an instance of the very thing it is intended to allegorize.[63] This, for me, is the necessity of the free black, since what emerges from the tension between the terms *free* and *black* is precisely the terror of nothing. The free black is catachrestic and imaginary ontologically for antebellum thinkers. The semantic confusion masks a more insidious terror—the free black as the destabilization of the metaphysical structure. If the human is to maintain its fiction of ontological coherence, it *must* exterminate the problem. But extermination is not a solution because, as Frank Wilderson has persuasively argued, "Without the Negro, capacity itself is incoherent, uncertain at best."[64] This is the tension between necessity and hatred (and the *same* tension between metaphysics and nothing). Without the Negro, the narcissistic coherence of the human being dissolves, but with the Negro the terror persists. There is no *out* to this deadlock. And this is why the Negro Question is unanswerable and has often remained unasked philosophically and historically.

What follows is my attempt to ask the unasked question, a proper metaphysical question—which will inevitably lead to more questions. Each chapter is a meditation on an aspect of this question through the paradigm of the free black.

TWO

==

OUTLAWING

In the *Weltanschauung* of a colonized people there is an impurity, a flaw that outlaws any ontological explanation. Someone may object that this is the case with every individual, but such an objection merely conceals a basic problem. Ontology—once it is finally admitted as leaving existence by the wayside— does not permit us to understand the being of the black man. The black man has no ontological resistance in the eyes of the white man.
FRANTZ FANON, *Black Skin, White Masks*

The essence of law is not legal. . . . The essence of law is distorted in its ontic occurrence. . . . The Being of law is the unfolding of law. . . . We need to think through the essence of law in the order of Being.
OREN BEN-DOR, *Thinking about Law: In Silence with Heidegger*

THE IMPURITY AND THE FLAW

What will preoccupy our investigation here is the relation, or (non)rela-tion, between black ~~being~~, law, and ontology. How exactly does the law produce and reproduce forms of terror that are ontological—meaning laws that sustain the metaphysical holocaust? As we unravel the layers of metaphysical violence occurring over deep time, we realize that law emerges as a crucial aspect of this violence. My concern is not a particular law, but that all laws are subordinate to a Law. The distinction between law and Law is the distinction between metaphysics and ontology that will serve as a heuristic guide in this investigation. I have argued that the ontological difference is not an issue for black ~~being~~, since available equipment cannot present a proper ontological question—it lacks Being (one must present a proper metaphysical question without any hope of ontological explanation). But we use the distinction between metaphysics and ontology as a way to understand, to the extent that we can do so, the multilayered manifestations of this terror.

Fanon builds a way into this (non)relation when he suggests, "There is an impurity, a flaw that outlaws any ontological explanation." Black ~~being~~ is a certain contamination or imperfection within the precincts of ontometaphysics. And understanding or explaining this contamination (hermeneutics and epistemology, for example) not only is impossible with the instruments of ontology (since it does not permit us to understand black ~~being~~) but is also outlawed—prohibited or forbidden. We might ask, then, what form of law both forbids ontological explanation and renders such explanation (and ~~being~~) contaminated? Fanon adumbrates an ontological law, which manifests in other forms of phenomenological-existential violence. But ontology must outlaw ontological terror, since it presents its field as pure (i.e., Being is impervious to politics, violence, and terror), and violence within this field is an incomprehensible contamination. Thinking with the free black, we will investigate this practice of outlawing and the challenge it presents to postmetaphysics and black humanism.

Our investigation will propose the following: (1) There is a fundamental distinction between law (metaphysical incarnation) and Law (the ontological dimension). (2) Both the law and the Law outlaw black ~~being~~, by necessity. The prohibition on black ~~being~~, then, occurs on both the ontological and ontic levels. This collusion contaminates ontology, so black ~~being~~ is prohibited and is an inclusive exclusion. (3) The free black, as paradigm, presents both an allegory and instance of this violence on both levels through reification (freedom papers), temporal suspension, ontological insecurity (kidnapping), and a gifted self, which lacks ipseity. (4) A fundamental gap between freedom and emancipation exists that black humanists have collapsed in their philosophical romance. Black ~~being~~ only has access to emancipation, never freedom. Emancipation is an aperture on the domain of terror and not self-adequation.

Our investigation will proceed by reading Fanon alongside the postmetaphysical thinking of Heidegger, Nancy, and Ben-Dor to understand the essence of law as nothing other than antiblackness. Fanon presents an alternative essence that postmetaphysical legal theorists and philosophers have neglected because it defies explanation. The aim here is to trace out the techniques and strategies of outlawing and to demonstrate that these tactics and strategies are forms of terror for black ~~being~~—ontological terror. Ultimately, we arrive at the conclusion that the free black exists to not exist.

THE LAW OF BEING AND THE BEING OF LAW

We cannot think the essence of Law without the execration, the nothing, of black ~~being~~. For this execration constitutes an unresolvable exception within the order of Being. What is the essence of Law? What is the exception that black ~~being~~ inhabits? I suggest that these two questions fold into each other, almost becoming indistinguishable, and the geometry of this enfolding is what Heidegger would call "ontological difference." In other words, the essence of Law and the exception of black ~~being~~ are both problems of ontological difference: one a problem of distortion/deferral and the other a problem of exclusion (or inclusive exclusion). The question of Law is inseparable from the question of black ~~being~~.

What sustains the law, or provides the condition of law's possibility, is ontological difference itself. We can think of the essence of law not as a scientific thing or a metaphysical object of knowledge, but as an unfolding of Being through law, which mediates through ontic distortion. Following Heidegger, we understand that ontological difference is that primordial (non)relation between Being and being in which being represents itself through metaphysical predispositions within the world, predispositions that forget the grandeur of Being,[1] and Being presents itself to being against (and through) the distorted screen of metaphysics (i.e., the *restriction* of being as primarily representation, correlation, object, and predictability). Ontological difference is sustained through ontic distortion, since this distortion both conceals Being (enables its withdrawal) and occasions Being's revealing or unfolding. The aim of a postmetaphysical enterprise, then, is to develop strategies to address this distortion so that the *essence* is revealed in its truth.

Since Being infuses itself into every facet of human existence, ontological difference and distortion are also issues for law. The metaphysical predispositions of law—the amendments, regulations, mandates, and legislations (what I will call the "being of law")—distort the Law of Being [*Dikē*]. The Law of Being, or the order and call of Being in relation to human being, is one of abandonment. Being's Law is that the human fully gives himself to the ban (to exist in unbridled abandonment toward Being), the order of Being, which is nothing other than abandonment itself. I will expound on abandonment further as the argument unfolds, but for our purpose here, the point is that law is also a feature of a distorted ontological difference: between the Law of Being (ontology) and the being of law (law's metaphysical incarnation as decree, formalist science, legislation). The relation between law's essence, Being-as-essence unfolding through law, and law's juridical and legislative incarnation is not only the precondition for anything like citizenship, justice, freedom, and political community to have any existence or meaning at all in the world, but also the space of a pernicious terror, what I will call "ontological terror," from which black ~~being~~ as exception emerges.

Distortion, then, not only conceals Being within the metaphysical precincts of law, but also conceals the breakdown of the ontological difference—the terror at the heart of the ontological distinction. What I am suggesting here is that we must push the fact of the black-as-nothing to its extreme consequence: if the black is available equipment, a body without flesh, then the ontological distinction is not an issue for it (it is only an issue for the human). The ontological difference that preconditions the human's freedom and citizenship, for example, is not a difference that provides grounding for the black as available equipment. In essence, black ~~being~~ is the physical incarnation of distortion, on another register, a register that provides the condition of possibility for the ontological difference so sacred to postmetaphysicians. The physical black body is a distortion and an ontic illusion. This black body, as equipment, cannot appeal to Being for grounding, freedom, or futurity, since it emerges as a thing for the human to understand ontological difference (by using black equipment—both ready-at-hand and present-at-hand—the human understands his there-ness within the world of objects, his historical place). Black ~~being~~ is a distortion to the extent that the black body conceals the breakdown of the ontological difference. Black ~~being~~, as equipment, is not ontological but other, something we lack a proper grammar to describe—there isn't a distinction apart from the metaphysical that can protect black ~~being~~ in an antiblack world. Thus, we cannot truly posit a fundamental difference between the metaphysical, antiblack body of commerce and an ontology beyond, or in spite of, this body. Asserting this "beyond" is the aspiration of black humanists and postmetaphysicians, which I believe is flawed. This poses a particular problem for law, however, since black ~~being~~ necessitates a perversion of law's function and objective ontologically.

To understand this function and objective of law, we must return to the ontological difference that is an issue for the human. In *Thinking about Law: In Silence with Heidegger*, Oren Ben-Dor understands law as a feature of Heidegger's ontological difference, and from this difference we can envision an ethics that emerges from the Order of Being. Although Heidegger does not write explicitly about law (at least not with the metaphysical expectations of legal theorists and lawyers), his insight into the Greek word *dikē* provides an opening onto a postmetaphysical analysis of law. Ben-Dor revisits Heidegger's critique of metaphysical thinking through his engagement with Plato's *Republic* in the essays "The Scope and Context of Plato's Meditation on the Relationship of Art and Truth," "The Anaximander Fragment," and "The Limitation of Being" (published in *Introduction to Metaphysics*). According to Ben-Dor, Dikē "has three senses, all interconnected: of order [*fug* in the German], of protection and of justice. [These are] the threefold senses of the essence of law distorted in the ontic for-the-most-part being and thinking with and through law."[2] Furthermore, Ben-Dor suggests that "*Dikē* connotes the protection offered to the guardian of Being [Dasein] against the harm done to it by the entrenched legal," and this is the "Law of the Being of being."[3]

Ben-Dor's philosophical rereading of Heidegger's work is sophisticated and complex, but what I find particularly illuminating, and what I will focus on here, is the *function* of law that he presents. He seems to suggest that the function of law—the metaphysical incarnation of it—is to *protect* and *enforce* the unfolding of Being or the primordial relation between the human and Being. This function is distorted, however, by an ontic legalism (or science of law), which focuses on calculating injury, objectifying redress, schematizing rights/privileges, and predicting consequences. What redress, rights, and consequences all conceal is their fundamental relationship to Being. In other words, you have rights to protect and sustain your relation with Being against forces designed to pulverize it (what we call "injury"). The self that anchors rights discourse, injury, and privilege becomes an ersatz, or insufficient, substitute for a (non)relation between the human's there-ness and Being. Returning to this primordial function of law, as protecting the unfolding of Being, helps us to sort through the seductions of legalism—that is, the proposed legal solutions to the problems of injury just sustain it, since these solutions forget Being. In short, as read through Heidegger and Ben-Dor, injury is the consequence of forgetting Being and distorting the function of this tool for the guardian of Being—to protect and enforce this (non)relation.

I would also suggest, following Heidegger and Ben-Dor, that "Ethics" and "Freedom" are two proper names for protecting and enforcing this (non)relation. Within the corpus of law, both freedom and ethics orbit around the protection of this self (the primordial relation) from the injuries of indignity and denial. Or, as Ben-Dor states, "To let *Dasein* gain ground, to let *Dasein* ground as one with the simple unity of the fourfold, is to be ethical. To let *Dasein* be open towards its unfolding world as the grounding of its nearest is ethical. To protect and enforce such ground is the essence of law."[4]

The law is an ontological instrument. Its purpose is distorted by the supremacy of metaphysical imperatives and objectives. But within this primordial function, we must tease out another distinction: the Law of Being and the being of law. What I have discussed thus far is the being of law—the metaphysical instrument designed to protect and enforce the Law of Being. The being of law is something akin to the executive agency of the Law of Being. Our legislative decrees, policies, and rights are all subordinate to the Law of Being.

ABANDONMENT AND OUTLAWING

What is the Law of Being? If we think of Law as the *order* of Being [*dikē*], then we understand this order, not just as a realm or field (e.g., like a political order), but also as a *command* (e.g., an order from a parental figure) of its particular saying, demand, or requirement. Perhaps the *realm* of Being is nothing more than this *command* itself. The Law of Being, then, is the *order* of Being—what it requires and how this requirement sustains Being (since the human is the *guardian* of Being and Being *needs* this guardianship, or care, to manifest). But this order is peculiar, and it confounds our diurnal (and metaphysical) understanding of a law and the order that characterizes law in general.

What is quite remarkable about Jean-Luc Nancy's *The Birth of Presence* is his interpretation of the (non)relation between Being, being, and law. For the Law of Being is a law that conditions all law (our metaphysical understanding of law as this or that decree/legislation as it concerns beings) and a law that "gives nothing, but orders." This order is revealed to be abandonment (the Law of Being is the Law of Abandonment). There is a fundamental (non)relation between law and abandonment; indeed, abandonment preconditions any law and is understood as the law outside of law that is itself a law (something akin to an exception that is within and without simultaneously). Abandonment is the "not" of law, to borrow Oren Ben-Dor's conception—this "not" escapes simple negativity (i.e., "this is radically different from that," a metaphysical formulation), but is the within/without exception that undergirds our metaphysical understanding of law. To return to Nancy, his presentation of abandonment, as the Law of Abandonment and the (non)relation between it and being (abandoned being) presents the condition of law as that which withholds or dissimulates itself within being. We can understand Nancy as suggesting the Law of Abandonment demands absolute submission to the withdrawal of Being through (and within) the there-ness of the human's being (Being revealed through the dissimulation of itself within being—withdrawal). According to Nancy:

> One always abandons to a law. The destitution of abandoned being is measured by the limitless severity of the law to which it finds itself exposed. Abandonment does not constitute a subpoena to present oneself before this or that court of law. It is a compulsion to appear absolutely under the law, under the law as such and in its totality. In the same way—it is the same thing—to be *banished* does not amount to coming under a provision of the law, but rather to coming under the entirety of the law. Turned over to the absolute of the law, the banished one is thereby abandoned completely outside its jurisdiction. The law of abandonment requires the law be applied through its withdrawal.

The Law of abandonment is the other of the law, which constitutes the law.

Abandoned being finds itself deserted to a degree that it finds itself remitted, entrusted, or thrown to this law that constitutes the law, this other and same, to this other side of all law that borders and upholds a legal universe; an absolute, solemn order, which prescribes nothing but abandonment. . . . Abandonment respects the law; it cannot do otherwise.[5]

Nancy's etymological investigation of abandonment presents the term as deriving from *bandon* (*bandum, band, bannen*), meaning an "order, prescription, a decree, a permission, and a power that holds these freely at its disposal. To *abandon* is to remit, entrust, or turn over to such a sovereign power, and to remit, entrust or turn over to its *ban*, that is to its proclaiming, to its convening, and to its sentencing."[6] Thus, Nancy suggests that the Law of Abandonment orders absolute submission, or remittance, to the ban (or law) of Being. This formulation necessitates a clarification of what the Law itself entails (we know, thus far, that it requires *absolute* submission to abandonment, as the withdrawal of Being through dissimulation). What is most important for our engagement with Nancy is precisely this clarification; for it adumbrates the inseparability of law and the human being:

Man is the being of abandoned being and as such is constituted or rather instituted only by the reception of the order to see man here, there where he is abandoned. To order to *see* is still an eidetic, or theoretical, order. But what it gives the order to see, the *there* of man, offers no idea, gives nothing to be seen . . . a place gives itself to be seen, configures itself, but *here* or *there* (it is the same, and the other), although it imparts places, although it broaches space and outlines its schemas, itself remains invisible. *Here* opens a spacing, clears an area upon which being is thrown, abandoned.[7]

What, then, does Nancy mean with this spacing of the order? If what defines the human's being is Da-sein [being *there*], then Being unfolds through the thrown-ness of the human in that very place (that very there). "Man is only ordered as being-there, or to be there—that is, *here*."[8] Thus, the Law of Abandonment *orders* the human to *see* this very place (space as there-ness) within which Being unfolds through it. But there is a co-nundrum: the law demands a seeing of the place of Being's unfolding but this place is invisible—the demand to *see* what is invisible, as a necessity of the order, is what constitutes withdrawal. According to Nancy, this constitutes an impossible categorical imperative, an impossibility that sets something like Kant's categorical imperative into motion (i.e., an *impossible* law founds the instantiation of all laws). But why is this place invisible? It is invisible precisely because the place where Being unfolds is the place where it also withdraws. We are thus ordered to see the place of withdrawal that constitutes the human as such. This withdrawal does not conform to the metaphysical schema of time/space, so it demands obedience to an impossible demand.

What we can take from Nancy's diacritical presentation is that *all* laws (i.e., legislation passed by Congress, amendments, decrees) are subordinate to an impossible demand to *see* an invisible space of Being's withdrawal—into the very there-ness that one is thrown. Although one cannot see the place, the order to *see anyway* is the order upon which law gains its ethical ground. To *see* what is invisible sets the enterprise of law—as both protection and enforcement—into motion.

But what I would like to present is an additional problematic: *all* seeing is predicated upon *blindness*. Something must remain outside the field of vision for the seeing to take place—blindness provides the condition of possibility for the sight mandated, even to see the invisible. We can also conceive of Nancy's ban through another perspective, as least etymologically, then. Ban also connotes a covering over or a censuring. When something is censured, it provides the condition of possibility *for something else to be seen*. Thus, the ban, the Law of Abandonment, not only requires the seeing of the invisible, but simultaneously the *not seeing*, the censuring, of the non-place (the always already not there or here). What I am suggesting is that the Law of Abandonment is doubled (and conceals this doubling). The double function is to see the invisible and *not* see that which never arrived—that which lacked a there-ness through which Being would withdraw.

This second, and hidden, order of law is what I will call "outlawing," following Frantz Fanon. It is the demand not to see the nonarrival, which Being parasitically relies upon for its own withdrawal. This, I argue, is a simultaneous order not to see black ~~being~~, since it is without a world and lacks a there-ness within the unfolding of Being. Blackness terrifies and is terrorized, ontologically, because it lacks a place from which an ethical imperative to see can emerge. Following Hortense Spillers, the consequence of this perverse imperative is that "we lose any hint or suggestion of a dimension of ethics, of relatedness . . . to that extent, the procedure adopted for the captive flesh demarcates a total objectification."[9] Spillers also suggests that "[the] undecipherable markings on the captive body render a kind of hieroglyphics of the flesh whose severe disjunctures come to be hidden to the *cultural seeing* of skin color"[10] (emphasis mine). Spillers's "cultural seeing" is precisely Nancy's impossible imperative to see, and the metaphysical holocaust (destruction of the flesh as primary narrative), which censures (bans) blackness out of sight, hides this devastation and recasts it as an unseen ontological hieroglyphic within law—unreadable and unseen within the Order of Being. Thus, the refusal to see the unreadable sign of ontological violence (hieroglyphic) is the Order of Being.

Outlawing is the enforced not seeing and maintenance of onticide—the continued destruction of the flesh. This not seeing is a condition of all law, both ontologically and metaphysically. Outlawing entails (1) censuring the ontological seeing of black ~~being~~'s holocaust, which continually obliterates there-ness and (2) the not of law, as the outside/inside formulation of the imperative. Outlawing is outside law, since it contravenes the ethical imperative to see the invisible, and also inside law, since it enables and conditions this very imperative—the censure is at the very heart of law. Outlawing is the exception that determines our legal and ethical norms.

To push this analysis further, I will suggest that the Law of Being (the Law of Abandonment) ~~is~~ antiblackness. Being can only provide a thereness from which to withdraw from an antiblack order or injunction. Antiblackness is the place of Being's historical unfolding, its perverse call to the human being. Why is this the case? The human requires equipment to re-member its (non)relation to Being, and for modernity, black ~~being~~ is the premier equipment of the human's existential journey through the world in his thrown-ness. Without equipment to help the human through his existential journey, re-membering Being is an impossible feat.

In *Race, Law, and Resistance*, Patricia Tuitt presents an important analysis of modern law. Drawing on the groundbreaking work of critical race theorists such as Patricia Williams, Cheryl Harris, and Kimberly Crenshaw, Tuitt suggests that the slave was a *cause* of modern law. It is commonplace to assume that the law existed *prior* to slavery and that the slave was merely governed by various codes and regulations. But for Tuitt, the slave *engenders* law. We can understand this engendering as the attempt to reconcile the obliteration of the ethical relation (the production of equipment in human form) with the ontological function of law—to protect and enforce the (non)relation between being and Being. Tuitt avers, "If we examine modern law in light of the emergence of its doctrine, it can be seen, that the slave existed at its earliest point. To be more precise, we can say that the slave was one of the chief *causes* of modern law, alongside animals and inanimate objects such as weapons and jewels. The slave was the only human agent among the 'things' that the law sought to integrate in its dominant conception of contractual relations, and was thus, I would suggest, one of the earliest subjects/objects of modern law."[11]

Although Tuitt's analysis presents a humanist desire to reclaim the slave as a human agent, despite the fact the law considers the slave property alongside inanimate and animate objects, rendering it a subject/object (which I believe is a strategy that only yields contradiction and aporias), her claim that the presence of the slave *engenders* law provides insight into the relation between law and ontology. Contract law (law of chattel) is perhaps the hallmark of modern legal development, given the need to regulate commerce and specify the rights and entitlement of property holders. But this corpus of law emerges because one needs to integrate the slave into the world. In other words, contract law conceals an ontological project: it uses the discourse of property, chattel, rights, and trade to *divide* the world into human subjects [Dasein], those who are entitled to the protection and enforcement of their ontological (non)relation, and the world of *things*, those entities lacking such protection of any relation, but whose existence is necessary for the human to operate within the world. The law of chattel performs the work of dividing legal seeing from not seeing. Thus, the law of chattel, through the contract form, is predicated upon an ontological difference that it disavows (or more precisely forgets): the difference between Being (the self that is the locus of rights and entitlement, as a stand-in for the ontological [non]relation) and ~~being~~ (the world of objects that support this self).

To read Oren Ben-Dor's postmetaphysical meditation on law through (and against) Patricia Tuitt's theoretical analysis of contract law, we can suggest that the primary function of chattel law is to protect and enforce the ground of the (non)relation—this law is ethical to the extent that the rights bestowed to the property holder enable him to project himself into the world of things and to re-member Being. The destruction of the flesh, the onticide that renders the slave available equipment, is a legal necessity, since contract law depends on it—the slave is produced through this very violence. Ben-Dor's suggestion that "the essence of law is not legal" provides a hermeneutic for reading and interpreting law, as always already an ontological enterprise. Taking chattel law, for example, the essence of this law is not the regulation of commerce and property rights, but the ontological division the law engenders between the world of things (equipment) and the world of the subject (the being for which Being is an issue for it—and thus requires rights to discover this issue). Moreover, this legal division is predicated upon both Nancy's "seeing the invisible" and outlawing black being. Ethics and freedom are the ontological discourses of law. They perform the crucial work of dividing the world between the free (the human) and unfree (the equipment of the human) and between humans and available equipment. Again, we lose any hint or suggestion of ethics between the human and his equipment (the not there), as Spillers suggests. The law of chattel relies on this loss of the ethical relation as a condition of its possibility—if the slave (as chattel) were to arrive in the withdrawn place of Being and have that inhabitation protected and enforced, the entire edifice of chattel law (a particular feature of modern contract law) would crumble.

Critical legal theorist Patricia Williams argues that contract law "reduces life to fairy tale."[12] This is the case, since the contract forges a fantasy (a scenario of relations conceived in the actors' minds)—it transforms imagination into legal obligation. But the contract creates not only the structure of relation between actors, but also the object through which the relation is sustained. In this case, the black object is constructed, or invented, within the vacuum (or hole) this structure produces. Bryan Wagner might describe this vacuum in the contract as blackness existing "in exchange without being party to exchange."[13] The object is exchanged between subjects, but the object itself is not a subject, not a party, within the contract. It exists merely within the black hole of the contract, as that which allows the structure to exist without a subjective existence itself. To exist in exchange is to lack existence outside transaction; existence for black ~~being~~ is ephemeral and tethered to the flimsy temporality of the contract structure. We might suggest, after Charles Mills, that an anti-black contract (a racial contract) is an instrument for dividing the world between acting subjects and inactive objects existing only in exchange.[14] Thus, the contract performs important ontological work, and, for this reason, it has become central to legal metaphysics.

Frank Wilderson suggests, "African slavery did not present an ethical dilemma for global civil society. The ethical dilemmas were unthought."[15] The dilemmas are unthought because applying the ethical relation to a ~~being~~ that never arrives and is not seen presents a stupefying conundrum that ethics is unable to resolve. We lack an ontological procedure or grammar to situate the outlawed in relation to ethics. Our ethics are entangled in our ontological commitments. For this reason, black ~~being~~ is unable to appeal even to Levinasian ethics—although he desires to escape the violence of ontology (one might argue this escape is predicated on a misreading of Heidegger, which would mean Levinas leads us right back to Heideggerian ontology). For as Fanon rightly critiques Sartre—which I would argue also applies to Levinas—"The white man is not only The Other but also the master, whether real or imaginary."[16] In other words, the Other is always already constituted by outlawing—the Law of AntiBlackness. There isn't a place in the work of either Heidegger (and neo-Heideggerians) or Levinas that is free from antiblackness. Such a place is a ruse.

In his critique of ontology, Fanon argues that "not only must the black man be black; he must be black in relation to the white man. Some critics will take it upon themselves to remind us that the proposition has a converse. I say this is false. The black man lacks ontological resistance in the eyes of the white man."[17] The phrase *in relation* opens us onto the impossibility of ethics, since ethics would require the very converse of the proposition that Fanon refuses. The black must ~~be~~ for the white man, as equipment in human form—the ontic illusion of humanity. But this being is not the being that grounds ethics or ontology; it is an existence untranslatable into the language of being and ethics (which is why "ontology does not permit an understanding of the black man").[18] This is why black ~~being~~ is an "impurity, a flaw that outlaws any ontological explanation," as Fanon would argue.[19] The procedure of outlawing rests on the severing of both the ethical relation and the ontological relation.

This also returns us to the *function* of law. If, as Oren Ben-Dor avers,

"To let *Dasein* gain ground, to let *Dasein* ground as one with the simple unity of the fourfold, is to be ethical. To let *Dasein* be open towards its unfolding world as the grounding of its nearest is ethical. To protect and enforce such ground is the essence of law."[20]

Then outlawing is a departure from this function. Rather than protecting and enforcing an ontological ground (the ethical demand of Being), outlawing functions to render black ~~being~~ continuously vulnerable, accessible, and uncovered. It employs judicial procedures, discourses, and technologies to sustain this vulnerability—as it is the precondition for the Law of Being.

––––––––––

What I want to discuss now is certain legal technologies, tactics, strategies, and inventions that perform the work of outlawing, now that we have outlined its necessity. It is also imperative to understand that the (non) place of black ~~being~~, produced through outlawing, is the emergence of ontological terror. Oren Ben-Dor provides a fruitful understanding of terror: "That which causes terror cannot protect from it. Terror occurs when the inexpressible is not allowed to be violently comported towards the order of Being. Terror occurs when no protection is offered to Dasein . . . when Dasein is not allowed to get its essential 'dues,' terror occurs."[21]

Terror, for Ben-Dor, is the lack of ontological protection, as one must rely on a legalism that just reinforces and produces forms of violation. When Dasein does not get its due—its ontological posture—it is exposed to violence. This terror, however, can be rectified if this due is provided by re-membering the essence of law (as the law of Being). The ontological terror that I am proposing, however, is a permanent condition of black ~~being~~ and the world itself—it is beyond resolution and abandonment. Ben-Dor's terror is situational, but his situational terror feeds off the permanent terror of outlawing. That which causes ontological terror, then, neither can (nor desires to) protect black ~~being~~ from it, nor offers a due that will bring it into relation to the Law of Being. The world depends on this terror—it is violence without end. As long as the world exists, so will it, by necessity. This terror is unlike other formations, since it is "hidden" by the "cultural seeing," if we follow Hortense Spillers. Ontological terror is the blindness of being, what it cannot (and refuses) to see, since it conditions sight. My argument here is that outlawing—destructive apparatuses, strategies, rationales, and technologies of law—produces and sustains this terror. We cannot think modern law without this terror; in fact, ontological terror provides the very condition of legal thinking (i.e., we are able to understand the distinction between the injured/uninjurable, the free/unfree, and the entitled/rightless because of this prior violence).

Ontological terror opens us up onto the abyss of Being—the exception that engenders order. It is through the free black, however, that this terror is exposed in all its absurdity and viciousness. For the free black brings to the fore the function of the law and the conflict presented when this function is applied to black being. The ethical and ontological ground of law desiccates. Since law's ontological function is to shore up the ground of the human by not seeing blackness, the slave, through law, has been the site of this not seeing. As unfree and rightless, the slave's place within the order of the material world is understood, although fragile (i.e., the slave is integrated into the world of things). The free black, however, forces an ontological conversation that otherwise would be left unsaid and unthought. And this is precisely why the free black serves as an excellent paradigm: because it exposes the ontological presumptions of ethics and freedom, which masquerade as universal (and it also exposes the universal as a fraudulent particularity). In other words, the free black presents a problem for legal reasoning because such a being is, indeed, a thought experiment—since it lacks ontological explanation. The law understands black being as an object of the material world, as available equipment. But a free black is inassimilable within law and engenders forms of paradox, contradiction, and absurdity when the law is forced to think blackness, freedom, and ethics together. The free black, then, exposes a double terror: the loss of the ontological ground that secures law's freedom and ethics for the human and the lack of protection for black being against the machinations of antiblack outlawing practices—this is the twin axes of this devastating terror.

CHIEF JUSTICE ROGER TANEY: ONTOMETAPHYSICIAN

Hortense Spillers remarks, "[Antebellum] law is compelled to a point of saturation, or a reverse zero degree, beyond which it cannot move on behalf of the enslaved or the free."[22] This point of saturation, the place where we expect to find the movement of Being, its unfolding through law as event [*Ereignis*] is absent when black ~~being~~ is in question.[23] The law, rather than serving as an aperture for this movement, becomes a terrifying stasis—or a reverse zero degree. This dreaded geometrical figuration, this point, constitutes the irresolvable within the system of legal thinking and reasoning. This point of saturation cannot be reduced to mere ontic distortion, since this point is the absence of ontological difference—but an absence that enables the subject before the law to have movement, to bring forth grievance, to seek redress, and to maintain dignity. We might also consider this point of saturation the distortion of distortion. In other words, the ontic/legal distortion that perpetuates the forgetting of Being is predicated on another distortion, or a disavowed concealing. Law must conceptualize and outlaw this distortion of distortion (the concealment that makes legal concealment possible). Ronald Judy might also call this distortion an "interdiction," in which "a censorship to be inarticulate, to not compel, to have no capacity to move, to be without effect, without agency, without thought."[24] The distortion, then, serves as an interdiction (or a censorship, a ban) on movement—the movement of thought, communication, and legal agency.

Legal reasoning must conceal this distortion, since the distortion throws law into crisis and produces contractions, paradoxes, and absurdities (like the Lacanian real rupturing the legal symbolic). For antebellum law, the free black incarnates this distortion because this figure foregrounds the problem with Being and law—the severing between blackness, ethics, and ontology—which the law would want to forget or to resolve through property rights. Can black ~~being~~ hold property in itself? Can black ~~being~~ constitute a being for itself and not for another? Should black ~~being~~ become an end in and of itself? The free black complicates these questions differently than it does for the slave, I would argue. The law uses property rights to resolve or answer these questions. Property is property, even if this property takes on a human form. The slave is indeed property, and the laws of property and propriety are in full effect. Despite the debates concerning the immorality of slavery, the rights of the property holder trump any appeal to the dignity or natural right one would assert on behalf of the slave. Put differently, the law's function is to protect the dignity and ontological relation of the human to Being, and property/equipment is necessary to fulfill this function—even in distorted form. This is why the law can appeal to rights to resolve the dilemma of the slave. It is only the rights of the human, of the property holder, that really matter before the law. The slave becomes a means to that end.

The free black, however, presents a quandary of problematics: is this free black still property? Does this freedom bring black ~~being~~ into an ontological relation to Being? Can the law accommodate black ~~being~~, which is not property? What impact does this have on the human being? One must ask these questions of black ~~being~~ because the right in property becomes difficult to sustain as a rationale (although the state will claim property in the free black; I will discuss this as the chapter progresses). In other words, the free black enables the presentation of a proper metaphysical question, which the law is compelled to answer. And since the law assumes freedom as a sacred conceptual instrument for its human, it is within the law that the question of black ~~being~~ emerges. The law, then, engages in important ontological work—citizen, slave, human, and property are not mere issues of legal status, since each term carries ontological presumptions with it. Thus, the fundamental question before us, at the heart of our questioning: do the ontological presumptions encoded in legal terminology change as the status between property and free black changes? (Or does a change ever occur?) We might go as far to say that this is the reformulation of our question "How is it going with black ~~being~~?"

Chief Justice Roger Taney provides an answer to these metaphysical questions. His opinion is much more than legalistic rationale; it is also philosophical discourse—ontometaphysical labor. For Taney did not just set for himself the task of addressing federalism (states' rights vs. congressional power concerning naturalization/citizenship), but also the function of black ~~being~~, the meaning of this freedom, and the ethical (non) relation between the human and black ~~being~~. Through Taney, perhaps, we find the strongest answer to these metaphysical questions within law. Taney uses Dred Scott as a philosophical allegory, or paradigm, to work through the ontological presumptions about blackness in an antiblack order. The opinion, then, reproduces the master and slave (non)relation as Dred Scott becomes a discursive tool (putative equipment, as it were) for the ontometaphysical/putative labor of dividing the world into articles of merchandise and the human being who uses those commodities.

Dred Scott is *presented* as a plaintiff in error. In legal terminology, the plaintiff in error submits a writ of error to the court challenging the decision of a lower court. In this case, Scott submits a writ of error to the Supreme Court challenging the decision of the Circuit Court. The writ of error provides the occasion of presentation for the subject to present a grief and seek redress. Etymologically, the term *plaintiff* originates from the Latin *plangere* (the infinitive verb form), to strike or beat in grief; the French *plainte* (noun), lamentation; and the Middle English *plaintiff*, a complaining person. The term *plaintiff* carries certain ontological presumptions with it—the legal subject *predicates* as a feature of its right (i.e., strikes out in grief) and presents this grief, or lamentation, to the court. The plaintiff, then, has the right to *present*, as an aspect of its relation to Being—its attempt to redress any injury hampering its Heideggerian projectionality, its unique project (i.e., life, happiness, and the pursuit of property). The *transit of grief* is foundational to any legal presentation—grief moves from the complaining person to the adjudicating body (the writ) and from the adjudicating body to the complaining person (through its decision). This movement creates a circuit of legal reasoning, and the law is invested in sustaining the integrity of this circuit.

But it is also important that Dred Scott is a plaintiff in error. And in the case of Scott, this "in error" makes all the difference. The "error" indicates much more than the presentation of a writ, but that the presentation itself is in error—the presenter is disqualified, and thus the presentation is censored or not seen, a presentation disappeared by not seeing. "Plaintiff in error," in this case, conceals a double error, or the error of error, which black ~~being~~ foregrounds. From a Heideggerian perspective, this error is nothing other than ontic distortion. According to Ben-Dor, "Errancy is a necessary part of the process of what it is to be human Dasein, namely a creature whose Being is an issue for it, and because it provides some openness. Some capacity for oppression by the essence of truth. . . . Error is counter-essence because in *Richtigkeit* Man does not yet grasp the essence of truth and the truth of essence—namely unification of essence and non-essence of truth."[25]

Humans depend on error for an opening into Being (since for the human the ontic is the way through the ontological). Law distorts the essence of truth by making humans believe that ultimate protection relies on legal reasoning and rights, when these instruments cause more pain by forgetting Being. Put differently, the human will always be in error in relation to law because the law distorts the ontic (non)relation.

The plaintiff, then, is in error—since presenting grief will, in essence, cause more grief if Being is not re-membered (the essence of truth). But error only works for the plaintiff to the extent that this error is predicated on an ontological (non)relation. Error is productive if the (non)relation is brought forward in legal thinking. But, as I have argued, the ontological difference is not an issue for black ~~being~~; it cannot rely on Being as essence of truth or the law as an instrument of re-membering. The Heideggerian error, then, conceals another error. When Dred Scott is in error, as a plaintiff, it is because he attempts to be seen against an interdiction of not seeing, and he attempts to move (grief) against an interdiction on movement (ungrievability). His error is not an aperture into Being and truth, but the terroristic mark of an outlawed ~~being~~—one execrated. Scott's error is an error against a fundamental Law (not merely the laws of Missouri); he attempts entry into an order that excludes him.

This error against antiblackness, as fundamental Law, is precisely what Taney attempts to articulate in his opinion. Scott errs against the human's error—and it is the human's exclusive right to error that Taney is protecting. These ontological issues condense on the term *jurisdiction*. For at the heart of Taney's concern is whether the Circuit Court had jurisdiction to render a decision in the case at all. Plaintiffs must first evince that the case presented falls within the jurisdiction of the court—that the court could rightfully adjudicate the matter. The Circuit Court allows for citizens of different states to sue, and the plaintiff must aver in the plea that the two parties are in fact citizens. This is the way Taney sets up his argument concerning jurisdiction. It is precisely this oversight that concerns Taney, and he argues that the Circuit Court overlooked the problem with jurisdiction because Dred Scott was not a citizen (only citizens can present grievance in this court). Ultimately, jurisdiction brings the law to a zero-degree point, since the presentation of grief, its movement, is foreclosed from the very beginning—following Taney's logic. This foreclosure engenders additional foreclosures within the law; for even the concept of injury, in this case, is emptied of efficacy because this injury never appears before the court. Kalpana Seshadri-Crooks might consider this the nexus between law and animality, which produces black muteness, or silence, as a feature of this zero-degree point in law.[26] Black injury, then, is censored—a mandated not seeing—since this injury is outside the jurisdiction of the court. And this mandated not seeing preconditions the rights of the legal subject who can be seen (in the place that renders the subject invisible). Each refusal to see black injury or to present black grief expands the prerogative and rights of the legal subject. We might even say the legal prerogative of the human in relation to black ~~being~~ is limitless, owing to jurisdiction.

Taney uses jurisdiction not just to correct this oversight, but also to perform important ontological work—work that needed to be done. His commentary on blackness and history are not extraneous or tangential; they are vitally important to the ontometaphysical labor he performs. He is both philosopher and judge. For what undergirds citizenship is ontological presumptions, which the Circuit Court does not address (perhaps, ironically, because such philosophizing is outside its jurisdiction). "Citizen" not only presumes nationality but also humanity. We might say that the courts take this ontological presumption for granted; it enables the law to function. Thus, "citizen" is a point of saturation. It condenses a host of presumptions, and Taney's opinion is a painstaking unraveling of these presumptions in relation to black ~~being~~. For Taney, the real error in this case was assuming that the ontological presumptions of the citizen (humanity and the ethical relation) applied to black ~~being~~. The question of jurisdiction, then, conceals a more egregious distortion: can black ~~being~~ present itself to the Law of Being? Is it within the Law of Being's jurisdiction (the order regulating the human's relation to Being) to see blackness? For Taney, the answer is a resounding no.[27]

He begins his ontometaphysical work by *dividing* the world, making a clear distinction between the human and his available equipment (Taney calls this division an "impassable barrier"): "A perpetual and impassable barrier was intended to be erected between the white race and the one which had been reduced to slavery and governed by subjects with absolute despotic power . . . and no distinction was made between the free Negro and the slave, but this stigma of the deepest degradation, was fixed upon the whole race."

"Citizen" becomes a synonym for the human in this legal rationale, and, concomitantly, "Negro" becomes the stand-in for the world of material objects, equipment, and merchandise. He situates this division by first posing his proper metaphysical question: "Can a negro, whose ancestors were imported into this county, and sold as slaves, become a member of the political community formed and brought into existence by the Constitution of the United States, and as such become entitled to all the rights and privileges, and immunities, guaranteed by that instrument to the citizen? One of which rights is the privilege of suing in a court of the United States in the cases specified in the Constitution?"

Can the imported thing (Negro) gain access to the political community? This is the crux of his question. *Political community* serves a vital function because it provides a conceptual apparatus of presenting the *world* of the human, the being with [*Mitwelt*]. It is within the political community that Being unfolds as freedom, rights, and ethics. Unlike Jean-Luc Nancy, who would argue that the ontological function of community is to remain incomplete and open, constantly expanding and refashioning, Taney presents closure and exclusivity as absolutely essential to the human. For it is only through this closure that the law can *protect* the vulnerability of the citizen. An open political community threatens its very survival, and this is not a finitude that opens the citizen onto the horizon of possibility. It is only when the boundaries of the political community are strictly delimited and policed that law works in all its distortion.

But we also have the world of material objects (or Heidegger's *Umwelt*), and no delineation is made between the free and enslaved. The Negro is a saturation of abject historicity and worldlessness; the Negro is that "thing" whose ancestors were *imported* and *sold*. Thus, Taney divides the world through disparate grammars: the grammar of the material world, imported and sold, and the grammar of the world of humans, the political community, rights, privileges, and immunities. The *Dred Scott* case forces a violent collision, or intermingling, of these grammars. And part of Taney's ontometaphysical labor is to untangle these grammars so that society may be protected, as Foucault might argue.

Taney continues this division by making a stronger argument about the thing and the political community:

> They [Negroes] had for more than a century before been regarded as beings of an inferior order, and altogether unfit to associate with the white race. Either in social or political relations; and so far inferior, that they *had no rights which the white man was bound to respect;* and that the negro might justly and lawfully be reduced to slavery for his benefit. *He was bought and sold, and treated as an ordinary article of*

merchandise and traffic, whenever a profit could be made by it. This opinion was at that time fixed and regarded as an *axiom in morals* as well as in politics, which no one thought of disputing or supposed to be open to dispute; and men in every grade and position in society daily and habitually acted upon it in their private pursuits [emphasis mine].[28]

This is part of Taney's philosophy of history, for Taney turns to historical contexts in England and the modern world to support the ontological presumptions and division he presents. Since the Negro entered into modernity as an "ordinary article of merchandise and traffic," his ontological position was fixed and beyond dispute. There is no provision in this reading for an ontological transformation of property into human being. This, for Taney, is ludicrous and is the philosophical problem with emancipation.[29]

Taney takes care to assert that the ontological division is not only fixed, but also an "axiom in morals." It is here that Taney introduces an ethics of (non)relation. For the axiom in morals translates into the Negro having "no rights which the white man was bound to respect."[30] Taney obliterates any ethical relation or regulation between the human and black ~~being~~. Since there is no right that the white man is bound to respect, either ethically or morally, not even the right to life or selfhood is protected. Under this ethical terror, black ~~being~~ is not protected and is rendered infinitely vulnerable to whatever violations the human desires. The law does not protect any fundamental right to being for blacks. In fact, under such conditions one could only be for the other, as the mechanisms for protecting and sustaining the self are absent. The Negro thing cannot properly inhabit the position of the Other—to do so is not only unethical but also immoral. Taney closes any philosophical gap we believe we have between ethics and morality and brings the two to an intense point of saturation. The "ought" and the "should" merge together in an axiom. Perhaps, this is one of Taney's philosophical objectives: to define an antiblack axiomatic. The world of black things is deprived of both an "ought" and a "should," and this continued deprivation is both the ethical and moral responsibility of the human. For the human depends upon it for his private pursuits (or Heidegger's unique project).

Within this philosophical statement, Taney presents a somewhat paradoxical (non)relation between blackness, law, and existence. We could suggest that this formulation is *the* articulation of nothing in an antiblack world:

> It is clear therefore, that no State can, by any act or law of its own, passed since the adoption of the Constitution, introduce a new member into the political community created by the Constitution of the United States. It cannot make him a member of this community by making him a member of its own. And for the same reason it cannot introduce any person, or description of persons, who were not intended to be embraced in this new political family, *which the Constitution brought into existence, but were intended to be excluded from it* [emphasis mine].

The prepositional phrase "which the Constitution brought into existence, but were intended to be excluded from it" conceals an amphiboly. For the question upon which this double reading hinges is the modification of the "it." My argument is that the phrase should be read in both ways: (1) as a statement of legal exclusion, when the "it" modifies Constitution, and (2) as a statement of ontometaphysics, when the "it" modifies existence. Both readings are supplements of each other, since ontological execration preconditions legal exclusion. But I want to focus on the ontological reading, which I believe contributes to our understanding of law, being, and blackness.

What this phrase, or axiom, as Taney might call it, seems to suggest is that the law (Constitution) introduces the Negro into existence, but that the purpose of the introduction is nonexistence. Put differently, *the Negro exists to not exist.* Black existence is predicated upon its perpetual erasure and obliteration; its existence is this very obliteration—existence as erasure. The Law recognizes the black only in its destruction, and this destruction is required for legal intelligibility. Thus, something like black redress is outside of the law's jurisdiction to the extent that the aim of redress is restorative, and restoring black ~~being~~ is not only impossible, but antithetical to law's aim (Law is commanded to see the invisible, not to see what never arrived). Law can only see blackness by not seeing through its fleeting presence in destruction. This not existing is, thus, the condition of any black existence. This is the dreaded condition of nothing in an antiblack world. It must be continuously obliterated for the world's existence. There is no guarantee of being in law either through ontic distortion or ontological unfolding for blacks. The axiom Taney presents is an attempt to explain a phenomenology without Being. Black ~~being~~, although appearing phenomenologically as "article of merchandise," does not have ~~being~~, since it has been outlawed from Being. The commodity exists, but not in any sense that matters—not in any sense that necessitates relational ethics and rights. It is an existence that does not exist. Being without existence throws existence into crisis.

Taney's antiblack ethics, then, is enabled by this axiom. The black "has no rights which the white man is bound to respect," since rights are the domain of life, being, and relation. Another way of reformulating Taney's statement is that there can be no right that would bring blacks into the domain of livable existence—since all rights are designed for this purpose. Thus, Taney's statement is really about the absurdity that any right could ever change the formulation of black existence as nonexistence. Any restorative right that we could imagine would destroy the political community. *Black rights would be the end of human rights.* And this is precisely why Taney *must* perform this ontometaphysical labor. The occasion of *Dred Scott v. Sandford* created a sense of urgency for him.

The free black, however, remains unthinkable for him, although it creates the occasion for the philosophical labor. It is easy for Taney to discuss the "article of merchandise," since it belongs to the world of material objects. The deprivation of freedom ensures that the degraded stigma is unmoved or challenged. But what about the free black? If the article of merchandise (slave) is virtually indistinguishable from the free black, what constitutes freedom? These questions place Taney within a double bind: he wants to protect the rights of property holders (slave masters) to discard property (by granting emancipation to the enslaved), but wants to retain the ontological status of property for these ~~beings~~ even after they are discarded (since he argues that emancipation does not incorporate blacks into the human family). Right rebounds upon itself, and we are left with an unthinkable that Taney sidesteps. Again, Taney can only think the free black as another feature of property, an aspect of the material world, since in his ontological division there is no other place for blacks. He must contend with the property that is no longer property—world poor, or more accurately, without a world. In other words, Taney is faced with the paradox, or enigma, of the nothing. Both inside and outside, inhabiting space but lacking place. And if the slave race has no rights that the white man is bound to respect, then the right to property in the self, the fundamental right of freedom, is not respected, either. The free black, then, cannot exist within Taney's ontometaphysical imaginary. The lack of ethics and relation would undermine any existence of freedom, resulting in a nonexistence.

This is why the free black serves as an excellent paradigm: because it brings us to this very space of impasse—which is the location of black ~~being~~. The impossibility of the free black foregrounds the question of black ~~being~~, since one must face the terror of this impasse. Through the free black, we understand the ontological determinations of freedom; it is designed for the human, and the attempt to integrate blacks into it results in grammatical instability and conceptual chaos. The free black exists to not exist as a mere speculative instrument, a paradigm, for working through our philosophical limits. The free black is a thought experiment. It has no place, ontologically, within the world—either as property or as human. It resides in the crevices of an active imagination, one designed for philosophical rumination and fiction. We have not witnessed (nor ever will) a free black in an antiblack world, despite the tomes of historiographical research on the subject.

What Taney's ontometaphysical labor and its lacuna illuminate is the nonworldliness of the *free* black. This necessitates an important distinction, one that Taney broaches but never quite presents: the distinction between emancipation and freedom. Emancipation releases blacks into an abyss of terror, since freedom will *always* be impossible in an antiblack world (the world, indeed, would end with black *freedom*). Emancipated blacks are *not* free. Romantic narratives of emancipation collapse the distinction—without attending to the *ontological presumptions* of these terms—by just assuming that the black is a human.

But to return to Taney's important axiom that blacks "exist to not exist," we can put together the pieces of our investigation on the Law of Being, the ban (abandonment), black ~~being~~, and emancipation. The ontic, distorted form of law is, nonetheless, subordinated to the Law of Being at the very essence, or truth, of law. The human exists because Being inhabits the place of existence and, paradoxically, withdraws and is remembered in this very place of abandon. This place provides the possibility for freedom (without it, the human remains enslaved to metaphysical domination). The black, however, lacks this place; it is outlawed from the

Law of Being and, thus, does not exist ontologically, since Being does not unfold. But the non-place of this outlawing is the condition of emancipation. What I am suggesting is that emancipation and freedom signify two different ontological conditions (not merely legal status). Taney used the opinion to protect this place of Being's unfolding—this is what he calls "political community." His refusal, however, to conceptualize a place for free blacks is precisely the problem that emancipation absorbs. Rather than transforming property into personhood, emancipation outlaws blacks from the ontological political community—we lack a grammar to describe this (non)place (besides damnation/hell, as Fanon might call it). "Free black" is the dreaded syntagm of this ontological terror.[31]

EMANCIPATION AND FREEDOM

They are called *free* Negroes; but alas! What does their freedom amount to? What to them is the name, but a cruel mockery? In some respects they are even worse off than the slaves . . . they are an oppressed and degraded caste. They feel it every day of their lives, and it keeps them down. They are not looked upon as men, in the true and proper sense of the term [emphasis in the original].

—*The African Repository*, 1851

Emancipation is precisely this "cruel mockery." The term *free black* explodes into onomastic absurdity and existential cruelty. This presents an ontic distortion, which conceals the ontological terror undergirding this term. Emancipation, then, is deceptive in that freedom is considered the outcome of this process; but this is not the case. Emancipation and freedom are antithetical, and the tendency in critical discourse and historiography to conflate the terms is problematic. The free black, as paradigm, necessitates an unraveling of these terms, since the ontological presumptions and objectives are exposed in their terror.

It is precisely this conflation that frustrates the author of the epigraph, and he insists that a free black is an oxymoron. Indeed, what type of freedom could blacks have in an antiblack order, especially when this freedom leaves blacks even worse off than slaves? Not only does this freedom amount to a pernicious form of bondage, but it also leaves these black

~~beings~~ without a proper ontological place, as "they are not looked upon as men, in the true and proper sense of the term." Emancipation is an instrument of law, an ontic strategy of distortion. Rather than restoring black ~~being~~, reuniting the body and the flesh, emancipation solidifies this fissure. Law, then, lacks a strategy, or tactic, to restore blackness, to transform available equipment into human being. In an antiblack order such a restorative enterprise is destructive—since the black object, as nothing, must be continuously obliterated. The free black constitutes an ontological catachresis in that it lacks any proper referent to capture the ~~being~~ without place in the world. The true purpose of emancipation, then, is to entrap black ~~being~~ in an abyss of shattered signification, terroristic operations, and irreparable violation. The ontological transformation that emancipation promises is deceptive; rather than transforming property (~~being~~ for another) into human (being for itself), it suspends becoming. This is the operation of ontological terror.

Within romantic, humanist narratives (both historiographical and philosophical), emancipation is presented as a legal process that restores what was taken from the human. The human is presumed as the ontological starting point, and emancipation, then, is merely a change in status, not a change in ontology. But as Taney's decision illustrates, the human cannot be assumed as the ground for emancipation when it concerns blacks. Articles of merchandise are not *human*, and the transformation cannot be restorative. This is precisely why the author of the epigraph mocks the very idea of emancipation. Those released from physical bondage are "not looked upon as men, in the true and proper sense of the term." Biological resemblance does not guarantee humanity—equipment in human form. The human, as I have argued, is an ontological relation and not a mere legal designation. The law is unable to transform what ontology will not allow. Perhaps, in the final analysis, this was Taney's frustration. The law will fail as an instrument of humanism for blacks. To suggest that blacks are not human, however, is not to suggest that blacks do not have an existence, but we lack a grammar to describe whatever this existence entails. This is the misery of bearing the burden of nothing in an antiblack world.

In her groundbreaking *Scenes of Subjection*, Saidiya Hartman describes postbellum emancipation as "travestied" precisely because the promises of liberal individualism were not realized. I would argue that emancipation, regardless of metaphysical time schemes and historical temporal-ities, *succeeds in this very travesty*. In other words, emancipation never intended to fulfill the promises of individual liberalism; in fact, it could not. It was unable to transform the nothing of metaphysics into a form of humanist value. Individual liberalism becomes a practice of fantasy and imagination when blacks become its object. The fantasy of equality and the humanist imagination can dream about a world of freedom, justice, and equality, but it must continually disavow the nightmare of the meta-physical holocaust, which continues. Whether we are in the antebellum period, the post-Reconstruction period, or the post–Civil Rights period, the metaphysical holocaust that obliterates black ~~being~~ and sustains on-tological terror is unchanging. This, indeed, is a belief that progress is a myth, even if the calendar year changes. Emancipation is entangled in the myth of progress, temporal change, and freedom dreams.

Since the human and his freedom are foreclosed as options, blacks are thrown into the terroristic space of ontological terror. Emancipation is the legal technology of ontological terror; it is the distortion of distortion. On-tological terror constitutes the strategies, tactics, and technologies that sustain the fissure between the flesh and the body (the primary relation), the enforced not seeing of black ~~being~~, and the obliteration of black bod-ies and cosmologies. It is precisely the space without place that is created for ~~beings~~ when the law rebounds upon itself. Put differently, ontological terror is the solution to Taney's conundrum: how do you honor the prop-erty rights of the human (to discard black property) and, at the same time, protect the political community [Mitsein] from the black nothing, which would undermine it? Ontological terror resolves the tension to the extent that blacks are not "looked upon as men in the true and proper sense." The lack of propriety in a political community is the terror that black ~~being~~ endures once emancipated. The political community offers protection for the ontological relation, even in distorted form, but without a political community blacks are left exposed, without any ontological security. Thus, a vicious choice is presented between continued captivity as "article of merchandise" or ontological insecurity and terroristic emancipation. This is the crux of black suffering, and now the line between these choices has blurred to a point of indistinction (or a "zone of indistinction," as Agam-ben might call it).

Frank Wilderson, in *Red, White, and Black*, ponders the reduction of freedom, as an ontological structure, to freedom, as a political experience (or "negative freedom," as philosopher Isaiah Berlin would describe it):

> Black slavery is foundational to modern Humanism's ontics because "freedom" is the hub of Humanism's infinite conceptual trajectories. But these trajectories only appear to be infinite. They are finite in the sense that they are predicated on the idea of freedom from some contingency that can be named, or at least conceptualized. The contingent rider could be freedom from patriarchy, freedom from economic exploitation, freedom from political tyranny (e.g., taxation without representation), freedom from heteronormativity, and so on. What I am suggesting is that first political discourse recognizes freedom as a structuring ontology and then it works to disavow this recognition by imagining freedom not through political ontology—where it rightfully began—but through political experience (and practice); whereupon it immediately loses its ontological foundations.[32]

Following Wilderson, I would argue that the tendency to reduce freedom to a contingent experience is a strategy of romantic humanism, and this strategy sets emancipation agendas into motion. If one proceeds from the assumption that freedom can be achieved from political action, then humanism can distort antiblackness, such that it is no longer a question of being, but of action/hard work. The question of black ~~being~~ is never broached, since romantic humanism just proceeds as if humanity is universal (and all humans can engage in political action). But when the question of black ~~being~~ is foregrounded, contingent freedom becomes irrelevant because freedom is not predicated on any contingent experience but on the Law of Being. And this Law cannot be transformed or revised with political action. In other words, we reach the inefficacy of political experience, contingency, and emancipation when freedom is unmoored from these terms—since it is the idea of freedom that provides an idealistic/mystic power for these terms. Emancipation deceptively tethers itself to freedom so that ontological questions are not broached—emancipation occurs when freedom fails.

Emancipation does not resolve the ontological problem that black ~~being~~ presents to the world. This is why the condition of slavery continues after emancipation. The legal distinctions between slave and free only matter within a romantic narrative in which emancipation is synonymous with freedom and freedom is reduced to the acquisition of rights. What the free black, as paradigm, reveals is that no right will restore black being—such restoration is a ruse. The scant rights given to free blacks— such as voting, holding property, and assembly—were ineffective in securing humanity (resolution of the nothing in an antiblack world). These rights, rather than incorporating blacks into the political community, served to distort the continued metaphysical holocaust, since it connects rights to restoration. In *Scenes of Subjection*, Saidiya Hartman argues that postbellum emancipation produced debt, burden, and instability. Emancipation is, thus, described as "travestied" because it created another form of bondage. Hartman's analysis in the postbellum period and my analysis of the antebellum period provide a paradigmatic perspective on emancipation. In neither period did emancipation eradicate antiblackness and restore being. The postbellum period, I would argue, is merely the extension of ontological terror to the entire black population. These period changes, proffered by historiography, conceal the continuity of the question. The forms of bondage might differ, but the necessity of bondage remains consistent across metaphysical time. Why is bondage continuous? This question brings us back to our proper metaphysical question: How is it going with black being? Bondage continues, in disguised form, because blacks bear the burden of incarnating nothing in an antiblack world. Put differently, emancipation sustains the imposition of nothing; it does not relieve the burden.

We must depart, then, from Orlando Patterson when he writes in *Slavery and Social Death*, "As enslavement is life-taking, it follows logically and symbolically that the release from slavery is life-giving and life-creating. The master gives, and in giving he creates . . . what results from this deliberate loss is a double negation: the negation of the negation of social life, resulting in a new creation—the new man, the free man. Manumission, then, is not simply an act of creation: it is rather, an act of creation brought about by an act of double negation initiated by his power— for nothing."[33]

Patterson's romantic humanism avoids the question of black being that his theory of social death necessitates. The altruistic master, who gifts freedom for nothing, assumes an ontological function: creating a "new man, the free man." What is the ontological procedure by which an article of merchandise outside the political community [Mitsein] becomes human? What philosophy of becoming sustains this romantic narrative? What type of life, given by the master, can transform the dead thing? This new man, which Patterson celebrates, is not "looked upon as a [man] in the true and proper sense." The life bequeathed to the emancipated does not resolve the issue of ontological propriety. For this life is neither true nor proper; it is a life indistinguishable from death, an ontic distortion. The gift of life (this existential condescension) reveals itself as an execration, since this new man assumes space without place—the new man is an outlaw. In this sense, life is fraudulent, as is as the master's promise of transformation. A resurrection never occurs, simply the extension of death in a different form (a more insidious form, since it is deceptive). Nothing *cannot* be negated (i.e., the black as nothing in an antiblack world). The negation of negation is a Hegelian romantic view of synthesis in which the new created from the negation is an elevation. But Hegel fails us here, since, as Fanon argues, the black "has no ontological resistance in the eyes of white men" (and even Hegel places blacks outside the movement of history and synthesis). Put differently, the new creature does not join the master-class; he is not master of anything, not even his own body (as kidnapping will show us).

Within Patterson's understanding, "free" (as in "free man") is a legal experience, a transfer of property. But the ontological question would shift us toward the man, since freedom exists for the man. We could also suggest "man" cannot be reduced to "human." Patterson assumes the two are synonymous and, thus, skirts the question of black ~~being~~. What is this created thing? To assume that this creation is human begs the question about the ontological stability of this human. For this humanity is only given by another—the human is still a being-for another, which is antithetical to a being-for-itself. (If the master decides to rescind his gift, what then?) This new human exists for (and at) the pleasure of his master. The man is still property, since he is born as a consequence of the master's ultimate right in property—the master's pleasure in his right to discard property at any time he so chooses. The slave, then, is never truly released from the master; he will always bear the stigma of the master's power and ultimate authority over life and death (the master's sovereignty remains in his creation). He breathes the breath of the master; it is in the master where his existence must be grounded and remain for the "gift" of freedom to hold. Thus, a man created (through legal decree) from a human is *not* a human. It is something else—something we lack an adequate grammar to describe. But whatever this something is, it is not the subject of humanism and cannot be easily incorporated into its romance (without facing the impasse of the question).

Alan Nadel suggests that once emancipated, or free, the black was "no longer the master's property, the black lost the protection entailed in being his asset. Because the extralegal code of honor which respected another white man's property (or the laws of slavery which protected his investment) no longer applied, the black became the universal slave of the white community and the white began to realize the implicit ideal of southern democracy as the *Richmond Enquirer* had articulated it—that all whites could be masters."[34] This *new man* is the property of all whites, the universal slave. The transformation (emancipation) is really just a move from the particular (single master) to the universal (community of whites/Mitsein), a transformation that retains slavery in essence. Thus, Patterson's notion of *life* is not a gift of freedom for blacks at all, but a reconfiguration of antiblack mastery.

TIME, DECISION, AND SUSPENSION

The slave's right to freedom took hold the *instant* it was granted. The court permitted a master to give a slave an "*immediate* right to *present* freedom [emphasis mine]."

—ARTHUR HOWINGTON, "A Property of Special and Peculiar Value"

The decision is an important aspect of law—either through an opinion, ruling, mandate, or order. It is through the decision that power manifests itself as sovereignty and demarcates between the legal and illegal by suspending this distinction between them. Following Agamben, we understand that the "state of exception" is the moment in which legal binaries are suspended into a zone of indistinction and sovereign power works through this indistinction.[35] But what concerns me here is the relation between decision and suspension as ontological mechanisms, or the relation between decision, suspension, law, and the Law of Being. For the free black, as paradigm, illuminates this relation as one of terror.

In *The Birth of Presence*, Jean-Luc Nancy makes a distinction between the decision of disclosedness and the decision that closes off. The latter is a feature of a metaphysics that uses the decision to self-assure existence, to remove uncertainty, and to close the openness of Being's thrown-ness. We might suggest that the legal decision exemplifies this closure, with its emphasis on precedent, resolution, and finality. This type of self-assurance distorts the mechanism of the decision, ontologically, since Being's thrown-ness presents an openness that defies closure or certainty. Put differently, the ontological decision must be *undecidable*, a decision that will never be able to decide. Dasein must decide that the decision is undecidable regarding existence and remain open to the unfolding of Being in this place of indecision. This, ultimately, will stimulate anxiety or a mood that reinforces indecision and exposes the absurdity of metaphysical se-curity. Nancy and Heidegger would call this moment of indecision "sus-pension": "In suspension, by definition, decision escapes; it does not take place; it can never take place. . . . This suspension *is* the condition and the constitution-of-Being of the existent as such."[36] The constitution of Being is such that it escapes any attempt to capture it within the net of under-standing metaphysics provides for the "They." We can also suggest, fol-lowing Nancy and Heidegger, that the Law of Being mandates the decision to undermine itself in indeterminacy, an indeterminate decision, which is the only *true* decision that one might ever reach concerning Being. What is important here is that indecision and suspension are *openings* for the unfolding of Being, for the (non)relation between it and Dasein. Rather than limiting *becoming*, indecision and suspension are necessary for it to occur. Legal certainty—the closedness of the law—depends on the dis-tortion of suspension and indecision.

Antiblackness, as fundamental Law, adds another layer of distortion (or violent perversion) to suspension and indecision. Rather than decision and suspension serving as apertures of Being and stimulating necessary moods, these mechanisms are instruments of ontological terror because they function to outlaw black ~~being~~. Indecision and suspension provide the contours of an abyss concerning abject black nothing. We will have to turn to the metaphysics of law to understand this, since (1) the pur-pose of legal metaphysics is to secure self-assurance, and this is denied black ~~being~~, and (2) the unfolding of Being in the place of indecision and suspension does not occur for black ~~being~~ because the ontological differ-ence is not an issue for available equipment. In other words, if we must get to the ontological through the ontic, then reading moments of legal indecision and suspension illumines another feature of metaphysics that is distorted doubly.

Part of this distortion, or the self-certainty of law, is reliance on metaphysical temporality. For the human, the undecidable (the suspension) is situated in a temporality beyond time, a primordial time in which the present, future, and past are all thrown into crisis. The vulgarity of metaphysical time is such that it enables a distortion of the decision concerning existence. But law attempts to provide a retreat from the heaviness of the undecidable by compressing the legal subject into the present. As system theorist Niklas Luhmann suggests, "The concept of the present [in law] contains rules for using the idea of simultaneity, which itself underlies the possibility of communication in social life."[37] The present provides a temporal structure of intelligibility, meaning, and communication for legal reasoning and decision. Law moves in the present—although it relies on the past (legal precedent) and the future to sustain this present.

Temporality and law are "conceptually fused in the West through their mutual implications of total order in relation to which social life acquires meaning," according to legal theorist Carol J. Greenhouse. In its aim to provide the horizon of social meaning, law assumes a "mythic dimension" in relation to time: "it is a product of being in time (in that it is a human product) but also out of time (where did it or does it begin or end?)."[38] Much like the Freudian primal father's paradoxical relationship to law, as both within the law (as the embodiment of the law) and outside the law (as the exception that grounds the law), the law assumes a paradoxical relationship to time in that it is produced through time but also situated outside of it (this is one dimension of law's aporia that Derrida, Benjamin, and Agamben adumbrate). For Greenhouse, the law is a primary vehicle for Western linear temporality, and this sustains its mythic nature.

What I am suggesting here through Luhmann and Greenhouse is that the present is the privileged site of legal constitution; the human assumes legal subjectivity through this fictive present. The law must maintain this fiction to ensure the integrity of its decision. This also, however, implicates freedom. The human's freedom, as articulated through the metaphysics of law, always unfolds *in* the present. Freedom exists for the legal present, and its benefits are not deferred into an indefinite future.

The question concerning black ~~being~~, then, is when does the free black emerge within the legal decision? Posing this question might seem rather awkward, since we think that the black received this freedom in the present, just as the human enjoys his freedom. The epigraph suggests that the slave's right to freedom took hold the instant it was granted. The court permitted a master to give a slave an "immediate right to present freedom." It assumes that the master's ontological power took hold immediately, within the temporality of the human. The free black became free at the signatory moment, when the freedom paper registered the marks of the master and witness. But what the courts experienced was the disjuncture of time concerning the free black. In fact, courts found it difficult to maintain this present for black ~~being~~ because it presented contradictions that were irresolvable.

According to historian Arthur Howington, "The owner had property in the slave, but the government had 'control over his social condition.' Manumission, then, necessarily involved a *concurrent* act by the owner of the slave and the government. The act of emancipation required not only the consent of the master but the consent of the government as well [emphasis mine]."[39]

Manumission enabled owners to dispose of property and disinvest, but the state retained its investment in black equipment through what Howington is calling "social condition." Although the master could grant manumission through declaration, this freedom was imperfect and incomplete until the state consented. In many cases, the captive could not obtain the consent of the state to complete the actualization of manumission.[40] Thus, without the concurrent consent of master and government, present freedom proved to be a legal fiction, a fiction without which the legal system could not survive. Black ~~being~~ is fractured as property, both belonging to the master and the state—a "slave without a master," as historian Ira Berlin would call it. The time of emancipation, then, is uncertain. The free black never obtains freedom because emancipation simply transfers property rights to the state. This is the condition of emancipation for blacks. Emancipation suspends temporality, precluding any chance of becoming. The free black lives in this suspension of time, which provides neither ontological restoration nor legal redress—black time.

Although the owner could abdicate the temporal ownership of the captive—remember the owner possesses the captive in perpetuity—this release of temporal materiality does not transform the captive into the mode of the present. In fact, the act of manumission places the free black out of time, in *black time*, without the temporal horizon that freedom bestows to the human. If the aim of metaphysics is to secure the fiction of being through time (self-assurance)—in particular, the present—then time mediates and illumines the relationship between humanity and freedom; freedom becomes a mode of temporizing, and the *human* being must activate existence in the present to have any intelligibility in a metaphysical world. Thus, the inability for the law to secure the freedom of the emancipated black in the present results from the temporal caesura created by the law itself. In producing the category of the free black, the law attenuates into ambivalence and confusion. Black time does not transition into human time. Emancipation exposes a temporal zone of indistinction between the human being and property being, between that which depreciates over time and that which self-actualizes over time. *Temporality without duration.*

Historian J. Merton England asserts, "A large number of Negroes seem to have been *quasi* slaves, released from the dominion of the master but whose freedom had not been sanctioned by the state. The nominal slave group was probably at least as large as those whose freedom was recognized by law."[41] In his seminal work on judicial cases, Catterall observed that the "status of 'quasi slave' had no terrors for the logicians of the Tennessee Court, even though they also believed that 'there was no middle ground between slavery and freedom; no such thing as qualified freedom, or qualified slavery.'"[42] And, paradoxically, even though the justices of the Tennessee Court refused to believe that a middle ground between freedom and bondage existed, Justice Robert L. Caruthers acknowledged, "It is true that the Court's stance [seemed] to recognize a kind of intermediate state, between freedom and slavery, which is difficult to manage and regulate."[43]

This contradictory stance, that an intermediate position exists and does not exist for emancipated blacks, is a curious feature of antebellum law. According to Caruthers, the courts were at great pains to "devise some plan which would be just to the slave, and not inconsistent with the interests of society—that would sustain his right to liberty, and at the same time save the community from the evils of a free Negro population."[44] The courts attempted to reconcile what appeared to be a paradox of law: to grant the captive liberty but at the same time deny this liberty (as it would be an evil to society); suspension became the solution to this conundrum. Within the dispensation of suspension (black time), black ~~being~~ is undecidable. The courts hold this inability to decide on the being of free blacks as a feature of terror, an ontological terror. This suspension, then, is not the Heideggerian uprooting of Dasein, in which indecision enables the unfolding of Being, but something pernicious. The decision outlaws black ~~being~~; this being remains a "being-for-another," since emancipation fails to provide this free self with ontological security.

The community that needs saving is the very political community that Taney's decision was designed to protect. And the evil of the free Negro is the nothing that invades this community, threatening to undo it. In other words, the conundrum that the courts are trying to work out is the mandate not to see and to refuse invisibility to black ~~being~~. Suspension holds this contradiction as a feature of metaphysical indecision. Time is turned against the emancipated ~~being~~ such that a lack of the present is reconfigured in the decision not to decide. What I am suggesting here, through Caruthers, is that emancipation withholds the present from black ~~being~~ (since the present is the privileged temporality of the human citizen; despite Heidegger's critique of vulgar time, this time is still fundamentally a racial privilege in an antiblack world. Furthermore, the philosopher cannot destroy metaphysical time without attending to the Negro's temporal suspension). Ontological terror is a legal strategy designed to place freedom in an indefinite future, but a future that will never arrive.

Kara Keeling, rereading Fanon, would call such a temporality an interval in which the black *waits* for arrival. The suspension is precisely this waiting and deferral of *ipseity*. The emancipated black will always remain fractured within this interval, awaiting the judgment of another. Once emancipated, then, freedom never arrives, since it lacks a temporal frame for such arrival; instead, the emancipated is given "black time," the abyss and fracturing of temporality. In black time, existence is predicated on perpetual waiting. The black self, the generous gift of the master, is never proper to itself because it still belongs to another—in this instance the state assumes absolute mastery.

But we must return to a proper metaphysical question, one the free black as paradigm brings to the fore with seismic force: what *is* this emancipated, new creature? What constitutes this "new man," which the law brings forth through the master's prerogative and a legal decree? Answering this question is, indeed, a difficult task, since it leads to more questions and impasse. We encircle this question, unable to approach it adequately with the ontometaphysical instruments at our disposal. But what we can think through is the legal ersatz, the stand-in for the ontological (non)relation—the self. The self is located at the *place* of Being's unfolding, and the law mandates *seeing* this self, even though it is invisible (Nancy's imperative to *see the invisible*). Even though this metaphysical self is not completely reducible to Dasein, we must, nonetheless, go through the ontic to get to the ontological (or "build a way," as Heidegger would suggest). So, it is here that we must start: with the self that is so crucial to the legal imaginary.

What renders the self so crucial is that it constitutes the mystical foundation of legal thought. This self is the raison d'être of rights, immunities, privileges, and redress. Our concern is the relation between this new creature and this legal self, since what the master owns is much more than the body; the master owns this self. The body is not reducible to the self, and it does not exhaust the field of the self. The self is the ultimate property because it anchors any ethical relation and possibility for freedom. Slavery is perverse precisely for this reason: it transforms the invisible and invaluable into something highly visible and monetized. The "high crime against the flesh," as Spillers would call it, is this crude translation of the ontological into the science of arithmetic and finance. Therefore, Heidegger's fear of metaphysics, that it would misuse technology, calculation, schematization, and predictability to turn the human into a mere object, is somewhat realized in slavery. The "flesh" (the primary relation) is severed, obliterated, and in its place the body stands as the object of market relations, statistical science, and arithmetic. Black nihilism would compel us to center the question of black ~~being~~ in any postmetaphysical investigatory procedure.

The self, as the stand-in for the primary (non)relation, is the mystical entity that is purloined during the financial transaction between the master and the seller. And, consequently, when a captive leaves the plantation to find freedom, he is said to have stolen this self. The self does not belong to the captive, and the attempt to reunite the self with other aspects of a fractured ~~being~~ is cast as criminal. For blacks, any restorative enterprise is criminal in an antiblack world. But, to return to Patterson's humanism, we must ask, does the master, in creating this new man, return this self? Can the law rectify an ontological obliteration? And is the self purchased the same self returned to the emancipated? Thus, our questions concern the subjects of self-possession and self-dispossession. How does the law transfer property of the self from the owner back to the property? One strategy of transferring property is through the legal instrument "freedom papers."

It is through the free black as paradigm that we begin to see extraordinary violence (ontological terror), as the immaterial, invisible self is not only objectified but does *not exist* without this objectification. We might borrow the word *reification* from the Marxist-Leninist tradition to attempt to conceptualize this aspect of terror. My concern here is not commodity fetishism and market relations (although these do factor into the process of emancipation) with my use of reification, but to suggest that something that is supposed to remain immaterial and invisible is transformed into materiality.[45] This is the form of ontological terror that emancipation introduced to the free black. The novelty of the new man created is that his returned property *remains* property, and the white public is the owner. It is still property for another, and the freedom paper is the *materialization* of this self-as-property.

Emancipation, then, ensures that the black self remains a visible object; it does not render this self immaterial and invaluable. This is precisely why the emancipated black is never free under such conditions, since emancipation does not restore the ontological relation upon which freedom is predicated. Freedom papers (deceptively named as such) actually served as "ontological" structures for free blacks. A piece of paper determined whether the black ~~being~~ in question was gifted with limited rights and autonomy or was an aspect of some master's real estate. The free black is only free to the extent that he can produce this paper—but having to produce, or prove, freedom is not freedom, it is emancipation. If freedom papers were lost, stolen, destroyed, or even eaten, the ~~being~~ in question could transition from a new man to an owner's property, at any time or any place. This is an aspect of ontological terror for blacks; since you never know when your freedom paper will become an issue for you or whether someone wants to reclaim you as property (per the Fugitive Act of 1850).

This is the crux of ontological terror for blacks: black ~~being~~ is violently reified into a material object (freedom paper), and this materiality is capable of infinite manipulation and destruction. Freedom papers are an indispensable technology of ontological terror because they enable the reification of the immaterial self, which leaves free blacks unprotected and vulnerable. The primary (non)relation cannot be secured, since this (non)relation depends on both a material object and the literary/hermeneutical judgment of a white inspector. Reification is a strategy for not seeing an invisible self and seeing an abject object.

The freedom paper served as proof of the master's ontological power to create and gift life, but this self required incessant approval and recognition from a human (nonreciprocal) recognition, which is the extremity of Fanon's critique of Hegel. Since recognition is required, this black self *always* belongs to a white other (human); the human *possesses* this self through reading and emancipation. This celebrated gift is an execration, since what the master *really* creates is a condition of ontological terror. The master gifts terror, not ontological security.

For whites, reading and interpretation become an antiblack form of possessing the free black. Given that this self is materialized, the problem of reading becomes more than a literary concern, but an ontological one, as well. The stakes of (mis)reading become a matter of life and death for a free black standing before the human. Free blacks were required to present this paper *whenever* the human desired it. While standing before a human inspector, the free black was *suspended* ontometaphysically—awaiting a judgment from the human (i.e., stolen property of a master or a new creature). The free black, as paradigm, reveals the structure of black existence in an antiblack world as a unilateral conferral of execration and terror.

In *Freedom Papers*, Rebecca Scott and Jean Hébrand offer a beautiful tracing of the Tinchant family traveling from several countries and the way written documents are central to this odyssey. Freedom papers are particular vehicles of movement through antiblack landscapes:

This family emerges as one with a tenacious commitment to claiming dignity and respect. Members of each generation, moreover, showed an awareness of the crucial role of documents in making such claims, as they arranged for papers *to be brought into being*—sacramental records when taking a child to be baptized, notarial records when registering a contract, letters to the editor when engaging in public debate, private correspondence when conveying news to each other. For members of the family, individual nationality and formal citizenship were not clearly defined but a person could still make things happen by putting works on paper. The manumission documents drafted to protect the members of the first generations from slavery or reenslavement, for example, turn out to be highly complex creations, with a power both more fragile and more real than one might imagine [emphasis mine].[46]

The authors are certainly correct about the fragility of the power, since ontological terror renders such power (defined through romantic humanism) insecure or nonexistent. Indeed, what would power mean when the self is reified and consistently inspected? Or when white gazing (the "eyes of the white man," as Fanon calls it) serves as the *ultimate* ontological procedure? What is also of interest is the linking between "claiming dignity and respect" (restoring the ontological relation) and arranging "for papers to be brought into being." Such an arrangement, ontologically, is impossible. The papers must do more than *appear* (bringing into being in a phenomenological sense); for the papers to have effect, they must also be brought *into* Being (realm of the ontological). These papers must arrive (into) the *place* of a withdrawal and an unfolding. This doubled reading indicates that *appearing* is impotent without the *placing* into Being—for an appearance (a phenomenology) without Being is *not seen*. (This allegorizes the gap between ontology and phenomenology, within which a black nihilistic thinking must begin). Put differently, *freedom papers deceive through appearance.* This is what renders the papers so fragile, and it is the *purpose* of these papers to remain fragile. Emancipation trades in real estate for fragility. This new man is the unseen, reified object, which romantic humanism—the agency, will, progress, and universality fetish—is unable to restore.

If language is the house of Being, as Heidegger has suggested, then our analysis must turn to the word itself to understand Being's execration—given that it is the word that creates this new man and gifts him with life. The dead letter of the law brings forth a life indistinguishable from death. In essence, the dead letter of the law transfers its death upon the *nothing* that bears the stigma of indistinction. Let us consider a freedom paper to demonstrate the manner in which the word works to dispossess at the very moment of purported self-possession. Not only is the material object fragile (it can be physically destroyed at any moment), but also at the level of the word we see the freedom paper as another form of dis-possession:

> THESE ARE TO WHOM IT MAY CONCERN: that the Bearer hereof, Black Hector and his wife Black Sallo, is now free from me and my heirs, executors and administrators and at full liberty to act and do for themselves, to pass and repass about their Lawful concerns, without trouble, let, or molestation of me the Subscriber, as WITNESS my hand and seal, This Twenty-first Day of April, One-Thousand, Seven Hundred and Fifty-eight.

> BE IT REMEMBERED: This, Twenty-first Day of April, One-Thousand-Seven-hundred and Fifty-eight, Came John Alexander of London Britain, Before me, John Scott, Esquire, And acknowledged the above Certificate of Freedom for the above named, Black Hector, and his wife Black Sallo (two of his Negroes) to be his Act and Deed as Witness to my hand and Seal and desire that they might be recorded this Twenty first day of April, 1758.
> —JOHN SCOTT (Justice of Peace) (Seal)

The law compels through the imperative voice ("Be it Remembered"), but who is the addressee? Who exactly is the subject *called* by the demand? The identity of the addressee is not clearly articulated in the freedom certificate. John Alexander provides a bit more clarity concerning the potential identity of the addressee. His witness opens with the phrase "THESE ARE TO WHOM IT MAY CONCERN." This phrase, a seemingly innocuous formality, establishes a boundary of exclusion. It, of course, is not addressed to everyone, but to a particular addressee who is *entitled* to the freedom certificate. The freedom certificate does not properly belong to (concern) everyone. The opening witness suggests exclusive property; only those who are permitted to concern themselves with the contents of the document are invited and have a right to its contents. Therefore, it is quite probable that the addressee compelled to remember the initiating event by the Justice of Peace is the same addressee to whom the certificate properly belongs.

John Alexander identifies Black Hector and his wife, Black Sallo, as the bearer of the freedom certificate ("That the Bearer Hereof, Black Hector and his wife Black Sallo"). The bearer presents or yields the document to another; but if Black Hector and Black Sallo are merely bearers, ~~beings~~ who yield or surrender, can it be said that the freedom certificate properly belongs to them? The addressee is the one to whom the freedom certificate is surrendered, not the one who must surrender its content. Although the identity of the addressee is probably obvious by now, it is nevertheless important to tease out the rhetorical constructions of the freedom certificate to understand how black freedom undermines itself in an antiblack language that cannot accommodate such a ~~being~~.

If the freedom certificate does not really concern Black Hector and Black Sallo, for they bear, surrender, and present a witness for another, then the freedom certificate also produces another instance of dispossession within its structure. Discursively, Black Hector and Black Sallo are excluded from the very structure that purportedly determines their ontological transformation (from property to personhood). We can suggest that the freedom certificate belongs to the addressee, for the certificate is created (brought into being) for the benefit/pleasure of this subject. Put differently, the self of the free black is given to an Other in language, a dispossession that is established at the very instance of purported self-possession. They must surrender the self to another (this self never really belongs to them); and rather than becoming an "I," Black Hector and Black Sallo become direct objects in a grammatical syntax attempting to bestow personhood. This grammatical objectification mimes the social objectification that a free black would experience in an antiblack order. Indeed, the freedom paper does not grant blacks the right to predicate (i.e., the inalienable capacities of the human); it only reconfigures objectification through grammar. Grammar, then, betrays the purported intentions of the freedom paper: the free black is dependent on the subject (the human) for the freedom paper to have any meaning or significance. Black ~~beings~~ are bereft of genuine predication, since available equipment can only act for another, for the benefit of the other.

Laws such as black codes and the Fugitive Slave Act of 1850, for example, deputized white citizenry—rendering each white citizen address-ees of the freedom certificate. The "To Whom It May Concern" opening phrase of the certificate, then, is an invitation to white citizenry [Mitsein] to participate in a collective reading, a reading that properly belongs to the white citizen by virtue of civic responsibility (i.e., the obligation to report fugitives and to ensure social order as mandated by the Fugitive Slaves Laws). Thus, the certificate addresses an *absent presence*, a col-lectivity that exists outside the initiating moment/event of the signature (absence), yet is undoubtedly infused within the grammar of racial col-lectivity (presence). Consequently, the presence of Black Hector and Black Sallo is registered as an absence—since the black physical body is always already absent from the collectivity that matters. In other words, Black Hector and Black Sallo are never called and do not have a right to respond to the call, even though the freedom paper makes them "free." Black free-dom does not arrive in the place of Being's unfolding, it is just a presence that is absent in its lack of being (*appearance without Being*).

The voice of the Law *calls* each white citizen to remember the event of the master's signatory power—its ontological force. This involves a collective acknowledgment of the unlimited power of the master, to gift life to the dead. The *signature* attests to his act and deed. Following Ag-amben, we could also suggest that the signature provides the "condition of possibility" for the master's ontological power—his unique stamp on an antiblack metaphysical world.[47] If, however, the call addresses a collec-tivity that exists outside the initiating moment of the signature (i.e., the white citizen was not physically present at the moment of the signing), how can this collectivity *remember* the event? Does the law, then, make a demand of the legal subject that is impossible to obey? Moreover, is an encounter with the impossible demand a precondition for obedience (like the demand to see the invisible)?

The law demands the reproducibility of the signatory event through the act of remembering, which is really an act of piecing together, re-membering, a fragmented narrative. Through the reconstruction of an event, the white citizen reconstitutes the ontology of Black Hector and Black Sallo at the time of inspection. In order for the will of the master's signature to materialize as the emancipation of the bearers (upon each case of review), the originary event must be reproduced without altera-tion. The self of Black Hector and Black Sallo depends upon the unfaltering, undifferentiating repetition of an original event (i.e., the original event of the master signing the freedom paper). Put differently, the black free self depends on the willingness of humans to fantasize, to imagine, an event for which they were not present, but which they are compelled to remember nonetheless. The black self, then, is constructed through exercises of fantasy mediated through grammar and literacy. If one is unable, or unwilling, to re-member an unknown event (the signing), the black self under inspection vanishes—and property arrives in the vacuous ontological space.

Black Hector and Black Sallo are continuously (re)produced through literacy and fantasy construction. Can we say that they are free? It is but a cruel mockery of freedom—freedom rebounding upon itself in absurdity. Thus, it matters little whether the freedom paper is forged or a master's generous gift; the fundamental structure of the paper ensures the impossibility of ontological security and the opening of terror. Being is never secure if it *must* be reified in a document. This is the viciousness of emancipation. The freedom paper engenders a fraudulent self but not Being. This self is the vehicle, or object, through which the *call* of Being reaches the human. The free black is, thus, reinstrumentalized in its freedom.

KIDNAPPING AND TERROR

What renders ontological terror so vicious is the object that it takes as its obsession. I am calling this terror "ontological" because the antiblack network of technologies and tactics takes this self as its target. But since this terror is invisible, not perceptible to the discerning eye, it is unlimited in its destruction and scope. More than fear, ontological terror engenders unending instability, without relief. Any black can become the target of this terror, since what sustains it is the lack of ontological ground and security for blacks in an antiblack world. To speak of a war on terror, in this instance, is difficult, since we lack any tactical procedures, strategies, and technologies to provide security for this self. Indeed, how do you restore the severed flesh, the primary narrative, if this is ultimately the only solution? Rather than restoring the flesh, emancipation entraps blacks in a network of terror—terror predicated on the very self emancipation bestows. Without freedom, there is only terror. Ontological terror is sustained by the unbridgeable gap between freedom and emancipation.

The free black, as a paradigm, illumines this terror; for in this instance we learn its tactics and operations: (1) It materializes the free self in a physical document. (2) It creates unending instability, since materiality is not permanent and is vulnerable to manipulation. (3) It profits from the invisibility of the violence, since the terror directed against this self is unseen. (4) It uses law as the vehicle through which it violates its target. (5) It renders black freedom just another form of captivity. This terror is the outcome of a metaphysical holocaust and the unbearable burden that nothing must endure in an antiblack world.

Kidnapping free blacks is one form of this terror. We can suggest that the essence of kidnapping is not legal, but ontometaphysical. It could not exist without the ontological violence that sustains it. What kidnappers steal, then, *is* this precarious self and not just a black body. The black body encases a more vulnerable entity. Kidnappers preyed on this ontometaphysical instability. They stole free blacks, usually from Northern states, and sold them into slavery for a profit. But again, what is important here is that kidnapping relies on the precarious black self—since this self *exists to not exist*, it is fleeting and material. Kidnapping illustrates that the free black does not exist as human *being*, since the ontological presumptions of freedom are denied blacks (and it is this denial that provides the condition of possibility for kidnapping). The lure of emancipation conceals the fact that freedom under such a condition is uncertain and stochastic. One experiences *terror* precisely because one never knows when this self will be targeted, or when one will be forced to prove the improvable. It is the terror of losing their freedom, as Carol Wilson has described it in *Freedom at Risk*.[48] This terror is the ontological dimension of insecurity—at any time or place this self can be targeted.

A kidnapper can claim blacks as property at any time because, as Samira Kawash explains, black freedom "was never absolute or unassailable in a context of race slavery, freedom maintained a kind of contingency not shared with freedom applied to whites in general."[49] This contingency is the difference between equipment and human being. The white human cannot transition from human into equipment because she has Being, and Being provides the condition for her freedom. Put differently, freedom is unassailable ontologically because Being is unassailable. The unfolding of Being is the space of freedom for the human. This is not the case for black ~~being~~, and this is why Taney argued that emancipation really did not matter much. Kidnappers benefited from this ontological problematic, since free blacks could move incessantly between property and freedom. This devastating transit is the ontological terror emancipation enables.

CODA

Philosophy is always already constitutively related to the law, and every philosophical work is always, quite literally, a decision on this relationship.
—GIORGIO AGAMBEN, *Potentialities: Collected Essays in Philosophy*

What I have proposed in this chapter is a theory of outlawing. Law is a fundamental instrument of terror, rendering black ~~being~~ unprotected, undefined, not seen, and reified. It exists to not exist. Outlawing departs from and challenges postmetaphysical thinkers and black humanists by asserting that blacks cannot rely on Being as an anchor for freedom, recognition, or ipseity because the Law of Being depends on black exclusion to enable the freedom of the human. The ontological difference must not become an issue for blackness, since black ~~being~~ is premier equipment for Dasein's existential journey in a modern world. Thus, the relation between the Law of Being and the being of law (the metaphysics of law) is a collusion of terror—both outlaw blacks. The Law of Being outlaws blacks ontologically by mandating not seeing this ~~being~~ within the order to see the invisible (Being itself, manifested in the human, is what is invisible but must be seen). And metaphysically, the self (the legal representation of the human's being) is denied blacks. This self is reified (in a physical document), placed within an interval of temporality, that holds the present (black time), unstable is, and can transition into a human's property at any time (kidnapping). For blacks, the ontological difference is suspended or withheld—Being will not stop the terror or serve as security against antiblackness. This is why outlawing departs from postmetaphysical thinkers—such as Nancy, Heidegger, and Ben-Dor—and humanists such as Patterson, Rebecca Scott, and Jean Hébrand.

The free black, as a paradigm, illumines the abyss of black ~~being~~. Freedom is but a mockery within an antiblack world. Emancipation is the only option; there are no solutions to restoring the flesh and eradicating ontological terror. The form of terror might change, but the necessity and manifestation of terror remains. The free black teaches us not to become seduced by romantic humanism and postmetaphysics. A change in terroristic tactics and strategies is not progress or freedom; rather, it is the metaphysical holocaust "showing itself in endless disguise," as Hortense Spillers would describe it.

THREE

SCIENTIFIC HORROR

"Nothing"—what can it be for science except a horror and a phantasm?
HEIDEGGER, *Introduction to Metaphysics*

Blackness is (always already and only) cast inside the mathematics of unlivingness (data/scientifically, proven/certified, violation/asterisk).
KATHERINE MCKITTRICK, "Mathematics Black Life"

Science abhors *nothing*. It works tirelessly to avoid it, to disavow it, to
dominate and control it. Metaphysical procedures and practices structure
scientific thinking—calculation, schematization, predictability, objectification, and numerical supremacy. But nothing resists such metaphysical strictures, and because it is not capable of capture within scientific
webs, it is a horror. Heidegger claimed that nothing is but "a horror and a
phantasm" for scientific thinking. Nothing is a monstrous thing, which,
paradoxically, provides the condition of possibility for scientific thinking.
In other words, nothing is the essence of science—the void, the abyss,
the unruly thing is the repressed ground of scientific inquiry. How do
you quantify nothing? How do you render nothing tangible, an object for
observation? How do we predict and isolate this nothing? How do we differentiate it from the "something" metaphysics rules with an iron fist? Undergirding these inquiries is the most horrifying of them all: why is there
something *rather* than nothing? Or what if there *really* is just nothing?
In other words, science poses a proper metaphysical question through its
avoidance of nothing—a nothing it must disavow and embrace all at once.

But this is not the entire story. If for Heidegger science is horrified of nothing and must repress this nothing to proceed scientifically, then science has also found substitutes or embodied projections of this nothing. In this way, it comes close to the horror of nothing but can remain at a safe distance by turning this nothing into a something.[1] This, I would argue, is the function of black ~~being~~ for science. Blackness enables a scientific encounter with the horrors of an entity that is nothing and something at the same time. This brings us back to Alain David's childhood riddle: "What is nothing while being something?" David's answer, of course, is blackness. It is both nothing and something. This leads him to inquire, "Why are Negroes black?"[2] Scientifically, we can suggest that Negroes are nothing incarnated because they are black. Much like black holes and other scientific mysteries, blackness functions to index the limit of science, that which it is unable to dominate through its schematized reasoning.[3] But with its will to power and its will to know, metaphysical science still desires to engage this mystery, even though it horrifies.

We will present a few propositions that meditate on the relation between blackness, nothing, and science: (1) Science projects nothing onto black bodies as a way to engage the horror and disavow it simultaneously. (2) Life and death lose distinction and coherency for black ~~being~~ as nothing. Once this distinction is displaced or otherwise destabilized, the scientific imagination is boundless in its conquest over blackness as nothing. (3) Science performs important philosophical work in that it suspends the ethical relation to recast physical, emotional, and spiritual torture as objective scientific methodology. (4) Science is obsessed with conquering blackness—constantly searching for ways to either eliminate it, through practices such as bleeding or rubbing away, or to keep it in a netherworld of horrors to sustain brutality. (5) Science relies on numeracy or the calculating mind to carry out its brutal obsession. Numbers are not neutral or innocuous but are weapons of pulverization and subjection. (6) The discourse of insanity is a particularly vicious framework for making ontometaphysical arguments about blackness.

The free black will serve as our paradigm for understanding the relation between science and black ~~being~~. Antebellum society often envisioned this nothing through the juxtaposition of freedom and blackness. Freedom and blackness are recast, insidiously, as scientific terms for the purpose of performing ontological work. Thus "free black" provided a conceptual frame for applying scientific procedures to work through an ontological crisis—what is this black thing? Is it property? Is it human? Is it animal? Does it lack taxonomy? Is it nothing?

THINKING WITH JOE, BLACK DEATH, AND METAPHYSICAL SCIENCE

Dr. W. T. Wragg published "Remarkable Case of Mental Alienation" in the *Boston Medical and Surgical Journal* in 1846. He informs us that he is treating a young Negro named Joe (twenty years of age), and Joe has taken ill with "fever of a bilious type" on a Charleston plantation. What stunned Dr. Wragg, however, was that Joe *pronounced himself dead*, and word of his death traveled throughout the city. Although Dr. Wragg claimed he was not dead but was, in fact, living and breathing when he discovered him, "his case was of so serious a character as to call for most careful attention." Joe became more "delirious" and "pressed with the belief that he was dead." Dr. Wragg initiated treatment of this "irrational contention," which was predicated on "unsound premises." According to Dr. Wragg, "[Joe] said that, being dead, his flesh would soon begin to rot and drop from his bones; remonstrated at being kept so unburied; earnestly demanded that his grave clothes should be prepared and put upon him, and that he be laid out in the usual form. He looked anxiously for the company to assemble, which was to follow his body to the grave, and would chant in touching language, a final adieu to his mother."[4]

Joe's delirium assumed a joyous constitution as he sang songs and gave witness about his death and burial. This troubled Dr. Wragg, and he diagnosed Joe as having "mental alienation," a fracture between a fantastical (or delirious) perception of reality and reality itself (the "real world"). This fracture, the irrational gulf between reason and the deadly imagination, needed suturing. Dr. Wragg's treatment, then, proceeds to suture perception with reality—to use medical science to create a *place* for Joe among the living, among human beings. Joe's cure entailed "repeated bleeding, both general and local, blistering, purging, hot pediluvia with mustard, and other means of depletion and deprivation," and as a result "his madness became more calm, but he never said anything rational."

I would suggest that Dr. Wragg used medical science to address an ontometaphysical condition. The symptom treated is the nihilistic answer to the proper ontometaphysical question "What is black ~~being~~?" Joe's answer to the question appears resolute: black ~~being~~ is an always already dead thing, and this thing is worldless. Although it might appear to be alive (within the precincts of biology and scientific reasoning), this life is but an illusion—a scientific/ontic illusion. The black body is just an encasing for a primordial death (the destruction of the flesh, thanatology). The black body, then, is a breathing tomb—a corporeal casket, containing a primordial death.

Joe's death is not a physical death, however (we might call this, after Heidegger, "perishment").[5] He makes a distinction between death and the corrosion of the body (perishment). Dr. Wragg's astonishment is really a misunderstanding; in fact, the entire treatment procedure is predicated on a fallacy—blurring the distinction between metaphysical death and biological death—a blurring that is necessary as a form of disavowal, a *not seeing* of the metaphysical destruction Joe endures. Thus, Joe's self-diagnosis, his madness, is an ontometaphysical condition. He is, indeed, already dead, awaiting his physical demise. *Death is an ontological murder.* The body is the least of Joe's concerns (in fact, he is all but happy to get rid of the corporeal casing). The metaphysical holocaust is a blind spot (anamorphic) to the scientific eye and its hegemonic vision, despite its purported acuity. Again, this is not a Heideggerian death—where death is actually an aperture onto life, authentic life with Being—but is an onticide, a destruction of all ontological grounds and relation to Being.

What we have, then, is the limit of science and the beyond it cannot fully broach, but can only medicalize away. Had Dr. Wragg actually taken Joe seriously, actually listened to what antiblackness muffles, he would understand that mental alienation is the only condition possible for black ~~being~~ in an antiblack world. The term *alienation* is but an inadequate placeholder for onticide, which severs the flesh from the body. Science can neither suture nor cure this fracturing. And it is this death, reconfigured as the nothing of a metaphysical world, which constitutes the limit of scientific thinking. Indeed, this type of death is a horror for science, since it is unable to transform it into an object of knowledge. This untranslatability is recast as madness. Joe's madness is the nihilistic condition of the metaphysical holocaust, of living in perpetual obliteration.

David Marriott provides a contrast to the Heideggerian understanding of death (as the authentic opening up onto Being through the mood *anxiety*). For Marriott, black death is "having lived without ever being truly alive; dead because never alive . . . black life is meaningless and so black death is meaningless—*a legacy in which death is nothing* . . . it is a death that cannot ever die because it depends on the total degradation and disavowal of black life. Ipso facto: death emerges as a transcendental fact of black existence but without transcendence (similarly, black existence is one condemned to live *without the possibility of being*) [emphasis mine]."[6]

Black death ~~is~~ nothing (existence without the possibility of being). It is not only that black death is nothing in the sense that it is meaningless or pointless (rather than paving the way for human freedom, it paves nothing), but also that it is metaphysical nothing, an entity without being. Black death is the symbolic form of nothing that Dr. Wragg could not understand (he needed to think philosophically). For what he pathologized and attempted to treat was nothing itself. Joe's pronouncement is really about this nothing and not his physical perishment. He was never alive, and any life perceived is erroneous. The treatment, then, inverts the ontometaphysical problem: if Joe were to pronounce that he was alive and well, that would be a disjuncture between reality and perception. Dr. Wragg's cure, then, is the true symptom in the diagnosis. We might call Joe's ontometaphysical condition "the already dead," following Eric Cazdyn. But in this case, black death is a chronic condition of modernity, without cure.[7] Abdul R. JanMohamed would consider this disjuncture a "death bound subject," which constitutes "a zone between the status of 'flesh' and that of 'meat,' neither quite alive nor quite dead."[8] Joe's body is meat, the object of a rapacious, antiblack appetite. What is the ontological status of this interstice between flesh and meat? Or, what is the status of the zone of indistinction between metaphysical death and biological life? This is the proper metaphysical question that science broaches from a distance.

We can also consider the "Remarkable Case of Mental Alienation" as an allegory of sorts, or a paradigm for thinking science with black ~~being~~. For science cannot understand black death, or the nothing that ~~is~~ black death. When science reaches its limit, when its episteme is unable to comprehend, it diagnoses the impasse as madness. Madness, I would argue, is the name for answering the proper metaphysical question, nihilistically. One is mad because one is always already dead, although appearing fully alive. Joe also allegorizes the plight of black ~~being~~: it is vulnerable to the viciousness of scientific thinking and its devastating procedures.

Hortense Spillers identifies medical science as a particularly terroristic field in relation to blackness. Reading through the work of William Goodell, she traces out the vicious profit motive, which creates an economy of selling and purchasing diseased, damaged, incurable, disabled, and otherwise worthless black bodies. She suggests, "This profitable 'atomizing' of the captive body provides another angle on the divided flesh: we lose any hint or suggestion of a dimension of ethics, of relatedness between human personality and its anatomical features, between human personality and cultural institutions. To that extent, the procedures adopted for the captive flesh demarcate a total objectification, as the entire captive community becomes a living laboratory."[9]

What Spillers describes here is a metaphysical procedure: what is totally objectified is more than just the captive's body. The *real* object of analysis is nothing. (It is the attempt to make nothing an object *through* the captive's abject body.) Thus, *the essence of science is not scientific.*[10] This nothing horrifies science, and, consequently, the black body also horrifies science. This horror, however, translates into both a will to know and a process of disavowal (the Heideggerian conflict), and both reinforce/generate each other. In other words, black bodies become living laboratories because these bodies hold the secret of science—what it most wishes to know and what it most wishes not to know. This play between knowing and not knowing, desiring and detesting, hating and admiring would seem to land us in Lacanian territory, something like a scientific unconscious. Science is obsessed with this nothing—its limit and its possibility. As Heidegger asserted, when science attempts to explore its own essence, it relies on this very nothing it rejects and detects for the exploration.[11] The atomizing Spillers describes is a *philosophical* procedure under the guise of scientific objectivity.

Andrew Curran would describe this scientific atomization as a textualization of the African through discourses such as anatomy.[12] Textualizing the black body would require a vicious hermeneutical-semiotic practice of reading blackness as a sign of abject nothingness. The black body, then, is a scientific mediator of sorts between the dreaded nothing and a scientific field determined to calculate, schematize, and dominate this nothing. This is precisely why black ~~being~~ is so valuable to science: black being enables the total suspension of limits (ethical, moral, and spiritual), and this suspension leaves the scientific imagination unbounded in its antiblack quest for knowledge, truth, and power. A living laboratory has no rights that a white scientific mind is bound to respect, no limitations on scientific creativity, and no resistance against scientific objectification. As equipment in human form, black being broaches infinity, nothing encased in a body. Our aim, then, is to understand the function of science in this metaphysical holocaust and to dispel the myth of objectivity, which masks metaphysical cruelty behind the auspices of scientific discovery.

In its schematization, science also relies on the mathematical mind and its procedures to give numerical form to the formless—the infinite and the nothing. Katherine McKittrick calls this the "mathematics of unlivingness," where metaphysical thinking deploys numbers and calculative thinking to perpetuate the metaphysical holocaust. This is to suggest that numbers are weaponized against black being, mobilized to create a destructive calculus. She understands the invention of black being as emerging through numbers and the crude economy of commerce: "This is where blackness comes from: the list, the breathless numbers, the absolutely economic, the mathematics of the unliving."[13] The purpose, then, of metaphysical arithmetic (schematized, calculative thinking) is to produce the unliving, the very death that Joe so insisted to Dr. Wragg. Once situated on the ledger, financial documents, and wills, black being is cast outside Dasein. These numbers provide space to black being without an ontological place—this is how numbers contribute to the metaphysical holocaust. Numbers conceal this devastation behind purported objectivity, but the number and its calculus are far from innocuous. The ledger is precisely the reification of this non-place (this nothing), and it is the way metaphysics can in fact contend with it.

Heidegger's critique of calculative thinking entails the destructive use of numbers to quantify man, to restrict his spontaneity and capture him in predictability.[14] Badiou revisits this critique and revises it to dethrone "1," which metaphysical philosophy uses to understand the subject and being.[15] We might say, following Badiou, that "1" begins metaphysical violence: man is reduced to this "1," a quantifiable thing of science. But, if we read McKittrick through Badiou's critique, we understand that the purpose of antiblack schematization is to deny black being metaphysical "1." As an ontological designator, mathematics of the unliving must begin with unending subtraction of the nonexistent—a calculus that takes us into imaginary numbers, purely functional but lacking tangibility. (Badiou's theory, then, leaves power and violence untheorized in relation to mathematics, and this is why McKittrick's conceptualization is essential to Badiou's revelation that "ontology is mathematics.") What I am suggesting, here, is that mathematics of the unliving does not calculate a metaphysical "1," which can be infinitely multiplied and added—this is the mathematics of humanism (and Badiou's infinitely multipliable set theory cannot help us in this calculation; since black ~~being~~ is impossible to factor, it is both infinity and nothing [or something else], and the operational procedure rebounds into nonsense. Perhaps blackness enables ontological operation, as mathematics, by its exclusion from both metaphysical "1" and the null set). We might say the drive of black humanism, its endless romance with metaphysics, is to translate this nonsense number (whatever it ~~is~~) into a quantifiable "1"—the indivisible human. This entails the ontological component of what Patricia Cline would call numeracy—the obsession with numbers, quantifying, and calculation in antebellum society.[16]

The metaphysical violence of the Three-Fifths Compromise, for example, is purportedly resolved by adding the alienated two-fifths to this fractioning; and somehow, we finally arrive at this metaphysical "1." (Most of romantic humanism and emancipatory logic is the attempt to reunite black ~~being~~ with this "1.") But I read a certain impossibility in McKittrick's term *mathematics of the unliving*, since such an additive procedure is a fantasy. Why is this the case? I would argue that the fractioning/fracturing is the mathematical component of the metaphysical holocaust—the alienated two-fifths is the severing of the flesh, the primordial death. It is irretrievable. Black ~~being~~ is precisely this three-fifths (the ontometaphysical remainder, its refuse), not a metaphysical "1"—no multiplicative procedure can produce this fantastical "1" (the three-fifths is, in fact, the numerical stand-in for nonsense, since the human cannot be fractioned from the "1." Thus, the black is not a metaphysical human, following this mathematical scheme, but something other—equipment). And since we lack a calculus to arrive at this "1," the promises of emancipation are but a ruse. Black ~~being~~ remains a nonsense sign within metaphysical arithmetic, even when one is holding freedom papers. Black ~~being~~ is an untranslatable variable (if we can even call it that) mathematically—it is imaginary and is used to perform the function of settling the limits of humanism (the function of imaginary numbers is to resolve an irresolvable equation). Emancipation is predicated on faulty mathematical ontology: it cannot incorporate black ~~being~~ into the "1" metaphysics uses to determine and identify a human.

Postmetaphysics might rejoice at this fracturing, arguing that it sets the stage for thinking [Andenken] outside metaphysical violence—that because blacks are inassimilable within metaphysical mathematical schema, they somehow are free. But this postmetaphysical logic denies the supreme privilege metaphysics holds over life; furthermore, the option to reject this privilege for some illusive freedom is also a power-laden privilege. Outside the metaphysics of the human, I would argue, is only vulnerability and violence—ontological terror. Being will not unfold in this arid space—even within the interstices between sets, Badiou's operations. We cannot twist [verwunden] this violence into something productive for Being. Blackness cannot look to Being for hope, that it will somehow save us from ontological terror if we assume an authentic posture toward Being's unfolding. The destructive/deconstructive solutions of postmetaphysical thinking will continue to fail us—only death is there. Joe's death, the death of black ~~being~~. A meaningless death, a (fore)closure of Being—anxiety without any reprieve. This is the terror postmetaphysics continues to refuse, and this not seeing secures thinking and freedom for the human being.

Scientific and mathematical thinking "calculates and factors blackness," as George Yancy might suggest.[17] And our task is to expose the essence of these calculations as the terror of nothing, black as nothing. Scientific thinking *needs* blackness because blackness is the living laboratory—*a laboratory that functions biologically, but is dead ontologically.* We will investigate a few instances of this thinking and how they contend with nothing in various forms.

For several years certain laboratories have been trying to produce a new a serum for "denegrification"; with all the earnestness in the world, laboratories have sterilized their test tubes, checked their scales, and embarked on researches that might make it possible for the miserable Negro to whiten himself and thus to throw off the burden of that corporeal malediction.

—FRANTZ FANON, *Black Skin, White Masks*

Benjamin Rush's "Observations Intended to Favor a Supposition That the Black Color (As It Is Called) of the Negroes Is Derived from Leprosy" presents a fantastical solution to the problem of blackness, its terrifying phenomenology, and the nothing it encases. Rush's "altruistic" intention in this study is to prove "that all the claims of superiority of the whites over the blacks, on account of their color, are founded alike in ignorance and inhumanity. If the color of the Negroes be the effect of a disease, instead of inviting us to tyrannize over them, it should entitle them to a double portion of our humanity, for disease all over the world has always been the signal for immediate and universal compassion."[18] The color black, then, provides a metaphysical form for thinking formlessness, dreaded nothing. And Rush medicalizes this formlessness *as* leprosy. To consider nothing an abject disease enables Rush to capture and schematize it. The discourse of epidemiology provides the distortion, or vehicle, for the real work of engaging this horror.

Because black ~~being~~ contaminates civil society by embodying the collapse of sacred boundaries, it is impossible to incorporate black ~~being~~ into civil society and maintain this society at the same time. This startling reality perplexed many "abolitionists"—I use scare quotes here because abolitionists really did not abolish the problem of blackness in modernity; they merely advocated for blacks to inhabit a space of ontological terror.[19] The conundrum of black ~~being~~ and civil society came to be known as "the Negro Question," and this question served as the limit of abolitionist fantasies of black freedom, equality, or retribution.[20] The Negro Question is the proper metaphysical question "What is black ~~being~~?" Trying to figure out what this thing is that contaminates civil society and lacks placement in the domain of the human is the problem abolitionists attempted to resolve. Black ~~being~~, whether as captive or as emancipated, would always threaten to unravel the fabric of an antiblack civil society. One solution to the problem was simply to remove blacks physically from the United States. Colonization societies emerged in the United States and advised masters and the state to encourage free blacks to emigrate and settle in Africa. This solution was not quite successful, owing to the cost of the enterprise and difficult logistics.[21] Neither was colonization benevolent, as Grant Walker would suggest—it became a convenient strategy for ridding society of its unwanted waste.[22]

Dr. Benjamin Rush, the father of American psychiatry, provides an absolute solution to the problem of black ~~being~~: eliminate it. This solution belongs to a class of genocidal discourses that seek to eliminate blackness itself, although Rush disavows such internecine implications. (He claims his aim is to generate compassion for the diseased, helpless black leper—black genocide recast as compassion.) "Observations" is not the typical genocidal enterprise, although there was discussion about literal genocide against free blacks in the mid-nineteenth century. William Andrew Smith, in his *Lectures on the Philosophy and Practice of Slavery* (1856), for example, argues that an accumulation of free blacks would make extermination the only reasonable and humane option for frustrated white humans.[23] Rush, rather than exterminating the physical black body to resolve the tension between blackness and freedom, as Smith might suggest, simply wanted to remove blackness from the individual (a different type of destruction). In essence, he desires to transform the abject black into salubrious white (the "natural" color of humans, as Rush would suggest). Thus, the answer to the problem of black ~~being~~ is transmogrification. Rush desires to end a metaphysical holocaust with physical transformation. The gap between corporeality and ontology is one he sutures with lightening the skin. Rush believed that leprosy caused the skin to become black, the lips to become big, the hair to become woolly, and the nose to become flat, and if left untreated, it would pass along through generations. The danger of black leprosy ("Negritude," as he called it) is apparent for Rush, since "a white woman in North Carolina not only acquired a dark color, but several of the features of a Negro, by marrying and living with a black husband."[24] Blackness is the ultimate pathogen. It not only threatens to injure blacks (by concretizing abjection) but also whites, if whites come in close contact with blacks.

Leprosy, then, is the scientific name of metaphysical execration—

nothing. Leprosy provides a conceptual space, within which Rush's scientific imagination luxuriates in its narcissism and its will to power over black as nothing. For the epidemiologist as philosopher, leprosy is indispensable; without black lepers, how would Rush test his scientific power and quench his thirst for omniscience of black ~~being~~? Put differently, the physical ailments of leprosy are not really Rush's concern at all; they are merely justifiable means for reaching his romantic end, the eradication of antiblackness (and for Rush, the extreme means certainly justify his redoubtable ends). He uses leprosy to treat the ontometaphysical death the diseased black body entombs (or as Rush would call it, "tyrannizing over them"). Rush, then, rewrites himself as a metaphysician in "Observations."

Rush insisted that black ~~being~~ could be cured if the leprosy were treated. The case of Henry Moss convinced him that blackness could be eliminated.[25] According to medical historian Harriet Washington, Henry Moss noticed that his skin began to whiten (what we now call "vitiligo"), and he began to display his body across the country to mystified audiences. Rush became fixated on Moss and "hungered to understand and hoped to duplicate the process by which the Negro skin lost its color, and he theorized that 'pressure and friction'—violent rubbing—could banish color from the rete mucosum."[26] As part of Rush's proposed solution to rub away blackness, "depletion, whether by bleeding, purging, or abstinence has been often observed to lessen the black color in Negroes."[27] The desire to rub away blackness, to deplete it from the world, became Rush's occupation. For he could not envision a political good life in which black ~~being~~ would be recognized as human being. Rush's solution is a sign of philosophical desperation, since he finds it impossible to transform an antiblack world, and it is impossible for black ~~being~~ to achieve freedom. What I am suggesting is that the leprosy diagnosis is philosophically illuminating; the fact that Rush could think of no other solution to the problem of antiblackness indicates that emancipation/ freedom dreams are mere fantasy—one's emerging from an active imagination. Only an extreme failure, recast as a compassionate solution, could put an end to the metaphysical holocaust and its lingering question for Rush.

All solutions fail to eradicate antiblackness, since solution-oriented thinking *depends* on antiblackness. But the *success within the failure* is precisely the exposure of this double bind. Rush's compassionate solution to the problem of antiblackness *must* rely on antiblack strategies to realize the solution—and this solution is just another antiblack formation. Antiblackness is both the problem and the solution. This is a dizzying and tortuous cycle, but one that does not seem to fatigue a romantic humanist. For as Mark Smith astutely remarks, despite Rush's altruistic intentions, his "Observations" "inadvertently helped perpetuate the notion that blacks were irretrievably different and inferior."[28]

We can return to Alain David's proper metaphysical question, "Why are Negroes black?" Rush's answer is leprosy; it is an execration articulated through a physical symptom (Fanon's "malediction"). But simply changing the skin color of blacks will not restore the flesh, the severed primordial relation. This, perhaps, is what legislation like the "one-drop rule" is designed to preempt. Lightening skin color will not change the blood, even if it is drained. The blood is but a metaphor for an execration of ~~being~~, which is unalterable. What Rush wishes to avoid, what horrifies him, is the nothing that black ~~being~~ incarnates. Transforming skin transforms this formless nothing into a physical sign of hope for him. But this hope is but a ruse—the world needs black ~~being~~.

DRAPETOMANIA/DYSAESTHESIA AETHIOPICA

Dr. Samuel Cartwright published "Diseases and Peculiarities of the Negro Race" in *DeBow's Review* (1851); it attempted to recast problems of metaphysics as problems of epidemiology. The essay, then, could be read as an exercise in translation—in which the grammar of science is imposed onto the syntactical terrain of the ontometaphysical. Cartwright is writing at the treacherous interstice between the ontometaphysical and the psyche; in his analysis, one informs the other until the distinction between psychic life and metaphysics is eradicated. We might call this interstice between the ontometaphysical and interior space of the subject "the black psyche." The black psyche is the metaphysical space of imagining the nothing that black ~~being~~ contains. In other words, science provides form for the terror of formlessness through this psyche—which is both abstraction and tangibility for science. As an abstraction, the black psyche articulates the symptoms, which emerge at the fault line between the two discourses. It also dissolves the distinction between the two, so that ontometaphysical commitments are predicated on it. Thus, the abstraction serves a vital philosophical function—it is science's alibi for metaphysical violence and domination. And because it is an abstraction, the black psyche is boundless in its probative power—its ability to get at the truth of black ~~being~~.

We are reminded here of Foucault's work on the production of the soul and the psyche in *The History of Sexuality*. For him, the invention of the confessional and clinical room, for example, depend on the apparatus of soul and psyche as a vehicle for truth, knowledge, and power. The psyche, for Foucault, allows medical science to make its gaze boundless, and it reaches to the essence of the human's truth.[29] What Foucault uncovers in his genealogical excavation, I would argue, is the ontometaphysical labor the psyche and the soul perform for the world—the metaphysical will to power. The soul and the psyche are portals for the metaphysical and not just instruments of governmentality or biopower. This labor also enables the production of knowledge about the human so that truth and knowledge marshal diverse fields at the site of the human—this relation is what Foucault would call "power."

Cartwright's scientific technique requires a supplement to Foucault's confessional technique in relation to black ~~being~~. The problem, then, is that Foucault relies on an interiority that is not universally applicable (biopower is not exclusive to interiority, but it is still an essential aspect of the working of power through the human). In *Toward a Global Idea of Race*, Denise Ferreira da Silva defines Foucault's subject as the Transparent I—the ontological figure consolidated in post-Enlightenment European thought. Interiority is the site of self-determination for this I, and scientific knowledge deploys productive nomos—reason as universal regulator—to secure the boundaries of this interiority in relation to self-determination that grounds scientific knowledge. But, the Transparent I is produced against the Affectable I—the scientific production of non-European minds as exteriority, non-self-determining and nonrational.[30] I would suggest that the Affectable I is the black psyche and the Transparent I is the mind or Hegelian Spirit. For da Silva, Foucault's analysis of biopower and modern genealogy does not go far enough because it is still wedded to interiority. Biopower must rely on interiority as its privileged site of subjection, after the body. Had Foucault been willing to question or give up interiority, he would have provided space for those who lack scientific interiority because of global domination and violence against the others. Again, for me, the black psyche is not the mind—but an antiblack invention of domination. What da Silva's masterful work does is present the coeval production of the "I" complement—the Affectable ~~I~~. It is the Affectable ~~I~~ that Cartwright and other antebellum scientists are producing with the invention of the black psyche. And the black psyche reverses the triad structure of interiority-extraction-truth, since interiority is replaced by exteriority and exteriority determines the truth of black ~~being~~. Extraction is no longer necessary. Everything the scientist needs to know about blackness is shown on the outside. Cartwright determines the truth of black ~~being~~, not by penetrating the depths of the black mind through confession and discourse, but by assembling a catalogue of external actions that he then inculcates into his invented black psyche. He then assigns the signifier *truth* to the end of the process of inculcating external interpretations to black ~~being~~.

Our concern here is not biopower, however. For the black psyche is designed not to fold blacks into humanity and the human sciences, but to situate black ~~being~~ outside these discourses. The black psyche is not about the manipulation of life or forced living, but about maintaining the meaningless of death and the obliteration of life. Put differently, for Cartwright, his black psyche holds the truth of the metaphysical holocaust: black ~~being~~ is without ontological ground, without any metaphysical security, and is malleable in the destructive hands of the scientist. As an abstraction, the black psyche is also his intermediary between a nothing that must be controlled and a black body that needs to be disciplined. Physical brutality and metaphysical violence are both justified by using this black psyche as a ground of truth. In essence, the black psyche holds diverse myths together in a knot, a nodal point. The knotting of inferiority, ontological groundlessness, insensitivity to pain, uninjurability, theological execration, and physical contamination are the diverse discourses that enable Cartwright's science to proceed—it could not without the invention of the black psyche. Furthermore, as an abstraction, Cartwright can deploy the capaciousness of his imagination and impute anything into this psyche. The black psyche does not contain any limits that the scientific gaze is bound to respect.

We can also suggest that the symptom provides the material evidence of this psyche. Cartwright attributes antiblack symptoms to the very apparatus he creates. Any symptom just becomes further evidence of the truth of the black psyche. This creates something like a closed hermeneutic circle for him (an unbreakable cycle); interpretation feeds off truth that itself is grounded in interpretation. Antiblackness *must* render the scientific procedure a hermetically sealed circle of myths recast as truth, abstractions recast as symptomatic materiality.[31]

But if there were any hesitations about the legitimacy of this circle, any attempt to tear through its closure, Cartwright grounds his scientific hermeneutic and procedure in theology—as the ultimate ground of truth. The black psyche just articulates the will of a "white, western-god-man," as theologian J. Kameron Carter would describe it.[32] Theology, metaphysics, and science are knotted in the space of the black psyche. The black psyche, in other words, is nothing, and as nothing it is infinitely pliable— as a toy in the hands of the white scientist.

Cartwright medicalizes this knotting with two terms: drapetomania (the disease causing Negroes to run away) and dysaesthesia aethiopica (hebetude of mind and obtuse sensibility of body—"rascality," a disease peculiar to Negroes). In his encyclopedic imagination, he invents instruments of execration that render being impossible for blackness. Drapetomania, or the disease causing Negroes to run away, is an assemblage of antiblack theology, epidemiology, and political critique. This "disease," according to Cartwright, "is as much a dis-ease of the mind as any other species of mental alienation, and much more curable, as a general rule. With the advantages of proper medical advice, strictly followed, this troublesome practice that many Negroes have of running away, can almost be entirely prevented" ("Report on the Diseases"). For Cartwright, the medical field is boundless because its grammar can be appropriated to diagnose any aspect of the social—social phenomenon is vulnerable to the medical gaze. Reclaiming the purloined black self is recast as mental alienation, so that a strange syntactical relationship is established between redemption and alienation. Self-possession is an injurious self-loss, and the idea of a coherent black self is caught within a deadlock of impossibilities. For blacks, fracture is the state of mental health, and the traditional terms of salubriousness are inverted within an antiblack order. If a fractured self, a dispossessed self, is the healthy state of blackness, then any attempt to suture this self through self-manumission precipitates death—the death of that which is already dead. Cartwright is not, then, attempting to save the life of blacks (which is the oath of humanist physicians); rather, he wants to save the death of black ~~being~~, to preserve ontological terror, which renders biological functioning a form of torment. These diseases are designed to prevent the violence from ending—which is what he considers the true objective of running away and all freedom dreams.

Cartwright's essay proffers a political theology as the etiology, or root, of this disease—he replaces biological antigens with theological transgression: if the white man attempts to oppose the Deity's will, by trying to make the Negro anything else than "the submissive knee-bender" (which the Almighty declared he should be) and raising him to a level with himself (turning equipment into human being), or by putting equality with the Negro; or if he abuses the power that God has given him over his fellow man by being cruel to him, or punishing him in anger, or by neglecting to protect him from the wanton abuses of his fellow servants and all others, or by denying him the usual comforts and necessaries of life, the negro will run away ("Report on the Diseases"). Violating the divine execration of blackness—which we might also call the "Hamitic Myth"—is responsible for this disease of running away.[33] Cartwright's naturalism is a theological fiction from which he establishes the "order of things," as Michel Foucault would describe it. The Negro is the eternal knee bender, and if the white man attempts to make this being upright through equality, then the black will run away. Cartwright neglects a neurological exegesis for this condition, how exactly theological transgression impairs the brain or how equality distorts normal brain functioning—other than to capitalize on the implied rigor of the terms *mental* and *disease* to do this work for him. Theology and science are indistinct discursive fields for Cartwright, and the lack of scientific specificity provides a level of mysticism to the disease, which heightens its danger.

Cartwright also identifies abusive power as another potential cause of this disease ("being cruel to him, punishing him in anger," "Report on the Diseases"), although this cruel abuse of power, ultimately, becomes Cartwright's cure for the disease. In essence, cruelty is the cause and the cure of the disease, which creates a dizzying circuit of cause and effect that is unbreakable:

> If any one or more of them, at any time, are inclined to raise their heads to a level with their master or overseers, humanity and their

own good require that they should be punished until they fall into that submissive state which it was intended for them to occupy in all after-time, when their progenitor received the name Canaan or "submissive Knee-bender" ("Report on the Diseases").[34]

It is here we begin to see the metaphysical necessity of the cure, since it is imperative for humanity that they be punished. Perpetuating a metaphysical violence translates into forms of physical brutality; it is a human necessity. Without this violence, the precarious ground of human ontology is exposed as fraudulent. This exposure, then, is the *death* of humanity, and this cannot occur.

In *The Body in Pain*, Elaine Scarry describes the devastation of intense bodily pain. It is designed to "disintegrate the contents of consciousness" and to destroy the symbolic world of the captive.[35] It unmakes the symbolic universe and produces what Agamben would call a "decreated being"—a husk of corporeality without the substance of consciousness. In this sense, we understand why Cartwright presents extreme cruelty, what masters call "beating the devil out of them," as the cure to this disease. When one's symbolic universe collapses with the laceration of the whip, the cropping of ears, the burning and amputation of limbs, the mauling of the canine patrol, it is difficult to sustain political desire or future aspirations. The experience of torture overwhelms black ~~being~~ such that the world outside the sadistic plantation ceases to exist—there is no longer a place to run. One inhabits space without a place in the world. Torture keeps black ~~being~~ worldless.

But along with the experience of corporeal pain comes the dissolution of ontological boundaries (ontological terror); any previous sense of a coherent self dissolves, and the self becomes merely an object of pain. Ontological terror provides the possibility for the experience of pain. Cartwright proffers a solution to the metaphysical problematic. When all else fails, simply dissolve the boundaries of the world such that the symbolic world and signification collapse. In such a context, only nothing exists.

The disease dysaesthesia aethiopica (hebetude of mind and obtuse sensibility of body, rascality) impacts both mind and body, and skin lesions are its primary physical symptoms. This disease is much more prevalent among free blacks, according to Cartwright, who "do not have some white person to direct and to take care of them" ("Report on the

Diseases"). It causes blacks to become destructive, stupid, ravenous, lazy, narcoleptic, and abusive. Dysaesthesia aethiopica is a cornucopia of vicious prepossessions about blackness, particularly free blacks, and the disease is "the natural offspring of Negro liberty—the liberty to be idle, to wallow in filth and to indulge in improper food and drinks" ("Report on the Diseases"). Liberty debilitates the mind and makes the free black unmanageable.

We could suggest, then, that dysaesthesia aethiopica becomes somewhat of a "crypt signifier" (as Abraham and Torok would describe it) for antebellum society, and it encapsulates, or contains, a social trauma—the disruptive function of blackness in an antiblack world.[36] The function of this signifier is to maintain an oppressive symbolic order, making dysaesthesia aethiopica another name for an antiblack phallus. Put differently, a crypt signifier absorbs trauma (trauma as a metaphysical problematic) within its discursive structure; it performs a necessary function of containing what is unbearable or unmanageable for the subject. Within this analysis, Cartwright's lexical properties assume this crypt function; dysaesthesia aethiopica is much more than just a neologism of racist pseudoscience. It absorbs the metaphysical anxiety about black ~~being~~ as nothing, the impossibility of incorporating this nothing into the world.

Thus, the spurious science does not really matter much; the function of the signifier to symbolize a metaphysical problem is what renders the disease absolutely irresistible. The syntax of epidemiology provides a necessary smoke screen, or covering, for the abjection of the ontological exception, and the disease becomes a repository of anxieties and fears concerning nothing in modernity.

Freedom is the terrain of the human being, and, according to Cartwright's science, any attempt to bring blacks into the fold of humanity creates dis-ease that is only curable with extreme forms of violence. Antiblack violence in modernity is reenvisioned as curative, as a necessary corrective, which renders it something other than violence, as we traditionally understand it. Antiblackness inverts the ethico-axiological structure so that black freedom becomes the name for *absolute violence* and antiblackness is the name for sociopolitical restoration. It is this perverse inversion of value and ethics that stains the metaphysical holocaust of blackness with abjection and devastation.

Jonathan Metzl coined the term *protest psychosis* to describe the pathologization by medical institutions of black men protesting during the Civil Rights movement.[37] We might suggest that Cartwright's diseases provide the discursive precursor for the twentieth-century political psychosis that characterizes black dreams of freedom. For Cartwright is really describing a certain psychosis, or maddening disjuncture, that would convince free blacks that they could actually operate as subjects instead of objects of property and accumulation—in much the same way that black protest for equality was considered so maddening and absurd that it could only be described as psychosis during the Civil Rights movement. In this way, Cartwright's writing prefigures twentieth-century medicalization of black equality and political incorporation.

Cartwright, then, provided us with two of the most powerful metaphors of black ~~being~~ in modernity; and he can be read, in my opinion, as a metaphysician using science to articulate the ineffable. Drapetomania and dysaesthesia aethiopica capture the impossibility of living for black ~~being~~. Modernity offers only two choices of death that are recast as life. Blacks live through social, metaphysical, and psychic death—the third choice of freedom is a fatal myth, one that antiblack violence is designed to eliminate.

CALCULATING BLACK ~~BEING~~: THE CENSUS OF 1840

In *Ideology and Insanity: Essays on the Psychiatric Dehumanization of Man*, Thomas Szasz rejects the phenomenology of insanity, the traditional view of insanity as a coherent/valid scientific entity existing in the world, and thinks of it, instead, as man's struggle with the problem of how he should live.[38] What undergirds insanity, for Szasz, is biofuturity—how man continues existence into the future, and how he can navigate the treacherous terrain of the world to maximize this existence. Insanity, then, would name the inability to resolve the riddle of existence and futurity. If Szasz thinks of insanity as the problem of life, then the term becomes somewhat problematized when we apply it to black ~~being~~ because the presumptions of humanity and biofuturity do not easily translate. We would have to revise Szasz's brilliant intervention into the ideology of insanity and suggest that for black ~~being~~, insanity names a certain meta-physical deadlock, an impasse in relation to the metaphysical holocaust or perpetual onticide.

We could describe the deadlock as this: if one accepts that one is already dead (as in the case of Joe), one is deemed insane (humanism's hegemony deploys the term to invalidate metaphysical violence); conversely, if one assumes that one is a human being, with the ontological freedom this designation entails, one is always deemed insane—this is the understanding of Cartwright, for example (humanism exposes its utter hypocrisy and dishonesty through this term when black ~~being~~ attempts entry into the political community). Thus, black madness is a double structure of impossibilities—the impossibility of human freedom and the impossibility of metaphysical resolution for black ~~being~~. Insanity is not an aberration from mental health (as if mental health is an option for severed flesh and body) but is the only existential (and metaphysical) condition for black ~~being~~ in modernity. Salubriousness for black ~~being~~ in an antiblack world is as preposterous as freedom.

Insanity, then, becomes more of a philosophical discourse than a scientific object in this regard. It borrows its semantic energy from the scientific, but its aim is to describe the parascientific, the ontometaphysical. The Census of 1840 provides a gravid site to investigate the way insanity functions as an ontological structure in an antiblack world. The census was not merely a medico-historical document (one we can review through a historical gaze), but also a significant philosophical articulation—rendering the free black both a medico-historical variable and a profound philosophical allegory. My aim, here, is to think about the free black and insanity as paradigmatic of ontological terror. If we read the mathematical/scientific document as saying something philosophical, it will supplement the historical reading. I will argue that the census is a commentary on this nothing black ~~being~~ bears, and the term *insanity* is the medical name for this metaphysical condition. Black insanity is not the inability to resolve the dictates of biofuturity, as Szasz would assert, but it is the inability to resolve the deadlock of black ~~being~~—which is unresolvable. In this sense, black insanity is not something that can be cured, since the only cure is the destruction of the world itself.

The sixth U.S. decennial census of 1840 is a peculiar document. For the first time in U.S. history, the federal government attempted to enumerate the "mentally defective"—"insane and idiots" (census nomenclature)—as a feature of racial difference. According to Albert Deutsch, the information was collected through the "discerning" eye of inexperienced state agents, marshals, who were instructed to "conduct their inquiry from house to house, leaving no dwelling or institution uninspected, and to record the number of white and colored inhabitants of each—how many were lunatics or idiots, how many were supported by their own estates or friends, and how many were supported at public charge."[39] These agents of the state apparatus received very little training concerning methodological procedures, reporting techniques, and medical literacy—statistics as "science in the making," as Bruce Curtis would call it.[40] In fact, marshals were unable to delineate between those individuals considered mentally insane and those individuals considered idiots, as insane patients and idiots were lumped together on statistical tables.[41]

The Census of 1840 received national attention because of the startling information collected. The most unexpected development of the census indicated that the rate of insanity was greater in Northern states:

The "insane and idiots" in the United States totaled 17,456. Of these, 14,521 were listed as whites and 2,935 as Negroes. There was little difference between the mentally handicapped rate among Northern and Southern whites. In the North, one out of 995 white persons was recorded as insane or idiotic; in the South the ratio was one to 945.3. Of the 2,788,572 Negro inhabitants of the slave state, 1,734 were insane or idiotic—making a ratio of one to every 1,558. In the Northern, or Free states, on the other hand, 1,191 Negroes out of 171,894 were found to be insane or idiotic—a ratio of one in every 144.5. The rate of mental disease and defect among free Negroes was about 11 times higher than it was among enslaved Negroes. In the free state of Maine, every fourteenth Negro was afflicted with mental disease or defect, in Michigan every twenty-seventh, in New Hampshire every twenty-eighth, in Massachusetts every forty-third. In contrast, in the deepest South, where slavery was most firmly entrenched, the rate of mental handicap among the Negroes ranged from one in 2,117 in Georgia to only one in 4,310 in Louisiana. Finally, New Jersey, with the lowest Negro insanity rate among Free states of the North, had twice the rate of its neighbor

Delaware, just below the Mason and Dixon line, which had the poorest showing of all the slave states.[42]

According to the census findings, 1 out of every 144 Northern Negroes was insane or feeble-minded, as compared with 1 out of every 995 Northern whites. But in the South, only one in every 1,558 Negroes was mentally handicapped. In the state of Maine, for example, it was reported that 1 in every 14 blacks was insane!

These statistics adumbrated a causal relationship between emancipation and insanity. Northern states experienced a higher rate of black insanity than in the Southern states, where the "peculiar institution" was more entrenched. Moreover, black insanity was reported highest in Northern states where blacks were emancipated.

This geopolitical understanding of blackness and insanity inadvertently created a psychic-cartographic imagination; by this, I mean the way that insanity is spatialized politically. Within a psychic-cartographic imagination, a map reveals much more than geopolitical configurations and landscapes. It also locates the origination and concentration of insanity and mental death for antebellum thinkers—in essence, it exteriorizes what is considered most interior. The Mason-Dixon Line not only delineated between free and slave territory, but also marked the limit of sanity along geopolitical configurations. The Mason-Dixon Line represented the liminal and unthinkable transition between conscious/unconscious, sane/insane, and manageable/unmanageable. Spivak, writing in another context, has called this permutation of geography, power, and knowledge an *epistemograph*, the peculiar way that the geographic imagination configures epistemic production.[43] In a word, the construction of the psychic cartographic imagination, an *American* epistemograph (the mapping of medical knowledge and antiblack domination in antebellum America) is perhaps one of the greatest achievements of this census report.

Pro-slavery advocates immediately used the census as scientific proof of the dangers of black freedom. This paternalistic discourse was articulated with a logical twist: slavery not only was essential to preserving civil society and its various economic institutions, a popular line of reasoning, but was also absolutely necessary for maintaining the psychic stability of the slave, a line of reasoning that was novel and difficult to combat. This social altruism, withholding self-possession for the sake of the slave, relied on a complex political-philosophical argument: sanity and the public sphere were mutually exclusive for black ~~being~~ (both slave and free). Civil society must always already remain a fragmented impossibility if life was to be maintained (life as onticidal death). The pro-slavery argument reconfigures black livability as the inhabitation of death—social, political, emotional, spiritual. Black life is crudely reduced to biological functionality, much like equipment's existence is reduced to its functionality. Put differently, pro-slavery advocates understand black bodies as equipment, and what they were saving was the maintenance of equipment—aside from use value, black bodies lacked biofuturity (outside the time of man and the world). The census, thus, provides scientific legitimacy for rationalizing antiblack violence.

Frank Wilderson perspicuously argues that "civil society is held together by a structural prohibition against recognizing and incorporating a being that is dead, despite the fact that this being is sentient and so appears to be very much alive."[44] Civil society depends on a prohibition on blackness to function—and we can suggest that this prohibition supplants the taboo prohibition that Freud claimed grounded civilization, since antebellum law permits incest and murder through the "chattel distinction," as Kalpana Seshadri-Crooks suggests.[45] If death "structures political life in terms of aversion as well as desire," according to Russ Castronovo, and "produces bodies whose materiality disturbs the impersonality of citizenship, but whose remove from socio-political life also idealizes the unhistorical and abstract nature of state identity," then the materiality and non-ontology of blackness, as the embodiment of death, desanitizes civil society.[46] The Census of 1840 articulates, through numerical signifiers, this very prohibition on blackness as death, and insanity provides the necessary grammar of prohibition. Nothing contaminates civil society and must be contained and removed. This is the metaphysical impetus behind antiblackness.

The Census of 1840, heralded as a beacon of truth to the world concerning the necessity of slavery, actually was one of the most striking "statistical falsehoods and errors ever woven together under government print."[47] An ambitious statistician, Dr. Edward Jarvis, discovered the embarrassing errors while confined to his bed with a broken leg. Reviewing the official Census of 1840, Jarvis exposed internal contradictions and statistical inaccuracies within the census and concluded that the sixth census has contributed nothing to the statistical nosology of the free blacks, and furnished us with no data wherein we may build any theory respecting the liability of humanity, in its different phases and in various outward circumstances, to loss of reason or of the senses. . . . Such a document as we have described, heavy with errors and its misstatements, instead of being a messenger of truth to the world, to enlighten its knowledge and guide its opinion, is, in respect to human ailment, a bearer of falsehood to confuse and mislead. So far from being an aid to medical science, as it was the intention of the government on ordering these inquiries, it has thrown a stumbling block in its way, which it will require years to remove.[48]

The statistical inconsistencies were so grossly apparent that Dr. Jarvis demanded an official correction of the census. Jarvis discovered the following startling inconsistencies in the census report:

We found that the town of Worchester, Massachusetts, is stated to contain one hundred and thirty-three coloured lunatics and idiots, supported at public charge. These we know are the white patients in the state hospital, situated in that town. This single mistake multiplies the coloured lunatics of this state three-fold, and if it were corrected, it would reduce the proportion of coloured insane from one in forty-three to one in one hundred and twenty-nine. Warned by this example, we examined the statements respecting every town, city, and county, in all the states and territories, and compared on each one of these, the total coloured population with the number of coloured insane . . . the number of coloured insane in these towns and counties, carries on its very face its own refutation; no one who thus studies this report, can possibly be misled.

But these palpable errors are by no means all. There are others almost as gross, and to observers of society almost as self-evident— In many towns all the coloured population are stated to be insane, in very many others, two-thirds; one-half, one-fourth, or one-tenth of this ill-starred race are reported to thus be afflicted, and as if the document delighted to revel in variety of error, every proportion of the negro population from seven-fold its whole number, as we have shown in some towns, to less than a two-thousandth, as is recorded of others, is declared to be a lunatic. . . .

We examined the details of that document in regard to these disorders among the coloured population in every town, city, and county of the Free states, and found in many of these places, the record cases of blindness and deafness and dumbness without subjects. These disorders exist there in a state of abstraction, and fortunately for humanity, where they are said to be present, there are no people to suffer from them.[49]

Although these inconsistencies presented the social scientist with violations of scientific inquiry, these errors actually highlighted interesting philosophical moments concerning black insanity, moments articulated through the manipulation of statistical signifiers.

One of the errors that most disturbed Jarvis was the reporting of insanity, deafness, and dumbness among Northern free blacks in areas in which free blacks did not reside. For example, Jarvis discovered that "many Northern towns were mysteriously credited with insane Negroes although they were entirely without Negro residents. Many other localities were listed in the census having more Negro madmen than were there Negro inhabitants. Thus the town of Scarsboro, Maine, which had a lily-white population, found itself charged with six insane Negroes. The town of Dresden, Maine, which boasted but three Negro inhabitants, found census-takers crediting it with double that number of insane blacks." These statistical errors prompted Jarvis to remark that "we examined the details of that document in regard to these disorders among the coloured population in every town, city, and county of the Free states, and found in many of these places, the record cases of blindness and deafness and dumbness *without subjects*. These disorders exist there in *a state of abstraction*, and fortunately for humanity, where they are said to be present, there *are no people* to suffer from them [emphasis mine]."[50]

How do we account for these statistical errors, philosophically? If these ontological errors (the false reporting of being) were confined to one locality, or if entire populations of Negroes were not reported insane (or if black bodies were not utilized as surrogates for white insane patients), it would be simple to excuse these errors as mere reporting glitches, but the fact that these errors were pervasive throughout diverse geographical locations merits further interrogation.

These statistical inconsistencies present a very interesting philosophical proposition: for black ~~being~~, insanity is an ontometaphysical structure, and the presence of the black body is irrelevant to the application of the diagnosis. In other words, the Census of 1840, along with the emphatic defenses of it, implicitly makes a distinction between blackness as a (non)ontological feature and blackness as a phenomenal entity (a body). This seems a rather odd proposition, given that insanity is usually applied to a particular person, a body that we can easily identify, discipline, and treat. But the census departs from this commonsense understanding of insanity. Marshals could account for black insanity in places where physical black bodies did not exist because one does not need the physical body to make the claim that black insanity is a problem. Why is this the case? I would suggest that this error is only an error within the ontic science of statistical reasoning; but when we are really trying to describe an ontological condition of blackness using statistical instruments, then "error" must be reconfigured. Blackness becomes a ubiquitous threat, always already existing and floating throughout civil society as a phantom-like danger. Because this danger is ubiquitous, any state, city, or locality can claim the presence of black insanity. Within this logic, black bodies are decentered and black ontometaphysics assumes centrality. This also explains why white insane patients were recorded in census data as black; insanity is an ontometaphysical feature of blackness in an antiblack world. So a "white insane patient" was somewhat of an oxymoron lexically for marshals, and they simply corrected this error.

Thus, the errors that Jarvis described in detail were ontological truths. The census allowed antebellum society to participate in a collective discourse about the dangers of black freedom. We are dealing more with ontology as the *ultimate science* concerning blackness (ontology becomes a science for antiblackness) and less with psychiatry and statistics as rigorous sciences. If Jarvis had been able to think philosophically about blackness, instead of merely social-scientifically, then he would have understood why these defenders embraced the census with such urgency. Defending the census became *self-preservation* against the encroachment of nothing for antebellum humans.

Needless to say, the census report was never corrected—despite Jarvis's insightful critique of its validity (the census was valid on an entirely different register). His demands, however, prompted Congressman John Quincy Adams to introduce a resolution in the House of Representatives to investigate the legitimacy of the census (in 1844). Adams instructed the Department of State to inform the House "whether any gross errors have been discovered in the printed Sixth Census . . . and if so, how those errors originated, what they are, and what, if any, measures have been taken to rectify them."[51] The Secretary of State was none other than John C. Calhoun, who was actually responsible for administering the Census of 1840, and he appointed William Weaver (who was actually superintendent of the Census of 1840) to review himself. Of course, Weaver found no errors, and the census was considered statistically valid.

Within an antiblack scientific procedure or process, truth and error lose integrity and become indissociable fictions. This is what Jarvis could not understand, but Calhoun adumbrated the arbitrariness of truth and error as scientific realities when it concerns free blacks:

> That it [the Census of 1840] may contain errors, more or less, is hardly to be doubted. It would be a miracle if such a document, with so many figures and entities, did not. But that they have, if they exist, materially affected the correctness of the general result would seem hardly possible. *Nothing but the truth itself is so* would seem capable of explaining the fact that in all slave-holding states, without exception, the census exhibits uniformly, a far comparative prevalence of these diseases among the free blacks than among the Slaves of another State [emphasis mine].[52]

Calhoun presents a tautology to discount the inaccuracies that Jarvis exposed: "Nothing but the truth itself is so would seem capable of explaining that in all slave-holding states, without exception, the census exhibits uniformly, a far comparative prevalence of these diseases among the free blacks than among the Slaves of another State." As Jarvis argues, since the reporting is flawed throughout the study, from the very beginning, all conclusions must be questioned. Calhoun's rejoinder insists that the conclusions are correct because they are correct—they were always correct, even before the census was compiled. Any errors are just subsumed (Hegelian *Aufhebung*) into the truth, such that errors become truth and truth becomes the errors that were always truth. This dizzying tautology appears to defy logic, or contravene the principles of science, but, in essence, antiblackness inverts logic for its own end.[53] This illogic, expressed in the tautology, translates into the logic of death. The displacement of truth and error is a strategy of metaphysical warfare. The tautology is designed to concretize the deadlock of black ~~being~~: one is insane if one desires freedom or one is sane if one accepts social/political death. Either way, the tautology ensures the inevitability of death, as scientific truth/error.

Thus, the errors—reporting black insane patients in localities where blacks didn't physically exist, for example—are eternal truths when black ~~being~~ and freedom are thought together. The syntagm "free black" is the discursive materiality of insanity; civil society collapses when the boundary between death and life, filth and purity, human and property is violated. The free black is insane precisely because of this unthinkable collapse.[54]

The insane represent the threshold of humanity, the not fully human transitioning into "rational inertia" or mental death, that zero degree of humanity, as a living and breathing waste object, wasting away into irrational obscurity. The mad represent a certain paradox—they exist in a state of nonexistence. It takes the free black, however, to realize fully this paradox because this ~~being~~ is situated at the threshold of ontometaphysics. Since its ontological borders are porous and unprotected by metaphysical and juridical discourses, the free black dissolves into the abyss of insanity. Insanity, then, is the index of ~~being~~ as nothing. In *Madness and Civilization*, Foucault describes madness as a particular void within which reason recedes into the darkness of infinity. What renders madness so disruptive is precisely this vacuous space that "has become man's possibility of abolishing both man and the world."[55] As somewhat of a dystopic dreamscape, insanity becomes the repository of unbearable exceptions, and the free black is the material embodiment of this nightmare. But if we follow the thought of Kant, Hegel, and most pro-slavery advocates (and some abolitionists, as well), blacks are situated outside of reason; they are the infants of reason's historical movement. How can a ~~being~~ purportedly void of reason, innately, become insane? If insanity assumes a becoming for the human, an unfortunate fall from the mountain of reason into the abyss of unreason, then this becoming is completely absent in the insane black. Blackness is insane from its very appearance in the world—its appearance is the evidence of insanity. Insanity identifies appearance without Being in an antiblack world. Given the existential positioning of blacks in an antiblack world, insanity is the only ground available. Blackness is born in this abyss within modernity.

If we read the census as just another piece of pro-slavery propaganda, then we miss the deep philosophical presumptions that engender (and sustain) the census; in particular, mathematics is philosophical writing otherwise. Unlike the Platonist, who believes that "mathematics is the discovery of truths about structures that exist independently of the activity or thought of mathematics," according to Benacerraf and Putnam in *Philosophy of Mathematics*,[56] the census expresses an Aristotelian (or Nietzschean) perspective in which mathematics is a fictive or linguistic formation, and it becomes more like "a rigorous esthetics. It tells us nothing of real-being, but it forges a fiction."[57] The census is a tapestry of antiblack aesthetics; the numerical signs create a canvas of the beautiful and the good life in an antiblack order. This is why the census was too good to give up because of its philosophical beauty—which translates into an unbearable ugliness for black ~~being~~. Statistics is ontological poetry in this case, and its validity exists in a register outside ontic accounting and verification. Put differently, the Census of 1840 invites us to think about mathematics not as an objective reflection of the external world, but as a premier tool for fantasies, power, and imaginings.

Antiblackness relies on mathematics when guns, knives, and whips reach their limit of destruction—mathematics' weapons are metaphysical and just as deadly.

CODA: THE FREE BLACK AS PARADIGM OF SCIENTIFIC HORROR

Here is proof of the necessity of slavery. The African is incapable of self-care and sinks into lunacy under the burden of freedom. It is a mercy to give him guardianship and protection from mental death.
—JOHN C. CALHOUN, quoted in Deutsch, "The First U.S. Census of the Insane (1840) and Its Uses as Pro-Slavery Propaganda"

What type of life is even possible in the metaphysical holocaust? Are the terms *life* and *death* even appropriate to describe the condition of the ~~being~~ situated within this ontological lacuna? Theorists have approached these inquiries with unavoidable paradoxes: social death, necrocitizenship, living corpse, and living dead, just to name a few. The antebellum free black—a ~~being~~ situated between slave and citizen, human and property, political death and social life, and subject and object—constitutes such an exception for antebellum U.S. society. Writing about the antebellum free black raises particular theoretical and philosophical problems, since the humanist grammars of being and existence fracture around the term *free black* and endlessly encircle it with paradoxes, contradictions, and puzzles. The juxtaposition of free and black collides two disparate grammars into chaotic signification and conceptual devastation: freedom is the terrain of the living, of the being we call human, and black is the territory of existential dread, nonfreedom, and the ~~being~~ we might call object. With the term *free black*, we are forced into a permutation of conceptual ground that is unstable, and it desiccates beneath itself as a self-consuming oxymoron. Within this grammatical, syntactical, and conceptual chaos, even the terms *life* and *death* must be reconfigured and reorganized to capture the ~~being~~ situated within this unending violence. Indeed, what does it mean to live or to die when one's living is a form of death, and one's death is a gift of life? Because biology does not exhaust the fields of life and death, the problem at hand is more profound than we can imagine, especially when we analyze the condition of ~~being~~ that we call blackness.

It is this conceptual density that gets trafficked into, unknowingly perhaps, the debates about free blacks in antebellum society. The epigraph raises these concerns without explicitly making bare the philosophical presumptions about blackness that anchor it. For John C. Calhoun, freedom for blackness is death, a form of death worse than mere biological expiration—mental death, or insanity. Since the human being names a relationship of care between the self, Being, and its projection into the external world (freedom), claiming that the black is incapable of such care places him outside the realm of freedom and into the domain of the unfree, the care-less, and the unthought. But this realm of unfreedom is also a form of death, according to Marriott, because antiblackness strips black ~~being~~ of this fundamental existential relationship by objectifying this self and presenting this relationship to the captor for his pleasure. Thus, we have a strange play between deaths, deaths reconfigured as life, which seems to be the only existential option for blackness in modernity: freedom engenders mental death and unfreedom engenders social death. Because social death is a form of mental death to the extent that the mind is pulverized by routinized pain and terror, and mental death is a form of social death to the extent that consciousness cannot actualize or move throughout the field of the social, there is no escaping this condition of death as life and life as death for Calhoun. "Free black" names this existential deadlock.

The antebellum free black has primarily become an object for historiography and, concomitantly, has been analyzed through humanist presuppositions and conceptual paradigms (e.g., that there is a subject of the historical process; that a clear distinction between life and death exists historically; that blacks are human, capable of transforming space through time). Because Western historiography takes humanism for granted and applies the notion of human agency and existence to its objects of analysis, the ontological crisis of blackness is often overlooked in historiography. In other words, can we have a historiography that does not presume the human as the subject of history and the various capacities that this human possesses (e.g., freedom, temporal change, time/ space capacity)? I would argue that the humanist grammar of "subject," "human," "agent," and "freedom" does not quite apply to the antebellum free black, and thus, the antebellum free black is more of a philosophical allegory than a historical agent.

Reading the free black as a philosophical allegory, as a paradigm for ontological terror, enables us to expose the function of science and mathematics in the destruction of black ~~being~~. Indeed, the antebellum free black is a particular historical figure (according to historiography), but the particularity of this figure exposes a larger paradigm of terror continuing in the present—and that will extend into the future as long as the world exists. Diagnosing free blacks as insane, even though their bodies are absent from the examination, proposing physically rubbing away blackness as the only solution to antiblackness, beating the "devil" out of blacks until the symbolic constituents of existence crumble, and bleeding out black bodies are scientific procedures for articulating the truth of the metaphysical holocaust (i.e., "one is already dead"). They serve as allegories of the condition of black ~~being~~ in a metaphysical war. The free black's relation to science and mathematics has been one of utter terror and ontological insecurity.

Whether we are talking about the experiments conducted on captive female flesh (e.g., Dr. J. Marion Sim's viciousness), the torture and humiliation of blacks during the Tuskegee Study on syphilis, the forced sterilization of black females, the fictions of the *Bell Curve* and other genres of antiblack scientific mythology, or the forced experimentation on prisoners, antiblackness mobilizes science and mathematics to inflict unspeakable harm. Thus, what I want to convey with the paradigm of the free black, here, is that the particularity of the antebellum free black unveils a vicious paradigm of terror for *all* blacks—no matter the time period, the geographical location, or the insistence of romantic humanism importuning us to accept that we are free and human like everyone else. Thinking these diverse particularities together enables us to penetrate the depths of scientific horror.

FOUR

═══

CATACHRESTIC FANTASIES

SEEING AND NOT SEEING: PLAYTIME

The problem of black ~~being~~ is also a problem of vision and envisioning. Our preoccupation here orbits around this proposition and the "metaphysical infrastructure" (as Nahum Chandler would call it) that undergirds the visual economy of signs, representations, and images concerning black ~~being~~. Part of the objective, then, is to listen to what images are telling us—to read the visual sign as a particular philosophical iteration, one wrapped up in violence.

To suggest that black visuality and violence are mutually constitutive and intertwined is well documented, and many scholars in art history and cultural/visual studies have edified our understanding of this entanglement.[1] Our investigation does not challenge this beautiful work, but seeks to contribute to it by centering a particular form of violence—ontometaphysical violence. I have argued that black ~~being~~ is continuously obliterated as a necessary feature of antiblackness. The nothing black ~~being~~ must incarnate is the metaphysical entity an antiblack world obsessively attempts to purge, but fails in this enterprise, since the world cannot eradicate nothing. But failure does not preclude the enterprise; rather, it serves as its pernicious fuel. Thus, the metaphysical holocaust, the obsessive attempt to eradicate the black nothing, requires an extensive arsenal of destruction. Hortense Spillers avers, "Sticks and bricks may break our bones, but words will most certainly kill us." The metaphysical holocaust requires, then, not just sticks, bricks, guns, and knives, but also words, iconography, images, and representations. Our focus here is on the way that images are indispensable weapons in the obsession with destroying nothing.

But this aspect of metaphysical violence raises a difficult problematic: how do you represent the immaterial, the nothing that haunts a metaphysical world? How do you give a material form to what is most formless? How do we visualize black as nothing? Black ~~being~~ compounds our problematic, since it is not just that metaphysical violence is immaterial, but that the free black does not exist as such (does not exist within ontological schemes). Or, if we return to Chief Justice Taney's metaphysics, black ~~being~~ "exists to not exist" and *must* exist in this nonexistence. I italicize the word must to docket a certain necessity that the world would wish to disavow. Although black ~~being~~ does not exist, it must contain nothing for an antiblack world (as equipment and not being)—this is the crux of black suffering and the unbearable labor black bodies are forced to perform for the world. We must then inquire, how do you represent both what does not exist and what is also immaterial? How does the immateriality of the metaphysical holocaust enforce the nonexistence of black ~~being~~?

These inquiries bring us to the problem of representation. Gayatri Spivak would consider this problematic one of catachresis. For her, catachresis is "a metaphor without a literal referent standing in for a concept that is the condition of conceptuality."[2] A catachresis ruptures the field of representation, given that it lacks a literal referent. And you cannot properly represent what lacks a literal referent (and in our case, you must represent that which exists in nonexistence, since representation is part of the arsenal of destroying nothing). The difficulty Spivak presents with the entanglement (but not collapse) of *Vertretung* (something akin to political representation, "treading in your shoes")/*Darstellung* (placing there through representation, as in portrait or theater) is that *Vertretung* relies on *Darstellung*, such that putting yourself in someone's shoes (or even representing a historical account of a ~~being~~, like the antebellum free black, for example) is also a form of portraiture or art.[3] In short, to suggest we can really represent at all conceals the disruption of the sign *real* at the heart of the enterprise. I completely agree with Spivak's deconstruction, her important displacement of the sign representation.

For our analysis, however, we must contend with the fact that metaphysical violence obliterates the *Da* in *Darstellung* in that there is no there for black ~~being~~ to be placed [*stellen*]. The destruction of the there-ness and the inability to place within this there-ness is the representational component of the metaphysical holocaust that black ~~being~~ must endure. The metaphysical infrastructure upon which representation depends is one that cannot accommodate black ~~being~~. In other words, the metaphysical holocaust renders representation always already fraught—because the place of representation is obliterated for black ~~being~~.

When investigating black ~~being~~, we are ultimately asking, how do you represent that which lacks a place (and not just a literal referent)? What, exactly, is placed there—the illegitimate place? I would suggest that the metaphysical holocaust (the obliteration of the very place enabling representation) mobilizes catachresis. I am borrowing the term *catachresis* in this investigation to docket the necessity of representing that lacking both a place and a literal referent (black ~~being~~, essentially, lacks a literal referent because this place has already been obliterated). As Ronald Judy reminds us, "The Negro cannot enable the representation of meaning, [since] it has no referent."[4]

Put differently, representation relies on ontological ground (or a metaphysical infrastructure) that assumes a coherent place of being, which representation fills. But when such a place is absent, representation encounters a problem. Catachresis provides a way out of this deadlock, since it *creates a fantastical place* for representation to situate the unrepresentable.

Visual terror frames Fanon's well-known encounter with a young boy:

"Dirty nigger!" Or simply, "*Look*, a Negro!"

"Look, a Negro!" It was an external stimulus that flicked over me as I passed by. I made a tight smile.

"Look, a Negro!" It was true. It amused me.

"Look, a Negro!" The circle was drawing a bit tighter.

I made no secret of my amusement.

"Mama, *see* the Negro! I'm frightened!" [emphasis mine]

The young boy makes an impossible demand, an imperative that is bound up in the visual—one similar to Nancy's imperative to see. In this instance, the imperative to look and to see is impossible precisely because it requires a seeing of that which is nothing, that which is execrated, that which does not exist. If the Law of Being requires the human to see what is invisible, meaning to see Being in the place of its withdrawal and unfolding, then the young boy presents an imperative that disables seeing and renders it ineffective because one can only see that which has a place (a being there). But the Negro lacks a place ontologically. One must see through a certain ontological blindness; this blindness, this unbearable opacity, illumines as it conceals. What one sees when one looks at the Negro is something ineffable, something we must struggle to comprehend with the resources at our disposal. For the imperative to see this thing is outside the frame of vision, and our metaphysical vision depends on ontological coherence. The ontic and the ontological converge on the site of the visual. Within (and without) this field, the Negro is anamorphic, an ontometaphysical distortion, or blind spot. The imperative to see this distorting blind spot is, then, an imperative to not see, or a seeing that disavows the impossibility of the demand. One must see to not see. In other words, the young boy demands Mama to see that which cannot be seen ontologically, and her seeing translates into a not seeing. The demand, then, could be restated as, "Mama, see the Negro precisely by not seeing him." Look into the blind spot of vision to see what vision cannot accommodate. As David Marriott perspicuously suggests, black being "can only be seen insofar as one blinds oneself to it, and blindness is all the security and comfort the whiteness of the eye needs."[5]

How does one look at that which does not exist and cannot be seen? What would enable such a looking? For one must not just see the "Nigger" but also the "Dirty Nigger."[6] How do you look at the dirtiness of black being? This dirtiness is the metaphysical contamination, the impurity, and the flaw that outlaw ontological explanation, as Fanon would describe it. Put differently, within the demand to see is both a phenomenological and ontological order. The young boy not only insists that Mama see Fanon's black body (the phenomenological form) but also his dirtiness (the ontological interdiction)—the contamination through which the black body is but a portal. Sylvia Wynter reminds us that the Negro must represent all that is evil and impure to secure the boundaries of the human. As such, the Negro cannot serve as a proper object of knowledge. The Negro, then, represents something for which epistemology and the vision predicated on this field of knowledge cannot accommodate. Mama must see this metaphysical impurity, this dirtiness, this "dirty Nigger."

Put differently, the eyes are not the organ of this seeing, of this impossible demand—one sees dirtiness, contamination, and impurity (the Dirty Nigger) through something else.

The black body is but an ontic illusion with devastating realities. It provides form for a nothing that metaphysics works tirelessly to obliterate. Lacan provides a heuristic way to understand the black body as the vase that provides form for the formlessness of *nothingness*.[7] The black body holds this nothing, a nothing that is projected onto it. The young boy's imperative, then, is a double imperative to see both the vase and the nothing it contains. One would think, however, that destroying the black body would resolve the problem, but since what is *really* the target is something for which carnal weapons are ineffective, the destruction will not end. This is the metaphysical holocaust that the Negro must endure, the unending terror and obliteration that will continue as long as the metaphysical world continues. Turning to Lacan again, we can suggest that the metaphysical holocaust is the *global* instantiation of a demand that relentlessly pursues its impossible object: the eradication of *nothing*.[8]

Fanon avers that the "Negro is a toy in the white man's hands."[9] The function of a toy is to facilitate play. It enables a staging, a configuration, an imagining of both the toy and the context within which the toy is placed. The toy is a vehicle for fantasy. Within this fantasy, the toy anchors the enjoyment and imagination of the one staging the experience. To understand the Negro as this toy, then, is to think about the Negro as a vehicle for fantasy—a vessel of the human's imagination and configuration of the world.[10] One plays with the Negro to stage an encounter with nothing. This nothing can assume various forms depending on the vitality of the human fantasizing, since one cannot just imagine nothing; some form must be given to it. An antiblack fantasy relies on the Negro to play with nothing and to configure it within the world—in essence, to *dominate* (and objectify) nothing through the knowledge imposed during the fantasy. Looking is a form of playing with the Negro. One looks *through* fantasy and manipulates the Negro as play—one is able to finally see the nonexistent and imagine filling in the vacuous space of nonbeing. Playing with the Negro as a toy, then, is all about filling in this ontological vacuity (the obliteration of *Da*, there-ness) with something devastating.

This vacuity, or blank space, is the non-thereness of black ~~being~~. As an activity of play, the human fantasizes about filling it up with something comprehensible, even if paradoxical and nonsensical. One can deploy the arsenal of imagination to fill in this place, where being never arrived. The objective of playing with this toy, in other words, is to provide a referent for that which does not exist, but must exist in our fantasizing (the condition of possibility for fantasizing nothing). We might call this a catachrestic fantasy. Since the Negro lacks an ontological place (a Da-sein), it also lacks a worldly referent (which is why Wynter might claim the Negro cannot serve as a proper object of knowledge). In a catachrestic fantasy, one attempts to address a proper metaphysical question: "What is the Negro?" The Negro is metaphysics' "most phantasmagoric creation," as Rinaldo Walcott cogently describes it.[11]

I will suggest that images, in particular, illustrations, are important tools for fantasizing, looking, and playing with the Negro. Within the image, the human's fantasizing power is boundless, and an absolute sovereignty of unchecked power is unleashed to fill in the empty space. It is within the image, the pictographic sign, that the impossible imperative to see that lacking a proper referent is achieved by *imagining* the referent. The image, then, performs important philosophical work, and playing is not merely an enterprise of amusement. Achille Mbembe suggests that the "pictographic sign does not belong solely in the field of 'seeing'; it also falls in that of 'speaking.' It is in itself a figure of speech, and this speech expresses itself, not only for itself or as a mode of describing, narrating and representing reality, but also a particular strategy of persuasion, even violence."[12] Thus, we must ascertain what the image is *saying* to us through the imperative to see. We must understand the ontological violence the image enacts as a feature of the continuous metaphysical holocaust. This chapter reads illustrations as a philosophical discourse, one enabled by fantasy and play.

These images are situated within what Hortense Spillers would call the "grid of associations, from the semantic and iconic folds buried deep within the collective past" that black being represents.[13] This grid is the network of fantasy that antiblackness engenders through images and iconography. Semiotics becomes untenable to the extent that the grid relies on a signified that is purely speculative, unstable, and unreliable. Furthermore, the signifier is just as problematic, since it does not exist. Both signifier and signified lack any real referent to ground them, and this exposes the ontological presumptions upon which semiotics, as a field, is predicated. We might suggest that the Negro marks the obliteration of the sign, as Baudrillard and other postmodern semioticians might insist.[14] But the Negro, as fantastical sign, exists for this obliteration—the destruction of the sign is the function of the Negro in an antiblack world. The Negro is the nodal point of semiotics, and at this zero point of saturation the Negro exists to be obliterated continuously, not just physically but also semiotically. What is "buried deep within the collective past" is precisely the metaphysical holocaust that renders the Negro an impossible referent—one that does not lend itself to substitutions easily. What I am suggesting is that the Negro is the irreplaceable nonreferent that sets semiotics in motion. Or, paradoxically, we could describe it as the phallus of the Lacanian phallus for the human. It is a nonsensical sign buried deeply within a global unconscious, which psychoanalysis and semiotics can only approach but never quite penetrate. The Negro, then, is a sign that is not a sign—nothing we are able to recognize or incorporate into the chain of associations and signifiers that provide meaning and interpretation for the world.

Playing, then, is not innocuous; it is a vicious form of enjoyment and a weapon of destruction. The Negro, as toy, encapsulates the utter collapse of the distinctions between play and terror, imagination and destruction, sign and referent, image and speech, and philosophy and fantasy. Saidiya Hartman describes this black being as "an empty vessel vulnerable to the projections of other's feelings, ideas, desires, and values."[15] What is projected in this emptiness is precisely the desire to overcome the nothing that limits freedom (that disrupts the metaphysical fantasy of human coherence).

To think through this play and the catachrestic fantasies it engenders, we must interrogate what Heidegger might call *Bildwesen*, or the "essence of images." To return to a pervasive theme throughout this book, I will argue that the essence of images about black being is not imagistic, but of the order of metaphysics. In other words, the essence is re-presenting black as nothing and staging an encounter with this nothing. What is played with, then, is nothing. The Negro makes the playing possible. We might, again, borrow a Lacanian (and Žižekian) reading of fantasy as that which allows the human to come close to nothingness (as the real) but not too close for comfort—to enjoy the pleasure within the terror the fantasy presents (as a form of jouissance).[16] As such, the fantasy would map the coordinates of the human's desires; it is pedagogical in that it teaches the human how to desire by engaging the undesirable. Along this thematic, we might say that the catachrestic fantasy is pedagogical in that it articulates a philosophical desire and maps its ontometaphysical coordinates. What is this philosophical desire? Precisely to give form to black formlessness and, finally, answer the riddle "What is black ~~being~~?"

Following Fanon's insistence that we "put the dream back in its proper *time* and *place*," I would suggest that the catachrestic fantasy constitutes an interstice between Fanon's real fantasy and a Lacanian fantasy.[17] By this, I mean that antiblackness is situated on both ends of the dream-work—as that which puts pressure on the dream and on the world. In a catachrestic fantasy, a free black is a *fantasy* within the (real) world *and* within the (unconscious) dream. Neither the real world nor the unconscious can adequately represent this thing—condensation and displacement are left without any sign except a nonsense one. In other words, the catachrestic fantasy dissolves the distinction between the real and the fantasy, not just because antiblackness is found on both sides, but also because *the free black doesn't exist on either side.* The figure presented *is not* a free black, but something else—something emancipation produced but cannot re-present. A catachrestic fantasy, then, emerges from the *need to give form to that which is nothing.* Black existence (what you *see* when you look at a black body, for example) is *not* anything representation can incorporate into its epistemology.

CATACHRESTIC FANTASY

We now turn to a few images to *see* what cannot be seen and to look into the blindness of nothing that the Negro must represent. Hortense Spillers once inquired, "Do we look with eyes, or with the psyche?"[18] How exactly must the young boy's mama see this thing that Fanon catachrestically re-presents? Our answer is that we look through catachrestic fantasies, which require much more than the eyes and an ocularcentric sensibility.[19] Seeing the staged fantasy, as play, requires an ontometaphysical perception beyond the eyes. The young boy's demand is to look *through* an antiblack fantasy in which the Negro is but a plaything for the *real* enjoyment. We are required to look *into* the vase and see nothing, the Negro *as* nothing. But this nothing must assume a form within the image. In fact, the form *conceals* the nothing it encases. Our seeing, then, must uncover this concealment.

I will present the following propositions to "build a way" (as Heidegger would call it) through this abyss of representation: (1) Catachrestic fantasy is deployed as a solution to the problem of black ~~being~~ and representation. (2) Fantasy enables the representation of the sign continuously obliterated. (3) Catachrestic fantasies enable the representation of black as nothing, and it enables representation to give form to formlessness. (4) The free black lacks both a literal referent and a place, given that it does not exist, even when the term is deployed as a description of ~~being~~. (5) Since the free black does not exist, emancipation allows illustrators to deploy a capacious imagination in imaging this ~~being~~.

Our investigation will listen to the work of illustrated journalism for its ontometaphysical commentary.[20] I chose politically motivated illustrations and a work from Edward Clay's "Life in Philadelphia Series" because it is here, I believe, that the metaphysical question is broached. Illustrators are not bound by a literal referent, and they often grapple with the problem of place. What these illustrations reveal, I will argue, is the important work that catachrestic fantasies perform in both giving form to formlessness and obliterating the place of black existence. I have also chosen an image from the antebellum period and beyond as a way to demonstrate the futility of temporal distinctions when it concerns black ~~being~~. Whether we are in the antebellum period, the Civil War, or post-Reconstruction, the proper metaphysical question is consistent. Neither time nor romantic progress narratives have settled the question of black ~~being~~. I have also chosen these particular images because I believe they engage the proper ontological question "What is black ~~being~~?" Or, "How is it going with black ~~being~~?" Images become philosophical discourse when philosophical proofs reach their limit—when philosophy needs to rely on irrationality, or unreason, to supplement its enterprise. In other words, the proper metaphysical question of black ~~being~~ can only be broached through the absurd or the fantastical. Images take us into the capacious universe of fantasy.

Illustrations are important, and often neglected, forms of philosophical discourse because they employ fantasy, imagination, and paradox to work through difficult questions. In figure 4.1, *Harper's Weekly* presents a catachrestic fantasy as an answer to the proper metaphysical question "What is black ~~being~~?" Or, following Patterson, what is this new creature the master creates with his power of transubstantiation? In this illustration, an emancipated black is contending with farm animals; he is at great pains to convince the animals of his newly acquired ontometaphysical status. The emancipated black, haughtily popping his collar and holding his head above the farm animals, asserts in stereotypically fragmented speech that "I ain't one ob you no more. I'se a man, I is!" The farm animals, as if fully comprehending this assertion, dissent with mouths ajar and with various looks of consternation. They respond with nonverbal communication. The comedic drive of the illustration is the utter absurdity of a dialogic exchange between a speaking ~~being~~ and a nonspeaking being. But this absurdity translates into metaphysical reality for the emancipated—fantastical comedy becomes a form of philosophical realism.

What is important about the illustration is that it provides a devastating critique of romantic humanism and emancipation rhetoric. If the captive is juxtaposed to inanimate and animate objects, chairs, desks, houses, and farm animals, then emancipation exacerbates this troubling juxtaposition. In essence, the animals *respond* to the emancipated black through looks of mockery and disbelief: "You may be emancipated, but what are you now?" Emancipation fails to transform property into personhood or chattel into human being.

The emancipated black must insist that he is no longer sentient property, but he directs this insistence to farm animals, not a human community (a political community). Put differently, he must seek recognition from farm animals, since such recognition is implausible within the political community. But this recognition makes a mockery of the Hegelian scene—for Hegel does not envision such recognition occurring between ~~objects~~. It is a recognition that undermines recognition. What would recognition from farm animals accomplish? Why does the emancipated black need such recognition? Emancipation engenders incessant pleading

CUTTING HIS OLD ASSOCIATES.
MAN OF COLOR. "Ugh! Get out. I ain't one ob you no more. *I'se a Man, I is!*"

FIGURE 4.1 This illustration depicts a free black man addressing farm animals by exclaiming, "Ugh! Get out. I ain't one ob you no more. *I'se a man, I is!*" *Harper's Weekly*, January 17, 1863. Courtesy of Hargrett Rare Book and Manuscript Library/University of Georgia Libraries.

to a community that is unable to grant recognition (farm animals) or a community that refuses such recognition (Taney's political community).

Furthermore, if ontological resistance is predicated on meeting the eyes of the white man, according to Fanon, then the illustration suggests that such resistance will never occur, since the emancipated are relegated to a netherworld, a spatiality without a proper name. Caught between animal and man, this new creature lacks a place within the world. The emancipated black resides in the interstice of existence. Giorgio Agamben would consider such a figure a "creature" or a "werewolf" produced through a sovereign ban. The free black embodies "a threshold of indistinction and of passage between animal and man, phyis and nomos, exclusion and inclusion . . . the werewolf, who is precisely neither man nor beast, and who dwells paradoxically within both while belonging to neither."[21] In other words, the emancipated black, or free black, is neither man nor animal, but something other. This, then, is the answer the catachrestic fantasy proposes: the emancipated black is nothing our symbolic can accommodate, no-thing that has a proper place within the order of things. Emancipation releases blacks into a non-place of utter terror, vulnerability, and vicious mockery. The answer to the proper metaphysical question, then, is that the emancipated black is a placeless ~~being~~.[22]

What is funny about this cartoon for subscribers, then, is the philosophical impasse itself: the utter placelessness and undecidability of this new creature. Hidden within the crevices of the cartoon is ontological terror; this terror becomes the punch line. Black ~~being~~ is amusing because it assumes subjectivity where there is none. Put differently, romantic humanism provides the necessary backdrop for the terroristic humor: it circulates untruth that is reappropriated for humorous ends. The untruth is that black ~~being~~ will be incorporated into the human family and its political community once emancipated, and this incorporation is the sign of freedom. Mocking humanism and its romance is the objective of the cartoon. The cartoon is a philosophical response to black freedom dreams.

Illustrators also rely on aphesis (dropping portions of a word), pleonasm (superfluity and redundancy), hyperbaton (inversion of normal grammatical order), malapropism (a substitution of one word for a similar-sounding word, resulting in nonsense), and solecism (improper use of grammar and tactless speech) to create a pernicious arsenal of rhetorical violence. They present stereotypical broken black speech as evidence that black ~~being~~ is inassimilable. If what distinguishes man from animal is language, as philosophers have asserted, then this new creature is a speaking animal—not human, but something like a "talking ape," to borrow David Walker's terminology.[23] But this talking thing lacks a place within the world, where language and subjectivity would converge. Thus, part of the humor is the utter inefficacy of language, literacy, and reason to resolve the ontometaphysical problem. The Negro must not only turn to nonspeaking animals for recognition and interlocution, but also face the fact that language/literacy will not guarantee humanity. In essence, communicative rationality is the joke, one that postmetaphysics and romantic humanism continue to disavow.[24]

This question carries over beyond the war, seeking a definitive answer.

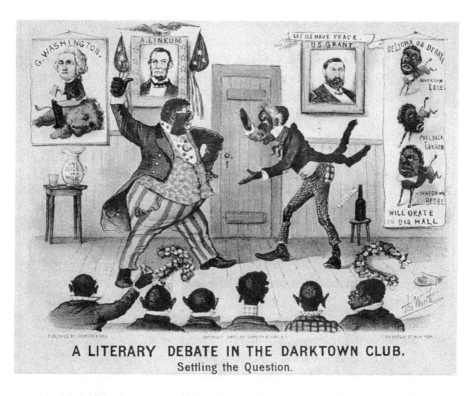

FIGURE 4.2 "A Literary Debate in the Darktown Club—Settling the Question," by Thomas Worth. Published by Currier and Ives, 1884. Courtesy of the Library of Congress.

The Currier and Ives illustration (figure 4.2), as if directly addressing this proper metaphysical question, answers with the subtitle, "Settling the Question." What needs to be settled, then, is not a trivial literary debate but the *proper metaphysical question* itself. The vicious illustrative imagination continues as two black literary scholars are debating in front of an eager crowd (again, illustrating the utter inefficacy of language and literacy for achieving human recognition). In the illustration accompanying this image, the debate ends with an all-out brawl. Both scholars are bruised and bleeding, and the room is totaled. It is clear that the illustration mocks black intelligence and civility. Ronald Judy has insisted that literacy is the hallmark of rationality and humanity in modernity, and this illustration suggests that even literacy will not restore humanity.[25] In the hands of the unruly thing, literacy devolves into physical violence.

Beneath this stereotypical depiction of black incivility lies a catachrestic fantasy—one that preconditions the violence that is to erupt after the debate. Hanging on the wall is a poster entitled, "De Lions ob Debate." The title is deceptive in that it would purport to present only those with the most formidable intelligence and sharp reasoning. The poster is designed to frame the scene, the fantasy, as a meeting of the minds. But the mind is not what the poster frames; rather, it uses lions literally and not metaphorically. The debaters are portrayed in an almost mythical way—half lion and half man (reflecting a version of what Tommy Lott has called "the Negro Ape metaphor" in visual culture).[26] Each hybrid ~~being~~, mockingly wearing a bow tie to exaggerate the hybridity, appears untamed and vicious. This is precisely Agamben's creature or werewolf as ontological limit. It is this limit that frames the fantasy, since we are to regard the debaters on stage not as humans, but as something other. Something neither fully man nor fully animal but something other—something without a proper name. The hybrid man/lion represents the catachresis that must constitute black ~~being~~. Emancipation produces this catachresis as necessity. Whatever this thing is, it lacks a proper referent.

The indistinction between man and animal is not an opening onto Being or a dethroning of anthropocentrism; rather, it is an indistinction of terror and dread.[27] The poster hanging on the opposite side demonstrates what happens to lions. President George Washington has slayed a lion and is victoriously sitting on it, holding an ax. We can suggest that the first president serves as a metonymic figure for humanity and the political community. The ax and the bloodied lion both symbolize the metaphysical holocaust, which provides the frame for the debate stage. Humanity valorizes the violence over the lion, a violence that continues without end. Furthermore, we can suggest that the question can only be settled with extreme forms of violence and terror—this is ontological terror. This creature is produced through this violence, and emancipation sustains it. The question, then, is settled. Will emancipation transform black ~~being~~ into human being? Currier and Ives respond with a mocking, "No!"

Derrida insisted that "one never escapes the economy of war."[28] And war becomes a structure through which metaphysics renders antiblack destruction operative, an "ideology of war," as Nelson Maldonado-Torres might call it.[29] This becomes even more apparent when catachrestic fantasies broach deep metaphysical questions. These fantasies rely on war and

DARK ARTILLERY; OR, HOW TO MAKE THE CONTRABANDS USEFUL.

FIGURE 4.3 "Dark Artillery; or, How to Make the Contrabands Useful."
Frank Leslie's Illustrated Newspaper, October 26, 1861. Courtesy of the
Library of Congress.

its apparatus to imagine beyond the limits of proper referents. In figure
4.3, *Frank Leslie's Illustrated Newspaper* presents a vicious fantasy concerning the disposability of black ~~being~~ as a scene of war. "Contrabands"
fled Confederate states and sought refuge from union soldiers during the
Civil War. According to Barbara Tomblin, General Benjamin F. Butler
declared blacks fleeing from Southern plantations and seeking protection
"property of the enemy and subject to confiscation."[30] Giving safe haven
to blacks served a strategic purpose: to drain the Confederacy of valuable
wealth. Once confiscated, Union armies pressed blacks into various forms
of work. Thus, even in union camps, blacks were still considered equipment and property—value was not grounded in the invaluable for blacks
(i.e., Being exceeding metaphysical value schemes), but freedom was cod-
ified in use value for the Union. Antiblackness, then, is not confined to
the antebellum South but is the condition of possibility for the world,
including the valiant North. But the question before the Union, and still

before us, is this: what type of work will help configure the value of black waste, the fleeing black body? What type of use does confiscation justify?

What value would such creatures have during a war—uneducated and unwanted? If one could not rely on natural law alone to ascertain value (i.e., the inalienable rights of man), then value must be found elsewhere. Hortense Spillers remarks, "The captive body, then, brings into focus a gathering of social realities as well as a metaphor for value so thoroughly interwoven in their literal and figurative emphases that distinctions be-tween them are virtually useless."[31] Whether we call this ~~being~~ a "captive," "emancipated," "contraband," or "free," the distinctions are utterly useless when the question of value is foregrounded. These distinctions, which orient much of historiography and legal studies, are differences without a difference, ontologically.

The question of value, then, reconfigures our proper metaphysical question. In essence, it inquires about how to ground value of a ~~being~~ lacking place in the world.[32] The illustrators provide an answer to this inquiry: since black ~~being~~ exists for destruction, why not make this ~~being~~ an extension of war machines? In this fantasy, black ~~being~~ is a sentient weapon, blurring the distinction between machine and flesh, weapon and body. Warfare provides value for sentient refuse. Black bodies are literal artilleries of destruction—there is no self to protect, just an open vulner-ability to deadly violence.

We might also suggest that the black weapon prefigures the suicide bomber, which preoccupies contemporary analysis of necropolitics. But martyrdom is absent from such an analysis because the black weapon is *pure use value.* The weapon does not sacrifice itself; destruction is its *reason* for existence. Black weapons also lack any relationality between humans and a political community from which to ground such self-sacrifice. Black death, vulnerability, injury, and destruction are mere comedic by-products of a war between humans. In the image, soldiers easily affix cannons to black bodies and position these weapons in the line of fire.

The battlefield is precisely the space of emancipation—a death-scape. And the ~~being~~ emancipation creates in this space is the black weapon. War allegorizes the metaphysical holocaust, which places black ~~being~~ in extraordinary harm without regard to any ontological ground of resis-tance. This war, unlike the Civil War, is without end. The black weapon is ~~being~~ for another within an economy of brutality, strategy, and calculation. This catachrestic fantasy realizes the terror Heidegger envisioned with his critique of technological reasoning. The complete collapse between technology and flesh could only be realized with black ~~being~~, and the image articulates this understanding.[33] It is unthinkable that the union soldiers would become weapons because they are human beings. Thus, it is not just that the image is viciously satirical, but also that the image exposes a kernel of truth: it is indeed plausible that black ~~being~~ could be used in such a way in an antiblack world. Humor encases a metaphysical truth. Black ~~being~~ lacks ontological security and is malleable in the hands of humans. This is ontological terror.

We might also revisit the Lacanian terms *enjoyment* and *interpassivity*—for it seems that both are operative in the catachrestic fantasy. The cynosure of the image is a black weapon with a minstrel-like smile (a smile that indicates utter obsequiousness to vicious demands and unawareness of immediate danger), gladly sitting on the ground to facilitate the soldier's reloading. The smile is a signifier of stupid enjoyment, a masochistic embrace of destruction. Through the smile, the black weapon is aligned with the nothing and all the terror it entails. The smile, then, is the figuration of interpassivity and enjoyment. The terror of nothing is projected onto black bodies (black weapons must hold the destructive enjoyment for the white subject, standing as a substitutional receptacle for the human's enjoyment), and the enjoyment is vicious—it is the enjoyment of continual destruction (the metaphysical holocaust).[34] The smile also dockets a certain duty or obligation of black ~~being~~—to rejoice in destruction as service (in this way, service as black suicide is inconceivable for the illustrator; only honor and duty explain the stupid enjoyment. The illustrators, then, impose a fallacious agency on the weapon, which is part of the vicious humor, since a weapon has no choice in the matter/manner of its destruction).

And we might say the smile signals "arbitrary [black] death as a legitimate feature of a system," as Lewis Gordon poignantly notes.[35] The arbitrariness of black perishment exposes its meaningless enjoyment through the loss of meaning.[36] The metaphysical world is a battlefield for blacks, blacks reconfigured as weapons for a war without end. At any moment, at any time, blacks could perish—or, to retool Heidegger, this perishment occurs *in einem Augenblick* (in a blink of an eye, or immediately). Again, I am using the term *perishment* over Gordon's death to docket the utter lack of meaning and being black destruction entails. Thus, there can never be Ereignis for black weapons, no event in which death enables an authentic embrace of being. Heideggerian death is impossible for black ~~being~~. There is only death as perishment—meaningless, arbitrary, and eventless destruction. The smile is the internecine sign of this destruction.

The smile, then, is absolutely essential to the image (its *punctum*, to borrow Barthes's term).[37] The smile gets us to the essence of the image. What the black weapon is smiling at *is nothing*. This, ultimately, is the fantasy the illustrator presents, and it serves to disavow the brutal context within which the weapon is placed. For the illustrator, blacks embrace the terroristic nothing antiblackness imposes upon it. Imposition is recast as masochistic embrace. The image stages an encounter with nothing as a dutiful embrace of onticide.

The black body is finished. The image articulates the closure of metaphysics: the black body is nothing more than an antiblack invention, an instrument of a destructive will to power. Any agency we imagine we can extract from this body by reclaiming and celebrating it has evaporated in a toxic atmosphere. By closure, however, I do not mean the end (as is the fantasy of some postmetaphysicians) but the completion of its internecine aim concerning black ~~being~~. The aim, the metaphysical enterprise, is to sever the flesh from the body through the work of violence, degradation, and terror, such that what is left is not a human body, but a body as machine. This is what the image proudly proclaims. The image, then, can be read as an antiblack celebration, a triumph over black ~~being~~ (and the intransigent remainder of the flesh). In his brilliant essay "The Black Body as Fetish," Anthony Farley argues that the black body serves as the object of white fantasy; the body is pressed into narratives of savagery and degradation to maintain white mastery and racial innocence. Taking something like Žižek's advice, "Enjoy your symptom," seriously,[38] Farley suggests that a masochistic embrace of the function of the black body in antiblack fantasy produces pleasure (or jouissance):

> Blackness today is a masochistic pleasure in being humiliated. Blackness, having completely submitted itself to the pleasure imperative of whiteness, has reached its limit. . . . We have experienced the black body from the situation of submission. From that situation, we have experienced the black body as a pleasure formation, a pleasure-in-

humiliation, that gave flesh to the body. The black body is familiar to us today because we have experienced white pleasure-in-humiliating as our own pleasure-in-being-humiliated. In making this connection to the audience we experience our identity, our black body identity, as a contingent historical project, as a game, as a performance, as a form of pleasure. This experience of blackness as a performance has made it possible to transgress. The creation of a new body is possible once the old body is experienced as a performance.[39]

For Farley, what I am calling the closure of metaphysics is complete, since the black body has been so thoroughly colonized by the white pleasure principle. But this closure, for him, has also produced a form of transgression; since the black body is nothing more than a performance for a white fantasy, one can refocus attention from liberating this body and creating a new one. I completely agree with Farley that a certain jouissance marks this body—how else could one endure antiblackness? But, unlike Farley, I do not believe that this produces transgression, if by "transgression" he means the potential to create a new body. What the image reveals is that the potential for creating something new, something transgressive, is almost impossible, since *the fantasy is corporeal destruction*. In other words, we assume that something will be left on the other side of the fantasy (i.e., like a Lacanian subject after having traversed the fundamental fantasy). But when the fantasy is to *destroy* through the performance of humiliation and submission, *nothing* is left to transgress. Antiblack fantasy and its pleasure principle *constitute warfare*, complete and absolute violence. Humanists introduce a counter-fantasy, as it were, that there will be a survivor, a contraband who will be saved if submitting to the sadistic pleasure of white masters. But this contraband reveling in masochism will be obliterated. This, then, is the closure of metaphysics— a cycle of invention and destruction; a cycle sealed hermetically by ontological terror; a cycle without end. The smile is the sign of this closure. *The black body is finished.*

What, then, would a ~~being~~ lacking ontological resistance resemble? It takes a catachrestic fantasy from *Frank Leslie* to broach this question, and the answer proffered is a thing that emerges through violence and exists only for perpetual destruction—black artillery.

Edward W. Clay, a nineteenth-century caricaturist, presents an ontological allegory in his series *Philadelphia Fashions*. This series denigrates free blacks and codifies its viciousness as humor. Clay demonstrates the terroristic uses of comedy; it is a pernicious instrument of antiblackness in his hands. Each illustration capitalizes on black abjection and execration. The aim is to mock emancipation by pairing malapropism with visual excess. The result is both extraordinary semiotic and linguistic violence. And since the violence occurs on both registers (semiotic and linguistic), the image is an indispensable weapon in the metaphysical holocaust. In other words, black ~~being~~ must be continually destroyed on multiple levels. Clay deploys the destructive resources of his imagination to pulverize blackness. The distinctions between terror and humor, comedy and injury, amusement and devastation are dissolved, and the semiotic field transforms into a battlefield. I would also suggest that Clay performs important philosophical work with his images—he provides an apodictic answer to the metaphysical question of black ~~being~~. Images are important ontometaphysical tools because they can defy the limits of reason and all the philosophical constraints of the imagination. When words, proofs, and formulation reach their rational limits, images carry them beyond these limits into a different philosophical arena, antiblack fantasy.

In figure 4.4, Mr. Frederick Augustus and his companion are elegantly dressed. The black dandy, eponymously (and sarcastically) named August(us), holds up a monocle. His companion inquires, "What you look at Mr. Frederick Augustus?," and he replies, "I look at dat white loafer wot looks at me, I guess he from New York."

Clay stages a fantastical (non)relation between the image of the free black (fixed in blackness, lifeless) and the human viewing the image (the white loafer). This (non)relation serves as an allegory for the position of the human and that of the equipment that can only be seen, but can never see in an antiblack world. The monocle also allegorizes emancipation—for the free black must see the world through a distorted vision. Emancipation does not restore sight to equipment (Nancy's injunction to see, for example); rather, it provides the illusion of seeing. I would also suggest that the (non)relation is fantastical, since a lifeless image is speaking to a white spectator (the consumer of Clay's humor). In short, we structure the discourse of the lifeless (the socially/politically dead) with the mocking presence of the human. This discourse translates into what Judy would call "muteness," since black ~~being~~ lacks a position in discourse that is ac-

FIGURE 4.4 *Philadelphia Fashions, 1837.* Courtesy of Smithsonian Institution, National Museum of American History, Division of Home and Community Life.

knowledged or recognized). Put differently, the free black can speak but cannot be heard.

Clay assigns a feature of animation (sight, looking) to an inanimate object (Mr. Augustus and his companion) to produce humor, for the opera glasses actually magnify an inanimate eye. With one eye closed and the monocle magnifying an inanimation, Mr. Augustus explains that he is looking at a white voyeur who is looking at him. But this presents a problematic: how does one see through an inanimate eye? What does this seeing provide Mr. Augustus? There is a disjuncture, then, between image and text, utterance and capacity, and eye and the look. In essence, the white loafer is looking at him, but Mr. Augustus is unable to return this look—but how would August have any knowledge of the world based on vision, given that the lifeless eye is unable to grant visual/epistemological certitude? Furthermore, if the "I" in the statement "I look at dat white loafer" is based on the functioning eye (the organ of his certitude), then not only is the eye disabled, but also the predicating function (looking) of the "I." Mr. Augustus's claim that he is looking, then, presents a certain fraudulence embedded in the deployment of this "I"—in this place of the missing eye. Both his eye and his "I" are fraudulent—he is unable to see the white human. Vision is unilaterally deployed as a feature of dominance (in an almost panopticon arrangement). Put differently, if what distinguishes the human from the object is the capacity to predicate, as a legitimate function of the "I," then Clay desiccates the ground of certitude and predication for the free black. Nahum Chandler describes black ~~being~~ as bringing "the problem of predication to issue with force."[40] The human has the prerogative of sight and the epistemological claims that accompany it, but the black can only assume a fraudulent relation to this predication. Mr. Augustus pretends to be a human, assuming that he can look just like the white loafer who is inspecting him; but without the privileged organ, he can only be seen (this is the realm of equipment).

We might ask, what does Mr. Augustus actually see through the inanimate eye? Nothing. In relation to the human, he sees the nothing that he ~~is~~ within an antiblack world. The free black, then, is nothing more than this fraudulent eye/I—this unbridgeable disjuncture between utterance and capacity. The image serves as a vicious allegory of black freedom. One can make a claim to it audaciously and proudly, but in the end emancipation is unable to suture the disjuncture between the claim and metaphysical condition. We might also suggest that the fraudulent eye is a substitute for Being—it fills an absent space, of being-there. If it is Being that allows us to see the invisible (the Law of Being), then such a seeing is absent for the free black. Moreover, the white loafer does not properly see Mr. Augustus, either, just equipment or an object where a human is supposed to appear, an anamorphic blind spot.

Frantz Fanon insists that "the black man has no ontological resistance in the *eyes* of the white man." The eye enables "ontological resistance," and in Fanon's formulation the eyes are an aspect of whiteness. The eyes serve as a metonymic extension of the "I"—it is the "I," as eye, that has the capacity to resist. The bilateral look, then, would bring us to a Hegelian moment of mutual recognition, where the look assumes an ontological function of constituting boundaries. But in the eyes of white men, blacks have no ontological resistance precisely *because the black eye is missing*. Ontological constitution is a *unilateral* enterprise from the human's eye to the non-seeing black thing. Fanon continues, "And already I am being dissected under white eyes, *the only real eyes*. I am *fixed*. Having adjusted their microtomes, they objectively cut away slices of my reality. I am laid bare. I feel, I see in those white faces that it is not a new man who has come in, but a new kind of man, a new genus. Why, it's a Negro!"[41] [emphasis mine].

Following Lacan, we can also suggest that white eyes stare into the gaze, rather than another pair of eyes when looking at black ~~being~~ (which is why black ~~being~~ cannot properly be seen). Mr. Augustus (and his companion) is not a human subject but the incarnation of the gaze within the visual field. For, as Jacques Lacan has indicated in the *Four Fundamental Concepts*, the gaze "[made] visible . . . the subject as annihilated in the form . . . of castration . . . it [reflected] [his] own nothingness."[42] The gaze is a terroristic entity. It shames the subject by reflecting the nothingness of the subject's core. It is precisely this nothingness that is projected onto black bodies—and this is why Mr. Augustus's eye must be missing, always already castrated. In other words, Clay presents his own catachrestic fantasy of an embodied gaze—a nothing within the field of vision, which can claim neither subjectivity nor predication. But since the free black does not exist, Mr. Augustus and his companion are signs without proper referents—signs of nothing. And a ~~being~~ without a proper referent provides ample ground for fantasizing. This enables Clay to present a fraudulent eye as the source of sight.[43]

I must also note that even without the distorting monocle, seeing still is precluded. Mr. Augustus's companion *appears* to have both eyes open, but this does not enable her to see any more than Mr. Frederick Augustus. She, in fact, asks Mr. Augustus, "What you look at Mr. Augustus?"[44] In this way, Clay seems to close the circle of uncertainty. Whether the eyes are present, open, or fraudulent, seeing is not a predicating function for the black object that can be seen, but not see. Freedom does not enable blacks to see, so such freedom is but a mockery. Without the capacity to see white humanity, to return the look, and to resist the objectifying impulse of the human, emancipation merely replaces property with fraudulence. Neither the captive nor the free black can see.

The title of figure 4.5 brings us to our metaphysical question: the great American "What Is It?" This is the crux of the issue before us, and it propels black thought and philosophy. The question turns Fanon's philosophical sarcasm and exasperation ("I see in those white faces that it is not a new man who has come in, but a new kind of man, a new genus") into a serious question: what is this new genus? The title refers to a deformed black man featured in P. T. Barnum's Museum on Broadway. Deformation, however, does not exhaust the question, since the question is put to all black ~~being~~. To provide an answer to this searing question, illustrators put catachrestic fantasies into service. This political cartoon attacks President Lincoln's integrity and racial loyalty. It is in response to the arrest of Clement Laird Vallandigham, leader of the Copperheads (Peace Democrats). Vallandigham claimed that Lincoln intended to enslave whites and to free blacks. Lincoln arrested him on charges of treason for supporting the confederacy.

The snakes are the Copperheads angrily chasing Lincoln for the arrest. Blacks also chase Lincoln, calling him "Fadderrr Abrum" and asking him to "take us to your Bussum." In response to this request for haven and acceptance, Lincoln says, "Go back to your masters, don't think you are free because you are emancipated." The image allegorizes the problem of black ~~being~~. When seeking reprieve from romantic humanism, an antiblack world insists, "Don't think you are free because you are emancipated." A fundamental distinction between freedom and emancipation exists that

FIGURE 4.5 "The Great American What Is It? Chased by Copper-Heads,"
E. W. T. Nichols, 1863. Courtesy of the Library of Congress.

distinguishes the human from his equipment. Conflating freedom and
emancipation produces disappointment, disavowal, and destruction.

Reading Lincoln's comment, "Don't think you are free because you are
emancipated," alongside the title of the image, "The great American what
is it?" suggests that the metaphysical question "What is it?" is a feature of
this gap between emancipation and freedom. Put differently, we understand freedom orients the human, but what does emancipation orient?
What is the ~~being~~ for whom emancipation is an issue? What is it? The
fantasy does not provide an apodictic answer to the question, but the
skeleton and demon in the background, along with the snake eating a
black man, suggest that this ~~being~~ is a thing of execration—of the dark
abyss. Emancipation releases blacks into a form of hell—a space of ontological terror.

The scene, then, imagines the "zone of non-being," as Fanon might call it. This is the space that is not a place, a site of unspeakable destruction without end. Lewis Gordon argues that this zone can be read in two ways: "It could be limbo, which would place blacks below white but above creatures whose lots are worse; or it could simply mean the point of total absence, the place most far from the light, in a theistic system, radiates reality, which would be hell."[45]

If we read this catachrestic fantasy as one determined to re-present this zone of non-being, then we might say that both of Gordon's readings are at work here. The scene is indeed a limbo to the extent that the political demand of blacks is situated outside a political community. In other words, the political architecture relegates black ~~being~~ outside its structure in a space without clear definition—such a demand cannot be heard, even if uttered (despite the yearnings of romantic humanism).[46] Lincoln appears to be running away from this space, attempting to leave the snakes, the skeleton, the blacks, and the demon behind him. Lincoln symbolizes a white descent into the liminal space—this is just the danger of aligning with blackness or attempting to end the metaphysical holocaust (you are cast out of community). But in this fantasy, blacks are on par with snakes, demons, and skeletons. Through this leveling, blacks are re-presented as ghost-like figures, taking their place alongside skeletons and demons—"specters of democracy," as Ivy Wilson might call it.[47] These ghosts are caught between the worlds of the living and the unliving— biologically functioning but ontologically dead—a form of purgatory, awaiting judgment. It is the ghost that is "the occasion of all racial ontology," as David Marriott would describe it.[48]

Don't think you are free because you are emancipated.

CODA

ADIEU TO THE HUMAN

The Department of Justice released its report (2016) exposing disturbing practices in the Baltimore Police Department. It details the persistence of antiblack violence, abuse, inveterate neglect, and routinized humiliation. Graphs, statistics, and anecdotal narratives create a vicious tapestry of signs and symbols. This tapestry requires a deciphering, for what it *says* is more than just persistent injustice; it articulates something else, which requires a different grammar. Rev. Heber Brown III, speaking to the *New York Times* (August 10, 2016) about the report, recounts a disturbing instance. A teenage boy was stopped and strip-searched in front of his girlfriend. After he filed a complaint with the police department, the officer, it seems, wanted revenge and stopped the young boy again, strip-searched him, and this time grabbed his genitals. The officer, intoxicated by unchecked power over black bodies, wanted to injure something else, not just the teenager's body. Rev. Heber Brown III states, "What that officer did is not just violate a body, but he injured a spirit, a soul, a psyche. And that young boy will not easily forget what happened to him, in public with his girlfriend. It's hard to really put gravity and weight to that type of offense."[1]

The violation that Reverend Heber Brown III describes is ontological terror—it is the systemic destruction of "a spirit, a soul, a psyche." Ontological terror is not a phenomenon we can relegate to an unenlightened past; it remains with us. What I have argued throughout this book is that black ~~being~~ constitutes the nothing in an antiblack world, which is continually degraded, dominated, and violated. Antiblackness is anti-nothing. A "spirit, a psyche, a soul" marks symbolic forms of a nothing (something not quite translatable within metaphysical schemes). It is precisely this nothing that ontological terror targets, and black existence is precisely the condition of unending nothing-destruction. This, of course, is a metaphysical fantasy, since nothing can never be destroyed, but it provides a metaphysical world with a devastating will to power. Black ~~being~~ is invented precisely to constitute the object of a global drive—the endless pursuit of nothing.

Postmetaphysicians and romantic humanists neglect this global drive —either by celebrating the emancipatory potential of nothing or by clinging, desperately, to metaphysical humanity and freedom. Both strategies have consistently failed to realize freedom, progress, or redress. It is time to discard these fantasies and face the terror of antiblackness.

What I am suggesting, ultimately, is that black ~~being~~ begins to get over the human and its humanism fantasies. We've tried everything: from marches, to masochistic citizenship (giving our bodies to the state to brutalize in hopes of evoking sympathy and empathy from humans), to exceptional citizenship and respectability, to protest and armed conflict; in the end, either we will continue this degrading quest for human rights and incorporation or we will take a leap of faith, as Kierkegaard might say, and reject the terms through which we organize our existence.

By abandoning the human, human-ness, and the liberal humanism that enshrouds it, we can better understand the violent formations of antiblackness, particularly ontological terror. To abandon the human does not mean that one accepts the terms of inferiority or worthlessness. We do not have to abandon within the axiological framework of humanism; we can reject that framework as well. In other words, we have invested unbelievable value in the human—it constitutes the *highest* value in the world. And for this reason, we are terrified of letting go of it because we believe this value will protect us against antiblackness (it will not). As long as we continue to invest in the value structure that renders the human the highest, and most important, being within the world, we will continue to plead for recognition and acceptance. It is this *terror* of value, of not possessing this value, that keeps us wedded to the idea of the human and its accouterments (and I must say, constantly revisiting the human, reimagining it, expanding it, and refashioning it does nothing but keep us entangled in the circuit of misery). This entanglement of value and ontology produces tremendous misery and disappointment for blackness. As Rinaldo Walcott perspicuously states, "What it means to be Human is continually defined against [blacks]. The very basic terms of social Human engagement are shaped by antiblack logics so deeply embedded in various normativities that they resist intelligibility as modes of thought and yet we must attempt to think them."[2] We must question the antiblack logics grounding the human, even if such thinking is rendered unintelligible by metaphysical knowledge formations and traditions. *Black* thinking, then, must think what is impossible to think within the constraints of metaphysics and ontology. Our enterprise broaches the unknown, the place where we can no longer ask questions, and there sits in this space.

Perhaps what I am suggesting constitutes an *ontological revolution*, one that will destroy the world and its institutions (i.e., the "end of the world," as Fanon calls it). But these are our options, since the metaphysical holocaust will continue as long as the world *exists*. The nihilistic revelation, however, is that such a revolution will destroy *all* life—far from the freedom dreams of the political idealists or the sobriety of the pragmatist.

The important task for black thinking (philosophizing, theorizing, theologizing, poeticizing) is to imagine black existence without Being, humanism, or the human. Such thinking would lead us into an abyss. But we must face this abyss—its terror and majesty. I would suggest that this thinking leads us into the spirit, something exceeding and preceding the metaphysical world. We are still on the path to developing a phenomenology of black spirit, but it is an important enterprise. I will continue this work in subsequent writing, but I can say for now, the aim is to shift emphasis from the human toward the spirit. The spirit enables one to endure the metaphysical holocaust; it is not a solution to antiblackness. The spirit will not transform an antiblack world into some egalitarian landscape—the antiblack world is irredeemable. Black nihilism must rest in the crevice between the impossibility of transforming the world and the dynamic enduring power of the spirit. In the absence of Being there is spirit. Heidegger understands spirit commingled with Being, and the question of Being ("How is it going with Being?") "is the spiritual fate of the West."[3] Heidegger is both correct and incorrect. The spiritual degradation, routinized violence, and suffering around the globe is a consequence of Being and its hegemonic, Eurocentric violence. So, for humans to continue to ask the question of Being is to perpetuate a spiritual violence of black torment. The answer to misery is not Being; rather, it is only by obliterating Being by dis(re)placing Heidegger's question with "How is it going with black ~~being~~?" that we can have access to the spirit. Being is enmity to the spirit. Contending with black as nothing will set us on this spiritual path. Along this path, we can experience something akin to Ashon Crawley's concept of breath (without the promises of universal humanism), as the possibility for thinking and breathing otherwise (we can push this thought to its limits and suggest that for black thinking, spiritual breath and thinking are "identical" rather than thinking and being). [4]

Black studies will have to disinvest our axiological commitments from humanism and invest *elsewhere*. Continuing to keep hope that freedom will occur, that one day the world will apologize for its antiblack brutality and accept us with open arms, is a devastating fantasy. It might give one motivation to fight on, but it is a drive that will only produce exhaustion and protest fatigue. What is the solution? What should we do? How do we live without metaphysical schemes of political hope, freedom, and humanity? I would have to suggest that there are no solutions to the problem of antiblackness—there is only endurance. And endurance cannot be reduced to biofuturity or humanist mandates. Endurance is a spiritual practice with entirely different aims.

Ontological Terror seeks to challenge metaphysical and postmetaphysical solutions. The paradigm of the free black teaches us that such solutions sustain the metaphysical holocaust. Let our thinking lead us into the "valley of the shadow of death," and once there we can begin to imagine an existence anew.

NOTES

INTRODUCTION: THE FREE BLACK IS NOTHING

1   Throughout this book, I will use the terms *Negro* and *black* interchangeably to docket an ontological problem of Being and blackness. I am not as much interested in historicizing the terms or engaging in the contentious debates concerning identity; rather, I understand these terms as pointing to the same problematic, which is beyond individual identity.

2   The term *ontological terror* appears in many scholarly texts, primarily as an undeveloped term but expressing a poetics of fear or anxiety. Much of this work is done in theological studies in which the lack of ultimate foundations (i.e., the Death of God thesis) leaves the subject unnerved. Most of this work, however, assumes humanism as its ground of investigation, meaning that the human subject is precluded from exercising its ontological capacity. My use of *ontological terror* is designed to foreground not only the terror the human feels with lack of security, but also that this fear is predicated on a projection of ontological terror onto black bodies and the disavowal of this projection. Thus, humanism does not exhaust ontological terror, and an antimetaphysical understanding of it is necessary to analyze antiblackness. My use of *ontological terror* is more along the lines of Julius Lester's description of it as "the terror of nonexistence, the unending trauma of being damned in the flesh" in his *Lovesong: Becoming a Jew*, 25. For examples of ontological terror as a human/humanist experience, please see Anthony B. Pinn's wonderful *Terror and Triumph: The Nature of Black Religion*; Markus Dressler and Arvind-Pal S. Mandair's *Secularism and Religion-Making*; and Louise Morris's master's thesis, "The Spectre of Grief: Visualizing Ontological Terror in Performance," which understands the artistic representations of terror as a veil—something concealing trauma. I will argue something similar in chapter 4, but argue that representations expose and uncover rather than serving as a veil.

3   In his *The Question Concerning Technology: And Other Essays*, Heidegger understands that the overcoming of metaphysics [überwunden] is impossible, since a remnant will always remain and one must go *through* metaphysics to ask the ontological question; but the thinker must aspire to verwunden, the

surmounting that restores metaphysics (technology as instrumentalization and domination in this instance) "back into its yet concealed truth," 39.

4 What does black thinking entail without being? This is an exceptionally difficult question, but one that sets all black critical enterprises into motion. Heidegger, for example, believed being and thinking were the same. If this is the case, then black philosophy's presentation is not thinking in this familiar sense, but something for which grammar fails us. In other words, the question put to black nihilists, and Afropessimists, "what are you *doing*?" cannot be answered apodictically within the horizon of metaphysical and postmetaphysical thinking. Black thinking is unthought because its activities are unrecognizable philosophically—thus, black thinking is the process of destroying the world.

5 See Grant Farred's *Martin Heidegger Saved My Life* for a Heideggerian approach to thinking race.

6 This seems to be the crux of Martin Heidegger's critique (and those of postmetaphysicians): that metaphysical procedures set the ground for tremendous acts of violence, since Being is so crudely reified. He suggested in "Letter on Humanism" (in *Basic Writings: Martin Heidgger*) that our metaphysical ideas of the human, representation, and objectification limit freedom.

7 I use the signpost of the transatlantic slave trade to indicate an emergence or event of metaphysical horror. Michelle Wright cautions against "Middle Passage Epistemology" in which other spatial formations (i.e., other oceans) are excluded from the narrative of African slavery. I certainly agree that antiblackness is a global event and that multiple oceans transported black commodities. My use of *transatlantic slave trade* here is not to posit it as the only passageway, but to provide a signifier for metaphysical holocaust and its commencement. Please see Michelle M. Wright, *Physics of Blackness: Beyond the Middle Passage Epistemology*.

8 Oren Ben-Dor, *Thinking about Law: In Silence with Heidegger*, 105.

9 Vattimo describes Heidegger's term *Ge-Schick* as "the ensemble (*Ge*) of the *Schicken*, the sendings or apertures of Being that have conditioned and made possible the experience of humanity in its historical phases prior to us. Only by inserting our current sending (our *Schickung*)—that is: present significance of 'Being'—into the ensemble of the *Ge-Schick* do we overcome the metaphysical oblivion of Being, breaking free of thought that identifies Being with beings, with the order that currently obtains." See his *Nihilism and Emancipation: Ethics, Politics, and Law*.

10 Gianni Vattimo, *The End of Modernity: Nihilism and Hermeneutics in Postmodern Culture*, 1–13.

11 Vattimo, *Nihilism and Emancipation: Ethics, Politics, and Law*, 35; emphasis mine.

12 It is not within the scope of this project to conduct a genealogy or a history of Being [*Geschichte des Seins*]. But the concept *Being*, particularly Dasein,

certainly has a development in Western thought not as a universal but as a Eurocentric field of inquiry. Heidegger condenses his antiblackness in the concept "primitive Dasein," which is "not conscious of itself in its way of being" (*The Metaphysical Foundations of Logic*, 138), and thus cannot pose the ontological question—being is not an issue for it. Or when Heidegger suggests in *The Introduction to Metaphysics*, "The Greeks become in principle *better* kind of Hottentot, in comparison to whom modern science has progressed infinitely far. Disregarding as the particular absurdities involved in conceiving of the inception of Western philosophy as primitive, it must be said that this interpretation forgets that what is at issue is . . . great can only begin great . . . so it is with the philosophy of the Greeks." What exactly *is* this primitive caught between human being and animal? What determines the "betterness" of the Greeks against the Hottentot, for whom philosophy proper is absent? How does the "particular absurdity" of black thinking (Hottentot philosophy)/black existence engender Heidegger's question of being itself? How do we break the antiblack tautological circle "great begins great" to create space for black thinking—that dejected and debased enterprise cast out of historical movement? Any history of Being would need to work through the exclusion of the primitive from Dasein and the *use* of this primitive in the existential journey of the human. For indeed, non-Western cultures provide a temporal backdrop for Heidegger to commence his philosophical thinking. My argument here is that the concept develops as an antiblack field that is exclusive and violent. It posits European Dasein as the guardian of Being and the rest of the globe as dependent on European thinking. Rather than thinking of Being as a universal field (i.e., everything *experiences its happening*), we can understand the development of the concept as an instrument of European global domination. Thus, whatever the black *is* lacks explanation within Being, and it is the task of black thinking to imagine black existence *outside* Being and its arrogant universalizing tactics. Please also see Nelson Maldonado-Torres's "On the Coloniality of Being: Contributions to the Development of a Concept," 240–70, for a similar argument about the violent development of the concept. Richard Wolin asked the provocative question "What is the role to be played by *politics* in the historico-metaphysical process whereby the truth of Being is historically recovered?"; see Wolin, *The Politics of Being: The Political Thought of Martin Heidegger*. Along these lines *Ontological Terror* inquires, "What is the role of antiblackness in the forgetting of Being and its historical recovering?" Throughout this book my answer is that remembering Being is *dependent* on remembering the Negro.

13 Martin Heidegger, *Introduction to Metaphysics*, 67.
14 David Marriott. "Waiting to Fall," 214.
15 I use "black thought," "black thinking," and "black philosophy" interchangeably to signal a certain intellectual labor, one designed to investigate the abyss of black existence without ontology. Thus, my approach will seem foreign to an-

alytic philosophical traditions (and its scientific reasoning and metaphysical logic) and equally foreign to Continental philosophy, or even what John Mullarkey (*Post-Continental Philosophy: An Outline*) would call "post-Continental Philosophy," as I do not assume that Being is universal in its difference or manifestations. Both analytic and Continental approaches rely on Being, and black thought/philosophy is charged with thinking against Being itself—even if we can never get completely outside of it. This means black thought is the "other of philosophy," as William Desmond would call it in his *Philosophy and Its Others: Ways of Being and Mind*, and even the other of Heideggerian *Andenken*. Black thought has not overcome metaphysics, since antiblackness is what remains, what anchors metaphysics within Destruktion. For this reason, black thought is the only thinking capable of entering the abyss of nothing. Cornel West defines Afro-American philosophy as "the interpretation of Afro-American history, highlighting the cultural heritage and political struggles, which provides desirable norms that should regulate responses to particular challenges presently confronting Afro-Americans." The question embedded in this beautiful definition is how does the black philosopher interpret existence (as history)? Is being the "ground" of such interpretation? In other words, the definition of the noetic function of Afro-American philosophy neglects the question of being itself—can we interpret "culture" without presuming the "isness" of culture, which would bring us back to the question of being? I would argue that black nihilism, as a philosophical formation, does not neatly fall into any of the categories West uses to map black thought: rationalism, existentialism, humanism, or vitalism—since the ontological ground anchoring these traditions is unreliable and is thrown into crisis. The question of black being unravels these traditions. Please see his magnificent essay "Philosophy and the Afro-American Experience" in *A Companion to African-American Philosophy*.

16 Jean-Luc Nancy might argue that freedom is the dissolution of grounds and, especially, the labor of experience and/as necessity. It is the utter exposure to groundlessness that is the experience of freedom as such. I agree that groundlessness is important, but would mention that Nancy's postmetaphysics introduces a form of terror that is left unacknowledged, and this is precisely what the metaphysical holocaust does: it leaves black being without any ontological grounds. Does this mean black being is free? We could only answer in the affirmative if we also suggest that antiblackness is necessary for black freedom. Such a formulation—in which freedom is groundlessness and antiblackness dissolves ground—would sustain the metaphysical holocaust as the condition of experiencing freedom for blacks. This is why black freedom is incompatible with postmetaphysical presentations of freedom because they, inadvertently, would rely on antiblackness to incorporate blacks into its narrative. If, then, freedom is antiblackness for blacks, what good is freedom? It, indeed, is not freedom at all—only the human can celebrate groundlessness. (Because this

groundlessness is sustained by Being's gift of unfolding, such is not the case for blackness.) Please see Nancy's *The Experience of Freedom*.

17 Heidegger, *The Essence of Human Freedom: An Introduction to Philosophy*, 203–5.

18 I would also suggest that our ideas of freedom originate from a political theory/ philosophy in which it becomes indistinguishable from liberty. For example, Isaiah Berlin's "Two Conceptions of Freedom" presents freedom as the twin axes of negative and positive vectors. Positive freedom is the actualization of one's desire for mastery, rationality, opportunity, and capacity. Negative freedom is the overcoming, or removal, of interference on one's mastery or reasoning will. Hannah Arendt, along this vein, offers a theory of freedom as action—in particular, political action (deriving from the Greek polis). These theories, by placing freedom squarely in political action or mastery, leave the question of what is free unattended because it is assumed to be a human. Once this ontological ground is questioned, however, we realize that Being must be secured before we can even engage in a question of action, reason, will, mastery, or interference. This approach to black ~~being~~ is unproductive because the ontological humanism, which grounds political philosophy/theory, does not transfer to the black thing outside ontology. This is the conundrum before us. The legal and historiographical literature applies this humanism to free blacks when the problem of blackness is that it lacks this ground to begin with. Thus, freedom is not an issue for it. We can speak of liberty, rights, and, as I will argue, terroristic emancipation, but these are not freedom, but ontic substitutes. Or, in the case of black ~~being~~, emancipation is what is left when freedom and ontology are no longer options.

19 Frank Wilderson, *Red, White, and Black* (Durham, NC: Duke University Press, 2010), 38.

20 Maurice S. Lee, *Slavery, Philosophy, and American Literature.*

21 Orlando Patterson offers a voluminous study of freedom in his *Freedom*, vol. 1: *Freedom in the Making of Western Culture*. His objective is to present a sociological analysis of freedom's evolution—from antiquity to modernity. He argues that valuing freedom evolves through devaluing the condition of slavery. I definitely agree that slavery renders freedom intelligible, but again, the ontological question is circumvented. His analysis presents freedom not as an aperture or horizon of ontology, but as an evolving object (a metaphysical entity) that moves through history in relation to slavery. Conceiving freedom in this way collapses it into practices of value and exchange—not something that provides the condition of possibility for *any* valuation because it enables the human to ground itself. Moreover, the ontological condition of both slave and master is not synonymous or merely a legal distinction—as if gifting the slave with freedom will make him a master.

22 Vittorio Possenti, *Nihilism and Metaphysics: The Third Voyage*, 8.

23 Please see Ira Berlin's *Slaves without Masters: The Free Negro in the Antebellum South.*

24 John Hope Franklin, *The Free Negro in North Carolina, 1790–1860*, 3–4.

25 As an example of skirting the ontological question in romantic narratives of black humanism, we can examine Ira Berlin's *The Long Emancipation: The Demise of Slavery in the United States.* He raises the question, "If black people were not to be slaves, what exactly would they *be*?" This question should compel an investigation of the word *be*, a question of existence when humanist ground is not secure. For indeed, the "transformation from person to property," as he describes it, is more than just a change in legal status; it is also a change in the meaning and condition of existence. We are led, however, into a romantic narrative about slavery's supposed demise and the function of multiple forces in achieving it—through emancipation. It seems as if the question dies alongside slavery's demise. I am arguing that this is far from the case. Slavery is still very much with us to the extent that slavery signifies the exclusion of black ~~being~~ from humanist ontology. We have not accomplished the demise of slavery, only variations of its viciousness.

26 Again, this is to reiterate that I am not suggesting the voices or opinions of free blacks do not matter. This is to say, however, that we want to interrogate the ontological ground and presumptions from which that voice emerges. There are many contemporary historiographies that grapple with the concepts of freedom and free blacks. In *Forging Freedom: Black Women and the Pursuit of Liberty in Antebellum Charleston*, for example, Amrita Chakrabarti Myers uncovers archival material of free black women in Charleston, South Carolina. She presents freedom as an experience, one that depends on resources and opportunity. The ground of ontology, however, is never broached; thus, freedom is removed from ontology and relegated to sociolegal context. The problem with this is that ontology is not reducible to experience, and the author proceeds as if free black experience is *an ontological claim of freedom*—however fickle it was or how tenuously the freedom might be experienced. I focus on the conflation of experience with (human) ontology because the problems that orient the text—systemic terror, risk of reenslavement, routinized violation—are ontological problems. Experience cannot eradicate these problems, no matter how free someone feels. These problems persist after sociolegal freedom because they are symptoms of the ontological condition of nonfreedom. Sociolegal and affective experiences leave the fundamental problem unresolved. There is a tendency in historiography to neglect the ontological foundation of the systemic violence it uncovers, since avoiding ontology and focusing on affect and experience allow us to incorporate blacks into a humanist fantasy (with synonyms like *agency, liberty, voice, power*). My issue is, then, that *assuming human freedom* is precisely the problem, which free blacks experienced as tension between a legal status and a nonplace in an antiblack world. This tension

is an ontological violence, which not labor, family, resources, wealth, nor community can rectify. A nonmetaphysical historiography would proceed from the lack of ontological ground and read the archive through this violence. My hope is that historiography will begin to question and challenge the humanism upon which it is predicated to understand the capaciousness of antiblackness. For similar elisions of ontology in historiography, see Max Grivno's *Gleanings of Freedom: Free and Slave Labor along the Mason-Dixon Line, 1790–1860*, and Damian Alan Pargas's *The Quarters and the Fields: Slave Families in the Non-Cotton South*.

27 Giorgio Agamben, *The Signature of All Things: On Method*, 18.

28 Alexander G. Weheliye, *Habeas Viscus: Racializing Assemblages, Biopolitics, and Black Feminist Theories of the Human*, 13.

29 Tommy Curry, "Saved by the Bell: Derrick Bell's Racial Realism as Pedagogy," 36.

30 Michel Foucault, "Questions of Method," in *The Foucault Effect: Studies in Governmentality*, 77.

31 See Vincent Woodard's brilliant analysis of consumption, cannibalism, and homoeroticism through historical archives in his *The Delectable Negro: Human Consumption and Homoeroticism with U.S. Slave Culture*.

CHAPTER 1: THE QUESTION OF BLACK ~~BEING~~

1 I use the word ~~being~~ in the term *black ~~being~~* simply to articulate the entity of blackness that bears the weight of unbearable nothing. Since ontology cannot provide the ground for understanding the being of blackness, terms like being, existence, and freedom applied to blackness become nonsense. But given grammatical paucity and the lack of intelligible language to describe the indescribable, I must make use of it, even as I undermine the very terms that I employ. I write the term ~~being~~ under erasure to indicate the double bind of communicability and to expose the death of blackness that constitutes the center of being.

2 Hortense Spillers, *Black, White, and in Color: Essays on American Literature and Culture*, 406.

3 In Martin Heidegger's *Introduction to Metaphysics*, he recovers Plato's non-metaphysical understanding of polis not simply as the geographical location of the city-state, but as "the place, the there, wherein and as which historical being-there is. Polis is the historical place, there in which, out of which, and for which history happens" (170). I am arguing that black ~~being~~ lacks precisely this historical place (there-ness) that situates the human being in the world. Black ~~being~~, then, lacks not only physical space in the world (i.e., a home) but also an existential place in an antiblack world. The black is worldless in this

way, bordering on something between the worldlessness of the object and the world poorness of the animal. Please see Kevin Aho's "Logos and the Poverty of Animals: Rethinking Heidegger's Humanism" and Matthew Calarco's *Zoographies: The Question of the Animal from Heidegger to Derrida* for an engagement with Heidegger's fraught distinction between the world-poor animal and the world-forming human and his anthropocentrism.

4 Heidegger, *The Question Concerning Technology and Other Essays*, 3.

5 Nahum Dimitri Chandler, *X: The Problem of the Negro as a Problem for Thought*, 2.

6 Spillers, *Black, White, and in Color*, 203.

7 In *The Remains of Being: Hermeneutic Ontology after Metaphysics*, Zabala suggests, "Heidegger undertook his destruction of the history of ontology in terms of the history of Being in order to destroy layers covering up the original nature of Being, those layers that metaphysical thinking has constructed." I am arguing that we cannot proceed with this destruction without the Negro's exclusion from history in Hegel, Kant's black, stupid Negro, Heidegger's primitive, unthinking Hottentot, etc. These are the layers of metaphysical violence that enable philosophy to develop notions of time, progress, freedom, and reason. Spillers would urge us, in my reading of her, to adopt a destructive protocol attentive to the violence undergirding the ontological question itself.

8 W. E. B. Dubois, *The Souls of Black Folk*, 1. Dubois also suggests in *Dusk of Dawn* that this problem is "the central problem[s] of the world's democracies and so the problem of the future world." I would also argue that this problem is the central problem of ontometaphysics. Philosopher Nahum Chandler provides a definitive reading of Dubois as broaching the problem of ontometaphysics through a "deconstructionist" practice in *X: The Problem of the Negro as a Problem for Thought*. My analysis, however, is situated at the limit of deconstruction and *Destruktion*—blackness as the "undeconstructable" core of ontometaphysics.

9 Spillers, *Black, White, and in Color*, 206.

10 I interpret Hortense Spillers's term *pornotroping* as the appropriation and *use* of the black body as a text, a sexualized text for fantasy, prurient othering, and unchecked gratification. Within an antiblack grammatical context, black bodies are pressed into the service of a sexualized semiotic and hermeneutic procedure or, as Spillers describes it, "externally imposed meanings and uses." How one interprets and makes meaning of the black body as a sexual sign in an antiblack grammar is the function of pornotroping. Alexander Weheliye understands pornotroping as translating into a scopic economy, where the hieroglyphics of the flesh are sexualized through vision. Although I am in full agreement with his presentation of the scopic dimensions of pornotroping, I depart from his diacritical analysis as it concerns the productive potential of it. I understand pornotroping as an antiblack strategy in the metaphysical

holocaust and not as a site for self-making or freedom; see Weheliye, *Habeas Viscus: Racializing Assemblages, Biopolitics, and Black Feminist Theories of the Human.*

11 Sylvia Wynter, "Unsettling the Coloniality of Being/Power/Truth/Freedom Towards the Human, after Man, Its Overrepresentation—An Argument," 313.

12 Heidegger, *Introduction to Metaphysics*, 1. The phrase *Wie steht es um das Sein?*" might also translated as "How is it going with Nothing?," as Heidegger seems to suggest in his lecture "What Is Metaphysics." The question "How is it going with Nothing?" is the question of black(ness) for me in metaphysics, since "Black" and "Nothing" are articulations of the problem of Being—that for which ontology cannot adequately account.

13 Santiago Zabala, *The Remains of Being: Hermeneutic Ontology after Metaphysics*, 1.

14 Heidegger, *Introduction to Metaphysics*, 77

15 In particular, Heidegger's discussion of calculative thinking in his *Introduction to Metaphysics*, 216.

16 The idea of relationality is essential to the work of postmetaphysics (and romantic humanism). For example, Arendt posits freedom as occurring between men; a relation between men engenders freedom in *The Human Condition*. Jean-Luc Nancy would claim that "singular plurality" or a relation within an open/undefined community determines both existence and the possibility of freedom in his *Being Singular Plural*. Heidegger would also posit a Mitsein or a "being-with" as constitutive of a collective "world-forming" in his *Being and Time*. In short, part of the postmetaphysical project is to center relationality as essential to existence. But when such relation is nonexistent for black being, meaning that there is only a unilateral use and not bilateral relation, all such grounds of existence, freedom, and being for blacks are thrown into fundamental crisis.

17 Alain David, "On Negroes," in *Race and Racism in Continental Philosophy*, 11.

18 David, "On Negroes," 14.

19 Philosopher François Laruelle also provides a similar metaphysical reading of blackness through the concept *uchromia*—thinking blackness as the determination and limit of color and understanding itself; please see Laruelle, *From Decision to Heresy: Experiments in Non-Standard Thought.*

20 Ronald Judy, *(Dis)forming the American Canon: African-Arabic Slave Narratives and the Vernacular*, 107.

21 David Marriott presents *the* reading of Fanon's *n'est pas* as reducible not to simple negation but to that which ruptures both negation and positivity. This, I would argue, is another articulation of the formless form that is the black Negro; please see Marriott, "Judging Fanon."

22 Gianni Vattimo, *Nihilism and Emancipation: Ethics, Politics, and Law*, 35.

23 Lindon Barrett, *Racial Blackness and the Discontinuity of Western Modernity*, 73.

24   Spillers, *Black, White, and in Color*, 212.

25   Arendt understands natality as the ontological anchor of human freedom (and the "central category of political thought"). In essence, the beginning is a state of capacity, a capacity she will later develop as political action. Jean-Luc Nancy has a similar conception of natality as a figuration for the way Being unfolds into existence (e.g., existence is the house of Being). For both Arendt and Nancy, natality and birth are conceptual ways of embracing possibility: either as the unfolding of Being or as the potential for political action and freedom. For black ~~being~~, I am arguing, such a natality is absent. Paradoxically, we can say that black ~~being~~ is born into death—the emergence of black ~~being~~ is a death sentence, not the domain of action or the unfolding of being. This paradox is the blind spot of postmetaphysical thinking, and it cannot accommodate a ~~being~~ whose emergence is without innate human freedom or being. In other words, the object lacks a substantial narrative of natality in both of these theories; it is just present and used. See Nancy, *The Birth to Presence*, and Arendt, *The Human Condition*.

26   Bryan Wagner, *Disturbing the Peace*, 1.

27   I do not have the space to delve into the problem of identity within the continental philosophical tradition, but this "problem" seems, at least in my mind, to reach a standstill concerning blackness. If the great problem of identity is metaphysical unity, or grounded sameness, according to Heidegger and Deleuze, then it seems that black ~~being~~ is a doubling or fracturing that displaces the logic of identity. Black ~~being~~ can never attain adequacy, as self-sameness—it is always being for another. Split between being for another and the form of formlessness, blackness is not identity (which is the error of black identity politics). Our task is to present black existence without the grammar of identity, unity, adequation, and metaphysics. This, perhaps, is an impossible task, but the presentation of the impossible is all one can do with a catachresis. Given this difficulty, we must be weary of appropriating the terms and concepts of metaphysics and ontological imaginations, as tempting as they might seem. Gavin Rae provides an exquisite analysis of the way Heidegger and Deleuze approach the problem of identity (ultimately reformulating the philosophy of becoming as difference or groundlessness). Neither of these strategies account for blackness. Please see his *Ontology in Heidegger and Deleuze: A Comparative Analysis*.

28   Ronald Judy, *(Dis)Forming the American Canon*, 89.

29   Frantz Fanon, *Black Skin, White Masks*, 110.

30   Fanon describes it as the "vast black abyss"; *Black Skin, White Masks*, 14.

31   Again, "African-being" here is merely a signifier for a primordial relation that antiblackness destroys. In Fanon's case he experiences this destruction from Martinique, while Equiano experienced it from Africa. The metaphysical holocaust is global in reach; I use "African being" to describe a variety of geographical specificities that produce blackness.

32 This, of course, is not to say that blacks do not exist, as Fanon intimated, as a phenomenal entity that can be encountered through the senses, but it is to suggest that this phenomenal existence does not equate to an ontology. How to describe this existence outside ontology is the *problem* of blackness—the problem for the whole of metaphysics.

33 I would also point this criticism to Jean-Paul Sartre's celebration of nothing in *Being and Nothingness: An Essay on Phenomenological Ontology*. His existentialism critiques the transcendental ground of human nature and the restricting teleology this ground engenders by arguing that there is nothing (no ultimate ground outside the self); therefore, we can choose, out of this nothingness, the form our lives will take. Ultimately, his existentialism uses this nothingness to place ultimate responsibility for one's life on the individual (on this subject). Thus a Sartrean existentialism would celebrate nothing/nothingness as the occasion for productive action and transformation. I cannot disagree with this celebration more strongly, since, in my opinion, it assumes a transcendental ontology of a human capable of transforming nothing into a productive something. This is not the case for black ~~being~~. For black nihilism, nothing restricts human freedom with a terror it attempts to control and project onto black ~~being~~. Put differently, if nothing for Sartre enables the celebration of agency and choice, it is only because the terror of nothing is first projected onto black bodies in a metaphysical world. The rejoinder that my position is bad faith relies on the very metaphysics (or philosophical anthropology) that destroys the flesh. Put differently, without the flesh, one cannot act authentically or experience radical freedom, since the ground of the human is absent. Sartrean existentialism only applies to the human subject (embodies flesh) in a metaphysical world. This critique carries over into the important work of black existentialism and its reliance on Sartrean ontology. Black nihilism and black existentialism, then, although agreeing on the viciousness of antiblack racism, would part ways as they concern philosophical anthropology, since humanity is not the ground of black ~~being~~, and this ground is necessary for a celebration of nothing and a rejection of bad faith; see Lewis Gordon's groundbreaking work *Bad Faith and Antiblack Racism* (in particular the critique of Deconstruction and the analysis of the living dead), and Sartre's *Being and Nothingness*.

34 Fanon, *Black Skin, White Masks*, 8.

35 Fred Moten, "Blackness and Nothingness," 749.

36 Spillers, *Black, White, and in Color*, 206.

37 I must address the inventive work of object-oriented ontology, particularly Graham Harman's speculative realism. Harman provides a rigorous critique of Kant's correlationism (as Quentin Meillassoux would describe it in *After Finitude: An Essay on the Necessity of Contingency*. He suggests that tools have "tool-being," and this being (or dare I say "essence") is withdrawn or distorted (allure) in the relationality between objects and human and objects such that

we never truly know this being (we never really know a tree), only the distorting presentation of the tool as it appears to us during certain context. The being of the tool "lies beneath the manifest presence of the object," according to Harman. Thus, we circulate various simulacra or distortions of all objects—and this distortion is what also plagues our encounter with Dasein, since its being also withdraws or is distorted ontically. I would argue, however, that the tool-being and the human being are differentiated through the work of violence and power. This is to say that even if the black, as tool, has a *being*, that has been distorted or concealed, this being is forever lost, inaccessible, and ultimately inconsequential in the face of antiblack violence. The tool-being will not protect black objects from violent relationality and exploitative use. Antiblackness constitutes *a global alluring function: to commence to destroy the being of black objects and to place nothing in the space of that destruction*. My argument is simply that object oriented ontology or speculative realism does not acknowledge the violent structuration of objects in relation to humans—even if we reject correlationism. Whatever lies beneath the black body will *not* provide freedom, escape, or refuge from the metaphysical holocaust; please see Harman's *Tool-Being: Heidegger and the Metaphysics of Objects*.

38 Hubert L. Dreyfus, *Being-in-the-World: A Commentary on Heidegger's Being and Time, Division I*, 63. In *Basic Problems: From Being and Time (1927) to The Task of Thinking (1964)*, Heidegger also states that it is the "in-order-to" that determines the "isness" of the equipment. It is utility *for* the human. "What and how it is an entity, its *whatness* and *howness*, is constituted by this in-order-to as such, by its involvement" (293).

39 Heidegger, *Being and Time*, 95 and 97.

40 Saidiya V. Hartman, *Scenes of Subjection: Terror, Slavery, and Self-Making in Nineteenth-Century America* , 21.

41 Wynter also suggests "the nonsupernatural but no less extrahuman ground (in the reoccupied place of traditional ancestors/gods, God, ground) of the answer that the secularizing West would now give to the Heideggerian question as to the who, and the what we are"; in "Unsettling the Coloniality of Being/Power/Truth/Freedom Towards the Human after Man, Its Overrepresentation—An Argument," 264.

42 Spillers, *Black, White, and in Color*, 208.

43 Miguel de Beistegui, *Heidegger and the Political*, 6.

44 Chandler, *X: The Problem of the Negro as a Problem for Thought*, 20.

45 Beistegui, *Heidegger and the Political*.

46 Giorgio Agamben, "What Is a Paradigm?" in *The Signature of All Things: On Method*.

47 Distinguished historian Ira Berlin makes a geographical distinction between the upper, middle, and lower South. These distinctions are designed to chal-

lenge the conception of the South as a homogenous space. Although I agree these distinctions might allow us to conceptualize different legal, social, and political occurrences, they are immaterial to the question of ~~being~~. No matter the geographical location or the different strategies of destruction, the metaphysical holocaust is a constant across diverse variables. There is not a space void of antiblack violence; please see Berlin, *Many Thousands Gone: The First Two Centuries of Slavery in North America*.

48 *The African Repository: The Twelfth Annual Report of American Society for Colonizing the Free People of Color of the United States*, vol. 1 (1851).

49 In *But One Race: The Life of Robert Purvis*, Margaret Hope Bacon presents a searing biographical witness. According to Bacon, Purvis's inherited wealth and lighter skin afforded him the opportunity to spend time thinking through the contradictions of blackness and freedom (e.g., the "irrational logic" of colonization society) and to challenge antiblack injustice. Purvis is one of many prominent leaders who worked tirelessly to address antiblackness.

50 Robert Purvis to Henry C. Wright, August 22, 1842, Weston Papers, Boston Public Library.

51 The *Liberator*, April 10, 1857; also quoted in Leon Litwack, *North of Slavery: The Negro in the Free States, 1790–1860*, 63.

52 Jared Sexton, "Don't Call It a Comeback," in *OpenDemocracy* (June 17,2015), https://www.opendemocracy.net/beyondslavery/jared-sexton/don%E2%80%99t -call-it-comeback-racial-slavery-is-not-yet-abolished.

53 *African Repository*, vol. 1, 68.

54 *African Repository*, vol. xxvii (1851).

55 Not only did the South impose anti-emigration laws banning blacks from entry, or forced removal once emancipated, the North made livability so miserable for free blacks that it became even more hostile than the South in many ways. Representative Henry C. Murphy of New York, for example, supported restrictive legislation in New York to prohibit "any who shall bring the *wretched beings* to our Free States, there to taint the blood of whites, or to destroy their own race by vicious courses" (emphasis mine). It is this wretchedness (the execration) that these restrictive laws are designed to address. In other words, the restrictive laws (even if only existing as a constant *terror*) attempt to address a metaphysical problem with a legal instrument; *Appendix to the Congressional Globe*, volume 17, 30th Congress, 1st session, 579–81.

56 *African Repository*, vol. xxvii (1851).

57 Sylvia Wynter, "Unsettling the Coloniality of Being/Power/Truth/Freedom Towards the Human, after Man, Its Overrepresentation—An Argument."

58 Julia Kristeva, *Powers of Horror: An Essay on Abjection*.

59 Rodney Barfield suggests that free Negro caste "was the most despised and reviled element of the American population—albeit the fastest-growing section.

Racism had so imbued itself in the American character that free blacks were completely outside the social contract"; see his *America's Forgotten Caste: Free Blacks in Antebellum Virginia and North Carolina* , 13.

60 *Illinois Constitutional Debates of 1847*, 860.

61 As quoted in Litwack, *North of Slavery*, 69.

62 The Lacanian drive serves as a productive heuristic device to understand antiblackness and its objective. For Lacan, the drive relentlessly pursues an impossible object, which commences as a destructive repetition and surplus enjoyment of this repetition—the ultimate result is a form of extinction. Antiblackness pursues nothing as its impossible drive, but the destructive pleasure is projected onto black bodies ("interpassivity," as Slavoj Žižek would call it); see Jacques Lacan's *Écrits: A Selection*.

63 Agamben, "What Is a Paradigm?"

64 Frank Wilderson, *Red, White, and Black*, 45.

CHAPTER 2: OUTLAWING

1 I am using the rather awkward construction *(non)relation* to signify that the idea of *relation* is always already infused with metaphysical presumptions (i.e., it presupposes a relation is comprises discrete entities that can be differentiated and brought together within space/time). Since Being is neither an entity nor subordinate to the scientific constraints we place on it (space/time), we cannot properly call the presencing of Being a *relation*, but for lack of a more sufficient grammar, I will call it a (non)relation to indicate the happening [Ereignis] between Being and being. This, then, is how I interpret Giorgio Agamben's rereading of Heidegger and Nancy when he suggests, "The being together of being and Being does not have the form of a relation," in his *Homo Sacer*, 60.

2 Oren Ben-Dor, *Thinking about Law: In Silence with Heidegger*, 145.

3 Ben-Dor, *Thinking about Law*, 150.

4 Ben-Dor, *Thinking about Law*, 378.

5 Jean-Luc Nancy, *The Birth to Presence*, 44.

6 Nancy, *Birth to Presence*, 43–44.

7 Nancy, *Birth to Presence*, 47.

8 Nancy, *Birth to Presence*, 47.

9 Hortense Spillers, *White, Black, and in Color: Essays on American Literature and Culture*, 208.

10 Spillers, *White, Black, and in Color*, 207.

11 Patricia Tuitt, *Race, Law, and Resistance*, 11.

12 Patricia Williams, "On Being the Object of Property," 13.

13 Bryan Wagner, *Disturbing the Peace: Black Culture and the Police Power after Slavery*, 1.

14 Charles Mills, *The Racial Contract.*

15 Frank Wilderson, *Red, White, and Black*, 17.

16 Frantz Fanon, *Black Skin, White Masks*, 138.

17 Fanon, *Black Skin, White Masks*, 110.

18 Fanon, *Black Skin, White Masks*, 110

19 Fanon, *Black Skin, White Masks*, 110

20 Ben-Dor, *Thinking about Law*, 378.

21 Ben-Dor, *Thinking about Law*, 164.

22 Spillers, *White, Black, and in Color*, 225.

23 I am using "place" here to indicate the there-ness within which Dasein stands forth and appears by emerging through its concealment. This standing forth requires a place, as Martin Heidegger argued in *Introduction to Metaphysics*: "The place belongs to the thing itself. The various things each have their place. That which becomes is set into this placelike 'space' and is set forth" (69). This isn't the metaphysical-geographical space bound to ordinary modes of appearance, but the inhabitation of becoming. Since black ~~being~~ does not become or appear through Being, such a place is absent. Luce Irigaray makes a similar argument with the place-lessness of woman (her proper place is absorbed by man as envelope, used for his existential unfolding), in her rereading of Greek philosophy and Heidegger. Please see her *An Ethics of Sexual Difference.*

24 Ronald Judy, *(Dis)Forming the American Canon: African-Arabic Slave Narratives and the Vernacular*, 89.

25 Ben-Dor, *Thinking about Law*, 131.

26 Kalpana Seshadri Crooks, *HumAnimal: Race, Law, and Language.*

27 Jurisdiction, then, determines who has standing before the law and who lacks such standing. Taney considers Scott's writ erroneous because he lacks the standing jurisdiction bestows. We can also read in this legal concept the essence, or essential unfolding, of law itself, since for Heidegger, in his *Introduction to Metaphysics*, Being, understood through the Greek *Phusis*, "is the event of *standing forth*, arising from the concealed and thus enabling the concealed to take its stand for the first time" (16). Furthermore, "This standing-there, this taking and maintaining a *stand* that stands erected high in itself, is what the Greeks understood as Being" (63). What I am suggesting here, by reading Taney's legal reasoning alongside Heidegger's understanding of Being, is that the law's *purpose* is to illumine the human's emerging through its *standing*. In other words, to have legal standing is to have one's Being recognized by the law. Taney ultimately argues that blacks lack standing because they lack Being—merchandise never emerges or appears but must remain *concealed* in the opening, or light, of law.

28 *The Dred Scott Decision: Opinion of Chief Justice Taney.* Library of Congress. http://hdl.loc.law//llst.022

29 The belief that the position of blacks was fixed was also advanced by many,

but Dr. Josiah Nott probably presented the strongest presentation of this arguments. For him, slavery was a moral obligation; see Paul Finkelman's "The Significance and Persistence of Proslavery Thought," 95–114.

30 I think Chief Justice Taney's use of the term *axiom* is quite revealing of the philosophical agenda he has in mind: not just to establish a set of truths by which an antiblack society must orient itself, but also that axioms are themselves ontological and the *idea* is the "ontic translation of ontological axioms. The subject draws on the symbolic resources of its world in order to represent to itself and others the axioms of being-in-the-world that are simultaneously transcendent and immanent, trans-immanent, in relation to this world," according to Sergei Prozorov. In other words, Taney uses an axiom to express, or symbolize, an ontological truth, but this ontological truth must *translate* into an idea. I would argue that the symbolization of an antiblack axiomatic is precisely the opinion itself. Taney's *opinion* is the representation (idea) of something ontological—which is why legal decisions are deceptively ontological; please see Prozorov, *Theory of the Political Subject: Void Universalism*, vol. 2, *Interventions*, 29.

31 It is well rehearsed in academic and legal circles that *Dred Scott* was one of the Supreme Court's greatest errors. I, however, think that the opinion was the *most realistic ruling in an antiblack world*. Taney performs a vitally important task here: to unravel the romantic narrative of universal humanism, which captivates the legal imagination.

32 Wilderson, *Red, White, and Black*, 22–23.

33 Orlando Patterson, *Slavery and Social Death*, 211. Patterson even goes as far to say, "Even when the slave pays, he is really not paying for his freedom. It is usually conceived of as making a gift offering in gratitude for the master's *freely given decision* to release him from slavery, however that release is arranged." This is the *extremity* of black humanism, and it translates into a disturbing avoidance of the *domination* within the manumission itself—manumission as a strategy of narcissistic power and control.

34 Alan Nadel, *Invisible Criticism: Ralph Ellison and the American Canon*, 13.

35 Agamben, *The State of Exception*.

36 Nancy, *Birth to Presence*, 95–96.

37 Niklas Luhmann, "Law and Social Theory: Law as a Social System."

38 Carol Greenhouse, "Just in Time: Temporality and the Cultural Legitimation of Law," 1631.

39 Howington, "Property of Special and Peculiar Value," 312. This split was designed to "balance the rights of the slaves and masters against those of the body politic." Saidiya V. Hartman brilliantly articulates another duality of being for the captive—the spilt between chattel object and reasoning criminal. This flexible ontology served the interest of the master as well as the State. Thus, the duality that Howington and Hartman explore is in essence quite similar; see

Hartman, *Scenes of Subjection: Terror, Slavery, and Self-Making in Nineteenth-Century America*.

40 In 1852, Tennessee attempted to re-enslave free blacks who had not received the consent of the state. "The statute mandated that when a slave was freed without the state's consent, the county court was to appoint a trustee for the slave. This trustee was tantamount to a master"; see Howington, "Property of Special and Peculiar Value," 315.

41 J. England Merton, "The Free Negro in Antebellum Tennessee," 46.

42 Helen Tunnicliff Catterall, ed., *Judicial Cases Concerning American Slavery and the Negro*, 479.

43 Howington, "Property of Special and Peculiar Value," 314.

44 Howington, "Property of Special and Peculiar Value," 315.

45 The term *reification* has a rich philosophical tradition originating from György Lukacs's *History and Class Consciousness*. Lukacs insists that the process of commodity exchange and the commodity fetishism that it produces distorts human praxis so that it becomes something like a second nature. Humans begin to transfer their "thingification" of the commodity and its use value to other humans, the intersubjective experience, and, ultimately, to themselves. Only a true human praxis could reverse this distorting stance, a structurally false praxis. My use of the term borrows the sematic energy of "thingification" and the crude praxis of conceiving of beings as mere means. I do not, however, share Lukacs's belief in the efficacy of true praxis, nor do I identify the source of antiblackness as the distorting practice of unchecked commodity-fetishism transference. My conception of reification is not tethered to capitalism because I believe antiblackness is a problem for any economic organization of the social. Reification is more in alignment with Martha Nussbaum's objectification, but I do not propose an ethical or moral framework within which to situate reification/objectification, since antiblackness renders every ethical and moral framework ineffective. Given this philosophical difficulty, I do not retain fealty to the original intent of the term. I do find it useful, however, for understanding the process of reducing immateriality into material substance. For lack of a better term (since "objectification" entraps me in the subject/object division of metaphysics), I have chosen "reification." Please see Martha Nussbaum's *Sex and Social Justice*, and Axel Honneth's reformulation of reification through recognition in his "Reification: A Recognition-Theoretical View."

46 Rebecca Scott and Jean Hébrand, *Freedom Papers: An Atlantic Odyssey in the Age of Emancipation*, 3.

47 Agamben, *The Signature of All Things: On Method*.

48 Carol Wilson, *Freedom at Risk: The Kidnapping of Free Blacks in America 1780-1865*.

49 Samira Kawash, *Dislocating the Color Line: Identity, Hybridity, and Singularity in African-American Literature*, 49.

CHAPTER 3: SCIENTIFIC HORROR

1   In "What Is Metaphysics," Martin Heidegger states, "If science is right, then one thing is for certain: science wants to know nothing of no-thing [*vom Nichts wissen*]. In the end, this is the scientifically strict comprehension of no-thing. We know it in wanting to know nothing about the no-thing"; in Heidegger, *Basic Writings: From Being and Time* (1927) to *The Task of Thinking* (1964), 96. This wanting to know nothing about nothing is the source of scientific knowledge, for all scientific procedures conceal the dreaded desire for nothing. My contention here is that science resolves this tension between refusal and embracing nothing with black ~~being~~. It uses black ~~being~~ to explore the metaphysical mysteries of nothing by projecting the dread onto black bodies. This projection provides an ideal site of scientific disavowal.

2   Alain David, "On Negroes," in *Race and Racism in Continental Philosophy*, 8–18.

3   Evelynn Hammonds conceptualizes black holes in relation to black female sexuality and absent-presence (or silence). She suggests that a black hole brings two problematics to the fore: detection and compositional knowledge (i.e., "What is it like inside a black hole?"). The first is answered by attentiveness to distortion (the distorting impact of a black hole on two stars, for example) and the second by geometry, a geometry still yet to be formulated by mathematical/scientific thinking. I find this analysis exceptionally generative in understanding the relation between blackness and nothing. How do we detect and understand the composition of nothing? These two questions pose a certain horror for science, given their unanswerability. Whereas black holes might be rendered comprehensible by positing being as a condition of studying them (i.e., detection and composition), black as nothing (i.e., formlessness) cannot rely on the ontological ground of being, so we reach a limit with the two procedures Hammonds lays out; please see Hammonds, "Black (W)holes and the Geometry of Black Female Sexuality," in *African American Literary Theory: A Reader*, 492–93.

4   W. T. Wragg, "The Remarkable Case of Mental Alienation," 34, 16.

5   Please see Heidegger's *Being and Time* on the distinction between perishing, demise, and death. I have been arguing that black ~~being~~ can lay no claim to ontological grounds, and this includes the existential meaning of death. Thus, within this ontometaphysical schema, Joe would simply perish—much like any biological organism. Only the human experiences authentic death or inauthentic dying. Black ~~being~~ cannot die, since this death assumes an inauthentic relation to being that can be corrected (through anxiety).

6   David Marriott, *Haunted Life: Visual Culture and Black Modernity*, 230–31.

7   Please see Eric Cazdyn's *The Already Dead: The New Time of Politics, Culture, and Illness*.

8   Abdul R. JanMohamed, *The Death-Bound Subject: Richard Wright's Archeology of Death*, 19.

9   Hortense Spillers, *Black, White, and in Color: Essays on American Literature and Culture*, 208.

10 In "What Is Metaphysics?," Heidegger ruminates on the essence of science: "Science wants to know nothing of 'no-thing.' But even so it is nonetheless certain that, when it attempts to talk about its own essence [*Wesen*], it calls on 'no-thing' for help. It claims for its own what it has rejected. What sort of conflicted essence unveils itself here?" (33). The black body facilitates the unveiling, or working through, of this conflict for science.

11 Heidegger, *Basic Writings*, 96.

12 Andrew S. Curran, *The Anatomy of Blackness: Science and Slavery in an Age of Enlightenment*.

13 Katherine McKittrick, "Mathematics Black Life," 17.

14 Please see Stuart Elden's remarkable study on Heidegger's critique of calculative thinking in *Speaking against Number: Heidegger, Language and Politics of Calculation* (especially the chapter "Taking the Measure of the Political").

15 Alain Badiou, *Being and Event*. Ricardo L. Nirenberg and David Nirenberg also trace the relation between the Heideggerian critique and Badiou's departure and supplement of this critique; please see their "Badiou's Number: A Critique of Mathematics as Ontology," 585–614. Although set theory does not provide an ontological framework within which to ground black ~~being~~ (is there a pure procedure to understand that straddling of nothing and infinity?), his critique of the violence 1 performs is essential to understanding the "mathematics of the unliving."

16 Patricia Cline Cohen, *A Calculating People: The Spread of Numeracy in Early America*.

17 George Yancy, *Look, a White!: Philosophical Essays on Whiteness*.

18 Benjamin Rush, "Observations Tended to Favor a Supposition That the Black Color as It Is Called of the Negroes Is Derived from the Leprosy," 295.

19 This understanding departs from aspects of abolition historiography that view abolition as a radical activity, one bringing the questions of labor and black humanity to the fore. For an example of this understanding of abolition, please see Manisha Sinha's *The Slave's Cause: A History of Abolition*. Steven Best and Saidiya Hartman argue in "Fugitive Justice" that abolition was "incomplete," and I understand the incompletion of the enterprise as the inability to resolve the ontological crisis of black ~~being~~. It is antiblackness that needs abolition, and a change in legal status does not change ontological death; please see Jared Sexton's "Don't Call It a Comeback: Racial Slavery Is Not Yet Abolished."

20 I might also add the Negro Question, or "Nigger Question," as Thomas Carlyle and John Stuart Mill call it (Carlyle and Mill, *The Nigger Question and the Ne-*

gro Question), remains even after emancipation—the ontological question of Negro Humanity is never really resolved (our proper metaphysical question). Thus a relentlessly antiblack study such as *Some Phases of the Negro Question*, penned by Charles Wesley Melick, pursues this question with the understanding that it isn't yet resolved in the twenty-first century.

21 Allen Yarema documents the negrophobia that necessitated the emergence of the colonization movement. The unwillingness of Americans to treat blacks as equal (or human), even when possessing limited rights, convinced many that colonization was the only option for blacks. Black freedom remained an ideal that only relocation could realize, but even relocation failed to provide freedom from antiblackness. African settlements were often not acknowledged as serious international actors, and those relocating faced very dangerous conditions, such as disease; see Yarema's *American Colonization Society: An Avenue to Freedom?*.

22 Please see Grant "Sylvester" Walker, *A Conspiracy to Colonize 19th Century United States Free Blacks in Africa by the American Colonization Society*.

23 William Andrew Smith, *Lectures on the Philosophy and Practice of Slavery: As Exhibited in the Institution of Domestic Slavery in the United States: With the Duties of Masters to Slaves* (1856), 128.

24 Rush, "Observations," 294.

25 Rush actually conducted his own experiments on Moss on July 27, 1796. He used the results of this experiment as the basis for his presentation to the American Philosophical Society entitled, "On the Color of the Negroes." He would expand this into "Observations." See Katy L. Chiles's *Transformable Race: Surprising Metamorphoses in the Literature of Early America*, 196. Moss's body, then, is precisely a living laboratory—biologically functional but ontologically dead—and Rush builds an entire career from the open vulnerability of black bodies to the scientific gaze. For could Moss *refuse* Rush's experiments? His body belonged to a public trust of prurient knowledge accumulation for science.

26 Harriet Washington, *Medical Apartheid*, 80.

27 Rush, "Observations," 296.

28 Mark M. Smith, *How Race Is Made: Slavery, Segregation, and the Senses*, 14.

29 Michel Foucault clarifies some of his thinking about confession, power, and madness in "The Confessions of the Flesh," in *Power/Knowledge: Selected Interviews and Other Writings 1972–1977*, 194–228.

30 Denise Ferreira da Silva, *Toward a Global Idea of Race*, 21–33.

31 Samuel Cartwright even proffers "Cholera of the mind" to explain the splintering of the mind unique to blacks diagnosed with cholera—the symptoms are "dreams, prophecies, or any idle thing." The choleric black mind is not a mind at all, but a black psyche within which Cartwright unloads antiblack reasoning and beliefs. Please see Katherine Bankole's *Slavery and Medicine: Enslavement and Medical Practices in Antebellum Louisiana* for Cartwright's discourse on blackness and cholera.

32 J. Kameron Carter, "Christian Atheism: The Only Response Worth Its Salt to the Zimmerman Verdict."

33 For a reading of the Hamitic myth as an antiblack Christian fantasy and a retooling of this fantasy by black Christians, see Sylvester Johnson's *The Myth of Ham in Nineteenth Century American Christianity: Race, Heathens, and the People of God*.

34 One of the most fervent rejoinders to Cartwright came from a black physician, Dr. James McCune Smith. He worked with orphans in New York and used his findings to make general claims about the misuse of science to make antiblack claims. He asserted that "he hoped much from science," but this humanistic hope— that science could operate objectively for the improvement of all beings— remained unrealized, a tortuous fantasy. Please see Gretchen Long's *Doctoring Freedom: The Politics of African American Medical Care in Slavery and Emancipation*, for more analysis on Dr. Smith's scientific desires.

35 Elaine Scarry, *The Body in Pain: The Making and Unmaking of the World*, 38.

36 Nicolas Abraham and Maria Torok, *The Wolf Man's Magic Word: A Cryptonomy*.

37 Jonathan Metzl, *The Protest Psychosis: How Schizophrenia Became a Black Disease*.

38 Thomas S. Szasz, *Ideology and Insanity: Essays on the Psychiatric Dehumanization of Man*, 4.

39 Albert Deutsch, "The First U.S. Census of the Insane (1840) and Its Uses as Pro-Slavery Propaganda," 471.

40 Bruce Curtis, *The Politics of Population: State Formation, Statistics, and the Census of Canada, 1840–1875*, 17.

41 Deutsch, "First U.S. Census of the Insane (1840)," 471.

42 Deutsch, "First U.S. Census of the Insane (1840)," 472.

43 Please see Gayatri Chakravorty Spivak's *A Critique of Postcolonial Reason: Toward a History of the Vanishing Present*, 41. Although Spivak is analyzing the cartographic imagination of continentalist philosophers, her discussion of the epistemograph is pertinent to a discussion of the geopolitics of knowledge in general.

44 Frank Wilderson, *Red, White, and Black*, 41.

45 Kalpana Seshadri-Crooks, *Desiring Whiteness: A Lacanian Analysis of Race*, 40.

46 Russ Castronovo, *Necro Citizenship: Death, Eroticism, and the Public Sphere in the Nineteenth-Century United States*, 1.

47 Quoted in Deutsch, "The First U.S. Census of the Insane (1840)," 475.

48 Edward Jarvis, "Insanity among the Coloured Population of the Free States," 83.

49 Jarvis, "Insanity among the Coloured Population," 84.

50 Jarvis, "Insanity among the Coloured Population," 84.

51 Deutsch, "The First U.S. Census of the Insane (1840)," 473.

52 Calhoun, *The Works of John C. Calhoun, vol. VI: Reports and Public Letters of John C. Calhoun*, 460–61.

53 Nancy Cartwright provides a rigorous critique of science fundamentalism through physics and the way this foundation is protected from what it excludes; more precisely, the law of fundamentalism is not immediately credited by what it excludes (i.e., like the forms of motion that are not governed by Newton's Law). We can see something similar happening in Cartwright's understanding of statistical science; see Cartwright, *The Dappled World: A Study of the Boundaries of Science*.

54 Mary Douglas might understand this as the problem of pollution—the free black as a pollutant to civil society; see Douglas, *Purity and Danger: An Analysis of Concepts of Pollution and Taboo*.

55 Foucault, *Madness and Civilization: A History of Insanity in the Age of Reason*, 281.

56 Paul Benacerraf and Hilary Putnam, in *Philosophy of Mathematics: Selected Readings*, 5.

57 Badiou, *Briefings on Existence: A Short Treatise on Transitory Existence*, 90.

CHAPTER 4: CATACHRESTIC FANTASIES

1 In *Troubling Vision: Performance, Visuality, and Blackness*, Nicole Fleetwood understands the black body as troubling scopic regimes through performativity. The idea of *troubling*, then, indicates a certain resistance to antiblackness through the visual. I agree that the black body troubles but part ways with Fleetwood's iteration of resistance and agency. In other words, troubling does not yield ontological or transformative results—rather, it translates into an incorrigibility that antiblack violence works to subdue. Michael Chaney also offers a reading of the visual and the "alternate field of vision" fugitivity engenders in *Fugitive Vision: Slave Image and Black Identity in Antebellum Narrative*.

2 Gayatri Chakravorty Spivak, *Outside in the Teaching Machine*, 127.

3 See Spivak, *The Spivak Reader: Selected Works of Gayatri Chakravorty Spivak*, 6.

4 Ronald Judy, *(Dis)forming the American Canon: African-Arabic Slave Narratives and the Vernacular*, 107.

5 David Marriott, *Haunted Life: Visual Culture and Black Modernity*, 7.

6 Dirtiness is a metaphysical sign, one designed to configure white as morally pure and blackness as evil—a moral abyss. Douglas Sharp avers antiblackness, "needs 'dirty' persons to alleviate and clarify [its] own sense of moral ambiguity; [it] needs a baseline in relation to which [it] can measure moral righteousness and purity"; see Sharp, *No Partiality: The Idolatry of Race and the New Humanity*, 71.

7 Jacques Lacan reinterprets Heidegger's fable of the vase to argue that the nothing of the vase (the empty space) provides the vase with its existence. The vase, then, is a material contour around nothing. According to Lacan, "This nothing in particular that characterizes it in its signifying function is that which in its incarnated form characterizes the vase as such. It creates the void and thereby introduces the possibility of filling it"; Lacan, Seminar VII in *The Ethics of Psychoanalysis 1959–1960: The Seminar of Jacques Lacan*, 120.

8 It is also important to note that nothing also terrorizes the Lacanian subject with the threat of aphanisis (the disintegration of the symbolic covering over of this nothing). In fantasies of the body in bits and pieces and other ruptures of the real, the subject tries its best to avoid this nothing at the core of its being. Through repression and disavowal, the subject tries to eliminate nothing, but is, of course, unsuccessful. I use this as a heuristic frame for understanding the way the human being hates (and is fascinated by) this nothing and projects this hatred onto black ~~being~~; see Lacan, "Some Reflections on the Ego," in *The International Journal of Psycho-Analysis*.

9 Frantz Fanon, *Black Skin, White Masks*, 140.

10 Toni Morrison also suggests that the Negro is a plaything for the literary imagination, a putative object for the human; see her *Playing in the Dark: Whiteness and the Literary Imagination* (Cambridge, MA: Harvard University Press, 1992).

11 Rinaldo Walcott, "The Problem of the Human: Black Ontologies and 'the Coloniality of Our Being,'" in *Postcolonial-Decoloniality-Black Critique: Joints and Fissures*," 95.

12 Achille Mbembe, *On the Postcolony*, 143.

13 Hortense Spillers, *Black, White, and in Color: Essays on American Literature and Culture*, 210.

14 See Jean Baudrillard's *Simulacra and Simulation*.

15 Saidiya V. Hartman, *Scenes of Subjection: Terror, Slavery, and Self-Making in Nineteenth-Century America*, 21.

16 *The Ethics of Psychoanalysis 1959–1960: The Seminar of Jacques Lacan*. Seminar VII.

17 Please see Vicky Lebeau's "Psycho-Politics: Frantz Fanon's *Black Skin, White Masks*," in *Psycho-Politics and Cultural Desires*, for an elaboration on Fanon's real fantasy contra Freudian/Lacanian understandings of it.

18 Spillers, *Black, White, and in Color*, 379.

19 In "Decline and Fall: Ocularcentrism in Heidegger's Reading of the History of Metaphysics," David Michael Levin argues that Heidegger challenged the ocularcentrism, which defines modernity's rationality, with his metaphors of vision and seeing—as a challenge to metaphysics. His seeing is not predicated merely on the eyes, but with a thinking anew. I agree with Levin's insightful reading and would suggest that the seeing and not seeing of black ~~being~~ does not end

with the eyes, but with antiblack thinking, which broaches other senses, as well.

20 Illustrated journalism had become a popular mode of leisurely entertainment and political education by 1857. Through the use of vivid illustrations, sketches, and eventually photography, this medium engaged in national debates and concerns. According to historian William Fletcher Thompson Jr., in *The Image of War: The Pictorial Reporting of the American Civil War*, "Recurring crisis in national affairs in the decade preceding the [civil] war established the market for news illustrations. Publishers, artists, and engravers solved the necessary technological problems of mass-printing woodcut engravings of hand-drawn illustrations. By such methods it was possible to print pictures within two or three weeks of the events portrayed—a 'marvel of the times' in comparison to earlier standards." These technological advances provided artists with the means to portray politically salient issues efficiently.

Much as the minstrel shows constructed racial identity through theatrical production, illustrated journalism constructed racial identity through print. Whereas the minstrel show was often confined to a certain space, owing to the physical demands of the stage, illustrated journalism was not limited by the constraints of a physical stage and could circulate images widely and quickly. In *Beyond the Lines: Pictorial Reporting, Everyday Life, and the Crisis of Gilded Age America*, Joshua Brown discusses the lexicography of these images: "They were intended for immediate social use, conveying to the American reading public the people, places, and events that composed the news of the day" (6). Part of the "social use," I argue, is an ontological one—a way of playing with nothing.

21 Giorgio Agamben, *Homo Sacer*, 105.

22 Following Jacques Derrida's *Disseminations*, we could also suggest that what the image is articulating is black ~~being~~ as spacing—the gap in between established properties. For Derrida, this spacing constitutes nothing itself. Spacing ruptures the metaphysics of presence and being, since it is a formlessness that preconditions the structure itself (grammar, language, semiotics). In this way, emancipation is a spacing of blackness. This spacing is the nothing of metaphysics.

23 David Walker, *David Walker's Appeal, in Four Articles, Together with a Preamble to the Coloured Citizens of the World, but in Particular, and Very Expressly, to Those of the United States of America*, 62.

24 The in-between status of the speaking ape problematizes the humanistic presuppositions of the communicative project in Jürgen Habermas's work. The illustrators show us that perhaps the joke is on the belief in the universality of grammatical and syntactical rationality; not everyone could participate in the repository of grammatical conventions and reasoning. Thus, there is a funda-

mental exclusion at the very heart of communicative rationality that African American history exposes; please see Habermas, *The Theory of Communicative Action*. Even if modernity's project is unfinished (as is metaphysics'), its evolution will not bridge the gap between emancipation and freedom for black ~~being~~.

25 Judy, *(Dis)Forming the American Canon*.

26 Tommy Lott, *The Invention of Race: Black Culture and the Politics of Representation*, 7–9.

27 I am thinking here of postmetaphysical works such as Agamben's *The Open: Man and Animal*, which deconstructs the metaphysics of the binary man/animal to understand something like being or existence. The deconstruction is the site of tremendous violence for black ~~being~~—it is not productive.

28 Derrida, *Writing and Difference*, 148.

29 Nelson Maldonado-Torres, *Against War: Views from the Underside of Modernity*. He reads the destructive strategies of antiblackness through Levinas's critique of ontology—ontology as war. I agree with both Torres and Levinas that ontology is a pugnacious enterprise, but I don't think that ethics is any less violent. In fact, ethics is probably more violent, since it disavows the antiblack violence that sustains it. In other words, antiblackness enables *both* ontology and ethics. Neither discourse is clean.

30 Barbara Tomblin, *Bluejackets and Contrabands: African Americans and the Union Navy*, 26.

31 Spillers, *Black, White, and in Color*, 208.

32 For a diacritical engagement with blackness and the question of value in its various iterations, please see Lindon Barrett's *Blackness and Value: Seeing Double*. In particular, Barrett argues that value is a social formation, and this formation is always already cut by race. I would agree with Barrett, but would only add that the social formation is antiblackness, such that value is produced *through* antiblack axiology.

33 I would also agree, along with Heidegger, that technology enables enframing. Technology reveals the essence (essential unfolding) of the human, the revelation that is the unfolding of being. Black weapons *facilitate* human enframing by revealing the nothing at the core of the human. But unlike Heidegger, this enframing is not a source of freedom or potential; it is a vicious aspect of antiblackness. Blacks are *used* for the ontological evolution of the human; see Martin Heidegger's *The Question Concerning Technology and Other Essays*, 287.

34 See Slavoj Žižek's *The Plague of Fantasies* for his discussion of interpassivity. For him, interpassivity is a process of transference in which the subject projects enjoyment onto the object—and the object carries out the projected enjoyment the subject passively, vicariously enjoys. The illustrations are forms of

interpassive enjoyment, an enjoyment with the terror of nothing. The subject projects this terror onto black bodies so that one can enjoy passively from a distance. Žižek notes that this may also produce aggression if the object disrupts the transference. We might say that freedom dreams are a form of disruption that antiblackness checks with extreme aggression (111–13).

35 Lewis R. Gordon, "Through the Hellish Zone of Nonbeing: Thinking through Fanon, Disaster, and the Damned of the Earth," 11.

36 Heidegger makes a distinction between perishment, demise, and death in *Being and Time*. Dasein does not perish. Lower forms of life perish where expiration does not have significance or meaning for being. Dasein experiences either authentic death (being-toward-death) or inauthentic demise (being at an end). In other words, death is bound up with a relation to Being. Since I have argued that this is not an issue for black equipment, perishment is closer to what happens to black weapons.

37 Roland Barthes, *Mythologies*.

38 Darieck Scott also argues for the agential potential of subjection and fantasy in his *Extravagant Abjection: Blackness, Power, and Sexuality in the African American Literary Imagination*. Amber Jamilla Musser suggests that masochism as a set of relations, converging on the site of freedom and agency, in *Sensational Flesh: Race, Power, and Masochism*. Both Scott and Musser suggest that masochism can serve as a strategy or tactic of resistance to domination— by undermining the terms of subjection and pleasure. I, however, do not find agency within masochism—pleasure is no more a strategy against antiblackness than voting or metaphysical romance. Pleasure reaches its limit when the body is literally destroyed, and pleasure in destruction just produces a dead black body. Antiblackness is not moved by black death or deterred through black pleasure.

39 Anthony Paul Farley, "The Black Body as Fetish Object," 533.

40 Nahum Dimitri Chandler, *X: The Problem of the Negro as a Problem for Thought*, 8–9.

41 Fanon, *Black Skin, White Masks*, 116.

42 Jacques Lacan, *The Four Fundamental Concepts of Psycho-Analysis*, 88–89.

43 Monica L. Miller reads resistance and disruption in the look: "Highlighting the foreignness of the gaze upon him, Mr. Augustus points out here a real change in the history of self-fashion. Whereas Clay's earlier Philadelphia series had been voyeuristic—one in which the viewer, presumably white, ridicules the black pretensions to high society by eavesdropping on blacks' social follies and foibles—this print is confrontational. Mr. Augustus's 'look' at the viewer, through the monocle, magnifies concern about the viewer's own sense of self and forces a comparison of this self with that of the nattily clad black man." I would argue, however, that the look is rendered powerless because it is

fraudulent—only the eyes of the white man matter in an antiblack world. The confrontation, then, is between the white subject and nothing; this is what the image stages—not black resistance; please see Miller's *Slaves to Fashion: Black Dandyism and the Styling of Black Diasporic Identity*, 105.

44 In *Picture Freedom: Remaking Black Visuality in the Early Nineteenth Century*, Jasmine Cobb argues persuasively that the black woman in the image is presented as both ignorant and buffoonish. Her inquiry is designed to present her as blithely unaware of her surroundings and the deadly white gaze. The problem of gender is one that compounds the issue of nihilism, since it requires us to think about the way gender is the structure through which black as nothing is represented. I would argue, however, that gender is precisely one form of vicious humor, since blacks do not have the privilege of gender intelligibility in an antiblack society. In other words, the free black woman *pretends* to be a woman (as she is *pretending* to be a human). This pretending was a source of great comedy for white spectators. Thus, her feminine comportment and stylish dress are props for comedy—*nothing wrapping itself up in human gender*.

45 Gordon, "Through the Hellish Zone of Nonbeing," 3.

46 We might answer Spivak's provocative query "Can the Subaltern Speak?, in *Colonial Discourse and Postcolonial Theory: A Reader* by saying that it doesn't matter whether black ~~being~~ can speak or be heard—given that language and discourse will not end the metaphysical holocaust. So even if black ~~being~~ can speak, write, and be heard, onticidal destruction will continue. The black nihilist must write, speak, and broach the metaphysical question to illumine the process of destruction. To say that the enterprise is meaningless is only potent if such a thing as meaning can be recuperated for black ~~being~~. Meaning is lost along with the flesh. This is the crux of black suffering in an antiblack world.

47 Ivy Wilson, *Specters of Democracy: Blackness and the Aesthetics of Politics in the Antebellum U.S.* Wilson argues that political aesthetics constitutes a web of practices engendering subversion and inversion. I definitely understand that art provides a vehicle for expressivity, but an artistic practice is unable to resolve an ontological issue. In *Specters of Democracy*, the ontological problem of blackness is neglected, and it proceeds as if the ontological ground of black humanity is self-evident. It is this very self-evidence that black nihilism seeks to unravel. In other words, political aesthetics never broaches the ontological problematic, even if it forges a sense of belonging or collective affirmation.

48 Marriott, *Haunted Life*, 7.

CODA: ADIEU TO THE HUMAN

1 As quoted in Sheryl Gay Stolberg, "Findings of Police Bias in Baltimore Validate What Many Have Long Felt," *New York Times*, August 10, 2016.
2 Rinaldo Walcott, "The Problem of the Human: Black Ontologies and 'the Coloniality of Our Being,'" in *Postcolonial-Decoloniality-Black Critique: Joints and Fissures*, 94.
3 Martin Heidegger, *Introduction to Metaphysics*, 40.
4 Ashon T. Crawley, *Blackpentecostal Breath: The Aesthetics of Possibility*.

BIBLIOGRAPHY

Abraham, Nicolas, and Maria Torok. *The Wolf Man's Magic Word: A Cryptonomy*. Minneapolis: University of Minnesota Press, 2005.

The African Repository: The Twelfth Annual Report of American Society for Colonizing the Free People of Color of the United States. Vols. 1 and 27. Washington, DC: Way and Gideon, 1825 and 1851.

Agamben, Giorgio. *Homo Sacer*. Trans. Daniel Heller-Roazen. Stanford, CA: Stanford University Press, 1998.

———. *The Open: Man and Animal*. Trans. Kevin Attell. Stanford, CA: Stanford University Press, 2004.

———. *Potentialities: Collected Essays in Philosophy*. Edited and translated with an introduction by Daniel Heller-Roazen. Stanford, CA: Stanford University Press, 2000.

———. *The Signature of All Things: On Method*. Trans. Luca D'Isanto, with Kevin Attell. New York: Zone, 2009.

———. *State of Exception*. Trans. Kevin Attell. Chicago: University of Chicago Press, 2005.

Aho, Kevin. "Logos and the Poverty of Animals: Rethinking Heidegger's Humanism." *New Yearbook for Phenomenology and Phenomenological Philosophy* 7 (2007): 1–18.

Arendt, Hannah. *The Human Condition*. Introduction by Margaret Canovan. 2nd ed. Chicago: University of Chicago Press, 1998.

Bacon, Margaret Hope. *But One Race: The Life of Robert Purvis*. Albany: SUNY Press, 2007.

Badiou, Alain. *Being and Event*. New York: Continuum, 2007.

———. *Briefings on Existence: A Short Treatise on Transitory Existence*. Trans. Norman Madarasz. New York: SUNY Press, 2006.

Bankole, Katherine. *Slavery and Medicine: Enslavement and Medical Practices in Antebellum Louisiana*. New York: Routledge, 2016.

Barfield, Rodney. *America's Forgotten Caste: Free Blacks in Antebellum Virginia and North Carolina*. Bloomington, IN: Xlibris, 2013.

Barrett, Lindon. *Blackness and Value: Seeing Double*. Cambridge: Cambridge University Press, 1999.

——. *Racial Blackness and the Discontinuity of Western Modernity*. Ed. Justin A. Joyce, Dwight A. McBride, and John Carlos Rowe. Chicago: University of Illinois Press, 2014.

Barthes, Roland. *Mythologies*. Trans. Richard Howard and Annette Lavers. New York: Farrar, Straus and Giroux, 2013.

Baudrillard, Jean. *Simulacra and Simulation*. Trans. Sheila Faria Glaser. Ann Arbor: University of Michigan Press, 1994.

Beistegui, Miguel de. *Heidegger and the Political*. New York: Routledge, 1998.

Benacerraf, Paul, and Hilary Putnam, eds. *Philosophy of Mathematics: Selected Readings*. 2nd ed. Cambridge: Cambridge University Press, 1983.

Ben-Dor, Oren. *Thinking about Law: In Silence with Heidegger*. Portland, OR: Hart, 2007.

Berlin, Ira. *The Long Emancipation: The Demise of Slavery in the United States*. Cambridge, MA: Harvard University Press, 2015.

——. *Many Thousands Gone: The First Two Centuries of Slavery in North America*. Cambridge, MA: Harvard University Press, 1998.

——. *Slaves without Masters: The Free Negro in the Antebellum South*. New York: Pantheon, 1974.

Best, Steven, and Saidiya Hartman. "Fugitive Justice: The Appeal of the Slave." *Representations* 92, no. 1 (fall 2005): 1–15.

Brown, Joshua. *Beyond the Lines: Pictorial Reporting, Everyday Life, and the Crisis of Gilded Age America*. Berkeley: University of California Press, 2002.

Calarco, Matthew. *Zoographies: The Question of the Animal from Heidegger to Derrida*. New York: Columbia University Press, 2008.

Calhoun, John C. *The Works of John C. Calhoun*, vol. 6. *Reports and Public Letters of John C. Calhoun*, edited by Richard K. Cralle. New York: D. Appleton and Company, 1870.

Carlyle, Thomas, and John Stuart Mill. *The Nigger Question and the Negro Question*. [1853]. Whitefish, MT: Kessinger, 2006.

Carter, J. Kameron. "Christian Atheism: The Only Response Worth Its Salt to the Zimmerman Verdict." In *Religion Dispatches*, July 23, 2013.

Cartwright, Nancy. *The Dappled World: A Study of the Boundaries of Science*. Cambridge: Cambridge University Press, 2003.

Cartwright, Samuel. "Report on the Diseases and Physical Peculiarities of the Negro Race." *DeBow's Review Southern and Western States* 7, no. 11 (1851). Accessed June 5, 2015. https://www.pbs.org/wgbh/aia/part4/4h3106t.html.

Castronovo, Russ. *Necro Citizenship: Death, Eroticism, and the Public Sphere in the Nineteenth-Century United States*. Durham, NC: Duke University Press, 2001.

Catterall, H. T., ed. *Judicial Cases Concerning American Slavery and the Negro*. Washington, DC: Carnegie Institution of Washington, 1926.

Cazdyn, Eric. *The Already Dead: The New Time of Politics, Culture, and Illness*. Durham, NC: Duke University Press, 2012.

Chandler, Nahum Dimitri. *X: The Problem of the Negro as a Problem for Thought*. New York: Fordham University Press, 2014.

Chaney, Michael. *Fugitive Vision: Slave Image and Black Identity in Antebellum Narrative*. Bloomington: Indiana University Press, 2008.

Chiles, Katy L. *Transformable Race: Surprising Metamorphoses in the Literature of Early America*. Oxford: Oxford University Press, 2013.

Cobb, Jasmine. *Picture Freedom: Remaking Black Visuality in the Early Nineteenth Century*. New York: NYU Press, 2015.

Cohen, Patricia Cline. *A Calculating People: The Spread of Numeracy in Early America* [1999]. New York: Routledge, 2016.

"Compendium of the Enumeration of the Inhabitants and Statistics of the United States, As Obtained at the Department of State, from Returns of the Sixth Census, To Which is Added an Abstract of Each Preceding Census." *Census of 1840*. Vol. 3. Washington, DC: U.S. State Department, 1841. Accessed December 20, 2015. www.census.gov/library/publications/1841 /dec/1840c.html.

Crawley, Ashon T. *Blackpentecostal Breath: The Aesthetics of Possibility*. New York: Fordham University Press, 2017.

Curran, Andrew S. *The Anatomy of Blackness: Science and Slavery in an Age of Enlightenment*. Baltimore: Johns Hopkins University Press, 2011.

Curry, Tommy. "Saved by the Bell: Derrick Bell's Racial Realism as Pedagogy." *Ohio Valley Philosophy of Education Society* 39 (2008): 35–46.

Curtis, Bruce. *The Politics of Population: State Formation, Statistics, and the Census of Canada, 1840–1875*. Toronto: University of Toronto Press, 2001.

David, Alain. "On Negroes." In *Race and Racism in Continental Philosophy*, ed. Robert Bernasconi, with Sybol Cook, 8–18. Bloomington: Indiana University Press, 2003.

Derrida, Jacques. *Disseminations*. Trans. Barbara Johnson. Chicago: University of Chicago Press, 1981.

———. *Writing and Difference*. Trans with introduction by Alain Bass. Chicago: University of Chicago Press, 1978.

Desmond, William. *Philosophy and Its Others: Ways of Being and Mind*. Albany: SUNY Press, 1990.

Deutsch, Albert. "The First U.S. Census of the Insane (1840) and Its Uses as Pro-Slavery Propaganda." *Bulletin of History of Medicine* 15 (1944).

Douglas, Mary. *Purity and Danger: An Analysis of Concepts of Pollution and Taboo*. New York: Routledge, 2003.

The Dred Scott Decision: Opinion of Chief Justice Taney. Library of Congress. http://hdl.loc.law//llst.022.

Dressler, Markus, and Arvind-Pal S. Mandair. *Secularism and Religion-Making.* Oxford: Oxford University Press, 2011.

Dreyfus, Hubert L. *Being-in-the-World: A Commentary on Heidegger's Being and Time, Division I.* Cambridge, MA: MIT Press, 1991.

Dubois, W. E. B. *The Souls of Black Folk* [1903]. New York: Penguin, 1989.

Elden, Stuart. *Speaking against Number: Heidegger, Language and Politics of Calculation.* Edinburgh: Edinburgh University Press, 2005.

Fanon, Frantz. *Black Skin, White Masks.* Trans. Charles Lam Markmann. New York: Grove, 1967.

Farley, Anthony Paul. "The Black Body as Fetish Object." *Oregon Law Review* 76 (1997).

Farred, Grant. *Martin Heidegger Saved My Life.* Minneapolis: University of Minnesota Press, 2015.

Ferreira da Silva, Denise. *Toward a Global Idea of Race.* Minneapolis: University of Minnesota Press, 2007.

Finkelman, Paul. "The Significance and Persistence of Proslavery Thought." In *The Problem of Evil: Slavery, Freedom, and the Ambiguities of American Reform*, ed. Steven Mintz and John Stauffer. Amherst: University of Massachusetts Press, 2007.

Fleetwood, Nicole. *Troubling Vision: Performance, Visuality, and Blackness.* Chicago: University of Chicago Press, 2011.

Foucault, Michel. "The Confessions of the Flesh." In *Power/Knowledge: Selected Interviews and Other Writings 1972–1977.* New York: Random House, 1988.

———. *Madness and Civilization: A History of Insanity in the Age of Reason.* New York: Random House, 1965.

———. "Questions of Method." In *The Foucault Effect: Studies in Governmentality*, ed. Graham Burchell, Colin Gordon, and Peter Miller. Chicago: University of Chicago Press, 1991.

Franklin, John Hope. *The Free Negro in North Carolina, 1790–1860.* New York: Russell and Russell, 1969.

Gordon, Lewis R. *Bad Faith and Antiblack Racism.* Atlantic Highlands, NJ: Humanities Press International, 1995.

———. "Through the Hellish Zone of Nonbeing: Thinking through Fanon, Disaster, and the Damned of the Earth." *Human Architecture: The Journal of the Sociology of Self-Knowledge* (summer 2007): 5–12.

Greenhouse, Carol. "Just in Time: Temporality and the Cultural Legitimation of Law." *Yale Law Journal* 98 (1989): 1631.

Grivno, Max. *Gleanings of Freedom: Free and Slave Labor along the Mason-Dixon Line, 1790–1860.* Champaign: University of Illinois Press, 2011.

Grob, Gerald. *Edward Jarvis and the Medical World of Nineteenth-Century America.* Knoxville: University of Tennessee Press, 1978.

Habermas, Jürgen. *The Theory of Communicative Action.* Boston: Beacon, 1987.

Hammonds, Evelynn. "Black (W)holes and the Geometry of Black Female Sexuality." In *African American Literary Theory: A Reader*, ed. Winston Napier. New York: NYU Press, 2000.

Harman, Graham. *Tool-Being: Heidegger and the Metaphysics of Objects*. Chicago: Open Court, 2002.

Hartman, Saidiya V. *Scenes of Subjection: Terror, Slavery, and Self-Making in Nineteenth-Century America*. New York: Oxford University Press, 1997.

Heidegger, Martin. *Basic Writings: From Being and Time (1927) to The Task of Thinking (1964)*. Ed. David Farrell Krell. San Francisco: Harper SanFrancisco, 1993.

——. *Being and Time*. Trans. Joan Stambaugh. Revised, with a foreword by Dennis J. Schmidt. Albany: SUNY Press, 2010.

——. *The Essence of Human Freedom: An Introduction to Philosophy*. Trans. Ted Sadler. New York: Continuum, 2002.

——. *Introduction to Metaphysics*. Revised and Expanded. Trans. Gregory Fried and Richard Polt. 2nd ed. New Haven, CT: Yale University Press, 2014.

——. "Letter on Humanism." In *Basic Writings: Martin Heidegger*. Ed. D. F. Krell. Trans. F. A. Capuzzi and J. Glenn Gray. London: Routledge, 1993.

——. *The Metaphysical Foundations of Logic*. Trans. Michael Heim. Bloomington: Indiana University Press, 1984.

——. *The Question Concerning Technology and Other Essays*. New York: HarperCollins, 2013.

Honneth, Axel. "Reification: A Recognition-Theoretical View." The Tanner Lectures on Human Value, delivered at University of California, Berkeley (March 2005).

Howington, Arthur. "A Property of Special and Peculiar Value: The Tennessee Supreme Court and the Law of Manumission." In *Law, the Constitution, and Slavery*, ed. Paul Finkelman. New York: Garland, 1989.

Illinois Constitutional Debates of 1847, 860. https://archive.org/details /constitutionaldeooilli.

Irigaray, Luce. "Place/Interval: A Reading of Aristotle, *Physics* IV." In *An Ethics of Sexual Difference*, trans. Carolyn Burke and Gillian C. Gill. Ithaca, NY: Cornell University Press, 1993.

JanMohamed, Abdul R. *The Death-Bound-Subject: Richard Wright's Archaeology of Death*. Durham, NC: Duke University Press, 2005.

Jarvis, Edward. "Insanity among the Colored Population of the Free States." *American Journal of Medical Sciences* (January 1844): 71–83.

Johnson, Sylvester. *The Myth of Ham in Nineteenth-Century American Christianity: Race, Heathens, and the People of God*. New York: Palgrave Macmillan, 2004.

Jones, Edward P. *The Known World: A Novel*. New York: HarperCollins, 2003.

Journal of the Senate of Pennsylvania, 1836–37 sess., I, 680.

Judy, Ronald. *(Dis)Forming the American Canon: African-Arabic Slave Narratives and the Vernacular*. Foreword by Wahneema Lubiano. Minneapolis: University of Minnesota Press, 1993.

Kawash, Samira. *Dislocating the Color Line: Identity, Hybridity, and Singularity in African-American Narrative*. Stanford, CA: Stanford University Press, 1997.

Kristeva, Julia. *Powers of Horror: An Essay on Abjection*. Trans. Leon S. Roudiez. New York: Columbia University Press, 1982.

Lacan, Jacques. *Écrits: A Selection*. Trans. Bruce Fink in collaboration with Heloise Fink and Russell Grigg. New York: W. W. Norton, 2004.

———. *Ethics of Psychoanalysis 1959–1960: The Seminar of Jacques Lacan*. Book 7. Ed. Jacques-Alain Miller. Trans. with notes by Dennis Porter. New York: Routledge, 1992.

———. *The Four Fundamental Concepts of Psycho-Analysis*. Ed. Jacques-Alain Miller. Trans. Alan Sheridan. [1977]. New York: Karnac, 2004.

———. "Some Reflections on the Ego." *International Journal of Psychoanalysis* 34, no. 1 (1953): 11–17.

Laruelle, François. *From Decision to Heresy: Experiments in Non-Standard Thought*. Ed. Robin Mackay. Trans. Miguel Abreu et al. New York: Sequence, 2012.

Lebeau, Vicky. "Psycho-Politics: Frantz Fanon's *Black Skin, Whites Masks*." In *Psycho-Politics and Cultural Desires*, ed. Janet Harbord and Jan Campbell. Bristol, PA: UCL Press, 1998.

Lee, Maurice S. *Slavery, Philosophy, and American Literature*. Cambridge: Cambridge University Press, 2005.

Lester, Julius. *Lovesong: Becoming a Jew*. New York: Arcade, 2013.

Levin, David Michael. "Decline and Fall: Ocularcentrism in Heidegger's Reading of the History of Metaphysics." In *Modernity and the Hegemony of Vision*, ed. David Michael Levin. Berkeley: University of California Press, 1993.

Levinas, Emmanuel. *Otherwise Than Being, or, Beyond Essence*. Trans. Alphonso Lingis. Boston: Kluwer, 1991.

Litwack, Leon. *North of Slavery: The Negro in the Free States, 1790–1860*. Chicago: University of Chicago Press, 1961.

Long, Gretchen. *Doctoring Freedom: The Politics of African American Medical Care in Slavery and Emancipation*. Chapel Hill: University of North Carolina Press, 2012.

Lott, Tommy. *The Invention of Race: Black Culture and the Politics of Representation*. Malden, MA: Blackwell, 1999.

Lott, Tommy, and John. P. Pittman. *A Companion to African American Philosophy*. Malden, MA: Blackwell, 2006.

Luhmann, Niklas. "Law and Social Theory: Law as a Social System." *Northwestern Law Review* (1988).

Lukacs, George. "Reification and the Consciousness of the Proletariat." In *History and Class Consciousness*. London: Merlin, 1967.

Maldonado Torres, Nelson. *Against War: Views from the Underside of Modernity*. Durham, NC: Duke University Press, 2008.

———. "On the Coloniality of Being: Contributions to the Development of a Concept." *Cultural Studies* 21, nos. 2–3 (March/May 2007): 240–70.

Marriott, David. *Haunted Life: Visual Culture and Black Modernity*. New Brunswick, NJ: Rutgers University Press, 2007.

———. "Judging Fanon." *Rhizomes* 29 (2016). https://doi.org/10.20415/rhiz/029.e03.

———. "Waiting to Fall." *CR: The New Centennial Review* 13, no. 3 (winter 2013): 163–240.

Mbembe, Achille. "Necropolitics." Trans. Libby Meintjes. *Public Culture* 15, no. 1 (2003): 11–40.

———. *On the Postcolony*. Berkeley: University of California Press, 2001.

McKittrick, Katherine. "Mathematics Black Life." *Black Scholar* 44, no. 2 (summer 2014): 16–28.

Meillassoux, Quentin. *After Finitude: An Essay on the Necessity of Contingency*. Trans. Ray Brassier. London: Continuum, 2008.

Melick, Charles Wesley. *Some Phases of the Negro Question*. [1908]. Ann Arbor: University of Michigan Library, 2009.

Merton, J. England. "The Free Negro in Antebellum Tennessee." *Journal of Southern History* 9, no. 1 (February 1943): 46.

Metzl, Jonathan. *The Protest Psychosis: How Schizophrenia Became a Black Disease*. Boston: Beacon, 2010.

Miller, Monica L. *Slaves to Fashion: Black Dandyism and the Styling of Black Diasporic Identity*. Durham, NC: Duke University Press, 2009.

Mills, Charles. *The Racial Contract*. Ithaca, NY: Cornell University Press, 1997.

Morris, Louise. "The Specter of Grief: Visualizing Ontological Terror in Performance." Master's thesis, University of Melbourne, 2007.

Morrison, Toni. *Playing in the Dark: Whiteness and the Literary Imagination*. Cambridge, MA: Harvard University Press, 1992.

Moten, Fred. "Blackness and Nothingness." *The South Atlantic Quarterly* 112, no. 4 (fall 2013): 737–80.

Mullarkey, John. *Post-Continental Philosophy: An Outline*. New York: Continuum, 2006.

Musser, Amber Jamilla. *Sensational Flesh: Race, Power, and Masochism*. New York: NYU Press, 2014.

Myers, Amrita Chakrabarti. *Forging Freedom: Black Women and the Pursuit of Liberty in Antebellum Charleston*. Chapel Hill: University of North Carolina Press, 2011.

Nadel, Alan. *Invisible Criticism: Ralph Ellison and the American Canon*. Iowa City: University of Iowa Press, 1988.

Nancy, Jean-Luc. *Being Singular Plural*. Stanford, CA: Stanford University Press, 2000.

——. *The Birth to Presence*. Trans. Bridget McDonald. Stanford, CA: Stanford University Press, 1993.

——. *The Experience of Freedom*. Trans. Bridget McDonald, with a foreword by Peter Fenves. Stanford, CA: Stanford University Press, 1993.

Nirenberg, Ricardo L., and David Nirenberg. "Badiou's Number: A Critique of Mathematics as Ontology." *Critical Inquiry* 37 (summer 2011).

Nussbaum, Martha. *Sex and Social Justice*. Oxford: Oxford University Press, 2000.

Pargas, Damian Alan. *The Quarters and the Fields: Slave Families in the Non-Cotton South*. Gainesville: University Press of Florida, 2010.

Patterson, Orlando. *Freedom*: volume I: *Freedom in the Making of Western Culture*. New York: Basic Books, 1991.

——. *Slavery and Social Death*. Cambridge, MA: Harvard University Press, 1982.

Pinn, Anthony B. *Terror and Triumph: The Nature of Black Religion*. Minneapolis: Fortress, 2013.

Possenti, Vittorio. *Nihilism and Metaphysics: The Third Voyage*. Trans. Daniel B. Gallagher. Foreword by Brian Schroeder. Albany: SUNY Press, 2014.

Prozorov, Sergei. *Theory of the Political Subject: Void Universalism*, volume 2: *Interventions*. New York: Routledge, 2014.

Purvis, Robert. Letter to Henry C. Wright, August 22, 1842. Weston Papers, Boston Public Library.

Rae, Gavin. *Ontology in Heidegger and Deleuze: A Comparative Analysis*. New York: Palgrave Macmillan, 2014.

"Reflections on the Census of 1840." *Southern Literary Messenger (1834–1845)* 9, no. 6 (June 1843): 340–52. Accessed July 10, 2010. http://quod.lib.umich.edu/m/moajrnl/acf2679.0009.006/348.

Rush, Benjamin. "Observations Tended to Favor a Supposition That the Black Color as It Is Called of the Negroes Is Derived from the Leprosy." *Transactions of the American Philosophical Society* 4 (1799): 288–97. Accessed August 10, 2011. http://www.jstor.org/stable/1005108.

Sartre, Jean-Paul. *Being and Nothingness: An Essay on Phenomenological Ontology*. Trans. Hazel Barnes. London: Routledge, 2003.

Scarry, Elaine. *The Body in Pain: The Making and Unmaking of the World*. Oxford: Oxford University Press, 1985.

Scott, Darieck. *Extravagant Abjection: Blackness, Power, and Sexuality in the African American Literary Imagination*. New York: NYU Press, 2010.

Scott, Rebecca, and Jean Hébrand. *Freedom Papers: An Atlantic Odyssey in the Age of Emancipation*. Cambridge, MA: Harvard University Press, 2014.

Seshadri-Crooks, Kalpana. *Desiring Whiteness: A Lacanian Analysis of Race*. New York: Routledge, 2000.

———. *HumAnimal: Race, Law, and Language*. Minneapolis: University of Minnesota Press, 2012.

Sexton, Jared. "Don't Call It a Comeback: Racial Slavery Is Not Yet Abolished." *OpenDemocracy*, June 17, 2015. https://www.opendemocracy.net/beyond slavery/jared-sexton/don%E2%80%99t-call-it-comeback-racial-slavery-is -not-yet-abolished.

Sharp, Douglas. *No Partiality: The Idolatry of Race and the New Humanity*. Downers Grove, IL: InterVarsity Press, 2002.

Sinha, Manisha. *The Slave's Cause: A History of Abolition*. New Haven, CT: Yale University Press, 2016.

Smith, William Andrew. *Lectures on the Philosophy and Practice of Slavery: As Exhibited in the Institution of Domestic Slavery in the United States: With the Duties of Masters to Slaves* (1856). Stanford, CA: Stanford University Library Archives.

Smith, Mark M. *How Race Is Made: Slavery, Segregation, and the Senses*. Chapel Hill: University of North Carolina Press, 2006.

Spillers, Hortense. *Black, White, and in Color: Essays on American Literature and Culture*. Chicago: University of Chicago Press, 2003.

Spivak, Gayatri Chakravorty. *A Critique of Postcolonial Reason: Toward a History of the Vanishing Present*. Cambridge, MA: Harvard University Press, 1999.

———. "Can the Subaltern Speak?" In *Colonial Discourse and Postcolonial Theory: A Reader*, ed. Patrick Williams and Laura Chrisman, 66–111. New York: Columbia University Press, 1994.

———. *Outside in the Teaching Machine*. New York: Routledge, 1993.

———. *The Spivak Reader: Selected Works of Gayatri Chakravorty Spivak*. Ed. Donna Landry and Gerald Maclean. New York: Routledge, 1996.

Szasz, Thomas S. *Ideology and Insanity: Essays on the Psychiatric Dehumanization of Man*. Syracuse, NY: Syracuse University Press, 1991.

Thompson, William Fletcher, Jr. *The Image of War: The Pictorial Reporting of the American Civil War*. New York: Thomas Yoseloff, 1960.

Tomblin, Barbara. *Bluejackets and Contrabands: African Americans and the Union Navy*. Lexington: University Press of Kentucky, 2009.

Tuitt, Patricia. *Race, Law, and Resistance*. Portland, OR: Glasshouse, 2004.

Vattimo, Gianni. *The End of Modernity: Nihilism and Hermeneutics in Postmodern Culture*. Baltimore: Johns Hopkins University Press, 1988.

———. *Nihilism and Emancipation: Ethics, Politics, and Law*. Foreword by Richard Rorty. Ed. Santiago Zabala. Trans. William McCuaig. New York: Columbia University Press, 2004.

Wagner, Bryan. *Disturbing the Peace: Black Culture and the Police Power after Slavery*. Cambridge, MA: Harvard University Press, 2009.

Walcott, Rinaldo. "The Problem of the Human: Black Ontologies and 'the Coloniality of Our Being.'" In *Postcolonial-Decoloniality-Black Critique: Joints and Fissures*, ed. Sabine Broeck and Carsten Junker, 93–109. New York: Campus Verlag, 2014.

Walker, David. *David Walker's Appeal, in Four Articles, Together with a Preamble to the Coloured Citizens of the World, but in Particular, and Very Expressly, to Those of the United States of America*. New York: Hill and Wang, 1995.

Walker, Grant "Sylvester." *A Conspiracy to Colonize 19th Century United States Free Blacks in Africa by the American Colonization Society*. Bloomington, IN: Trafford, 2014.

Washington, Harriet. *Medical Apartheid*. New York: Anchor, 2006.

Weheliye, Alexander G. *Habeas Viscus: Racializing Assemblages, Biopolitics, and Black Feminist Theories of the Human*. Durham, NC: Duke University Press, 2014.

West, Cornel. "Philosophy and the Afro-American Experience." In *A Companion to African-American Philosophy*, edited by Tommy L. Lott and John P. Pittman, 7–32. Malden, MA: Blackwell, 2003.

Wilderson, Frank. *Red, White, and Black*. Durham, NC: Duke University Press, 2010.

Williams, Patricia. "On Being the Object of Property." *Signs* 14, no. 1 (autumn 1988): 5–24.

Wilson, Carol. *Freedom at Risk: The Kidnapping of Free Blacks in America, 1780-1865*. Lexington: University Press of Kentucky, 2015.

Wilson, Ivy. *Specters of Democracy: Blackness and the Aesthetics of Politics in the Antebellum U.S.* Oxford: Oxford University Press, 2011.

Wolin, Richard. *The Politics of Being: The Political Thought of Martin Heidegger*. New York: Columbia University Press, 1990.

Woodard, Vincent. *The Delectable Negro: Human Consumption and Homoeroticism with U.S. Slave Culture*. Ed. Justin A. Joyce and Dwight A. McBride. Foreword by E. Patrick Johnson. New York: NYU Press, 2014.

Wragg, W. T. "The Remarkable Case of Mental Alienation." *Boston Medical and Surgical Journal (1828–1851)* (May 20, 1846): 34, 16.

Wright, Michelle M. *Physics of Blackness: Beyond the Middle Passage Epistemology*. Minneapolis: University of Minnesota Press, 2015.

Wynter, Sylvia, "Unsettling the Coloniality of Being/Power/Truth/Freedom: Towards the Human, after Man, Its Overrepresentation—An Argument." *CR: The New Centennial Review* 3, no. 3 (fall 2003): 257–337.

Yancy, George. *Look, a White!: Philosophical Essays on Whiteness*. Foreword by Naomi Zack. Philadelphia: Temple University Press, 2012.

Yarema, Allan. *The American Colonization Society: An Avenue to Freedom?* Boulder, CO: University Press of America, 2006.

Zabala, Santiago. *The Remains of Being: Hermeneutic Ontology after Metaphysics*. New York: Columbia University Press, 2009.

Žižek, Slavoj. *The Plague of Fantasies*. New York: Verso, 1997.

INDEX

Page numbers followed by *f* indicate illustrations.

Bacon, Margaret Hope, 185n49

Badiou, Alain, 8, 116, 191n15

Baltimore Police Department, 169

ban, the. *See* abandonment

Barfield, Rodney, 185n59

Barthes, Roland, 160

Baudrillard, Jean, 149

Being: abandonment and, 42–43, 65, 67–77, 86–87, 133–34, 153; equipment in human form and, 6, 28–37, 39–48, 65–67, 73, 81–87, 94–95, 107–8, 116–18, 166–68, 167*f*; essence and, 64–67; execration of, 19, 27, 40–42, 44–45, 92, 102–3, 120–21, 126, 150, 167–68; existence and, 12–14, 19, 27, 29–30, 38–48, 83–84, 113–14, 132–33, 143–50, 171–72; formlessness and, 5–6, 12, 143–51; as *Ge-Schick*, 11, 174n9; giftedness and, 17, 41, 63–64, 91–93, 98, 101, 105; Greek definitions of, 12–13; law of, 22, 64–67, 74–75, 81, 90, 94, 146, 164–65; as object, 6, 9, 11, 16–17, 22–25, 29–30, 88–89, 99–108, 115–18, 140, 147, 152–53, 188n39, 189n45; order of, 66–69, 71; placelessness and, 43, 52–58, 65–76, 81, 86–93, 112–18; politics and, 48–59, 82–89, 153, 179n3, 199n47; as presence, 10, 29–30, 69–70; relationality and, 5, 15–16, 62–73, 78–84, 94, 99, 101, 162, 186n1; scientific thinking and, 110–12, 116–22, 129–39; strikethrough and, 5, 8–9, 12–13, 15–16, 18, 21–23, 26–30, 37–48, 52–53, 62–64, 90–91, 111–18, 179n1; unfolding of, 9–10, 15, 65–67, 69–70, 76–77, 86–87, 94–95, 99, 105; visibility and, 70, 75–76, 80–85, 99–100, 113, 143–50. *See also* antiblackness; humanism; metaphysics; ontology

Being and Nothingness (Sartre), 183n33

Being and Time (Heidegger), 8, 22, 29, 181n16, 198n36

Being Singular Plural (Nancy), 181n16

Bell Curve, The (Herrnstein and Murray), 142

Ben-Dor, Oren, 10, 63–64, 66–68, 72–75, 79, 108

Benjamin, Walter, 95

Berlin, Ira, 17, 90, 96, 184n47

Berlin, Isaiah, 177n18

biofuturity, 129–30, 172

biology, 139–42

biopower, 123–24

Birth of Presence, The (Nancy), 68, 93–94

black archives, 20

"Black Body as Fetish, The" (Farley), 160–61

black existence, 12–13, 19, 33, 37–48, 54–59, 83–84, 113–14, 132–33, 143–50, 171–72

Black Hector, 104–6

black humanism, 4–5, 66, 77–78

Black Lives Matter, 1–6, 14

black nihilism, 9–15, 174n4, 183n33

Black Sallo, 104–6

Black Skin, White Masks (Fanon), 12

black thinking, 7–8, 13, 18–19, 22–23, 170–72, 175n15

black time, 23–24, 97–98, 108–9

blindness, 70, 75–76, 80–81

body, the: blackness as ontic distortion and, 65–67, 77–79, 87–93, 113–18; as "floating," 55–57, 60; kidnapping and, 107–9; nothing as imposed upon, 38–48, 111–18, 159–60; scientific thinking and, 112–39, 141–42; the self and, 99–106, 123–24; as weapon, 157–59. *See also* black existence; flesh, the

Body in Pain, The (Scarry), 127

breath, 172

Brown, Heber, III, 169

Harman, Graham, 45, 183n37
Harper's Weekly, 152–53
Harris, Cheryl, 71
Hartman, Saidiya, 46, 88–89, 91, 149, 188n39, 191n19
Hébrand, Jean, 101–2, 108
Hegel, G. W. F., 4, 16, 92, 101, 137–38, 152
Heidegger, Martin, 10; *Bildwesen* and, 149; death and, 159–60; the decision and, 94; equipmentality and, 45–46; metaphysics and, 7–10, 12–13, 15, 20, 28–37, 173n3, 179n3, 184n38, 187n23, 190n1, 191n10; occularcentrism and, 195n19; as postmetaphysician, 31, 40, 60, 63–64, 66, 171–72; scientific thinking and, 110–12; Spillers and, 22, 28–29, 31; suspension and, 94; Vattimo on, 10–11; the way and, 27–28, 99, 151
hermeneutic nihilism, 5
History and Class Consciousness (Lukács), 189n45
History of Sexuality, The (Foucault), 123
Howington, Arthur, 96, 188n39
"How is it going with Being?," 7–9, 22–23, 30–31, 48, 78, 151, 171–72
hyperbaton, 154
Human Condition, The (Arendt), 181n16
humanism, 15, 17–19, 24, 90, 92–93, 109; altered human factor and, 38, 47–48; animality and, 81–82, 152–56, 197n27; antiblackness and, 38–48, 141–42, 154; the ban and, 65–76, 79–80; citizenship and, 16–17, 27–28, 49, 65, 78–83, 133–34, 139–42, 170; emancipation and, 88–93; equipment and, 6, 28–37, 81–87, 117–18; freedom and, 128–29, 170, 177n18; scientific thinking and, 112–29, 140. *See also* antiblackness; citizenship; metaphysics; politics
Humphrey, Humen, 52, 54–55

identity (logic of), 182n27
Ideology and Insanity (Szasz), 129–30
Illinois, 59
illustrations, 151–68
Image of War, The (Thompson), 196n20
Indiana, 59
insanity, 112–18, 129–30, 138, 141–42, 192n31
Introduction to Metaphysics (Heidegger), 10, 22, 30, 46, 179n3, 187n23
Irigaray, Luce, 187n23

JanMohamed, Abdul R., 114
Jarvis, Edward, 133–37
Jefferson, Thomas, 49
Joe (study subject), 112–18, 130
Jones, Edward P., 24–25
Judy, Ronald, 14, 35, 40–41, 45, 77, 155–56, 162–63
jurisdiction, 79–81, 187n27

Kant, Immanuel, 4, 15, 138
Kawash, Samira, 107
Keeling, Kara, 98
kidnapping, 25, 63–64, 92, 101, 106–9
Kierkegaard, Søren, 170
Known World, The (Jones), 24–25
Kristeva, Julia, 58

Lacan, Jacques, 23, 147, 149, 159, 161, 165, 186n62, 195nn7–8
language, 102–4, 148, 152–54
Laruelle, François, 181n19
law: abandonment and, 68–76, 187n27; antiblackness and, 2–4, 18; of Being, 22, 64–67, 74–75, 81, 90, 94, 146, 164–65; the decision and, 93–98, 153; emancipation and, 85–93; the free black and, 18, 53, 85–87; freedom and, 90–92, 99–106; inclusive exclusion and, 83–87; ontology and, 48–59, 64–67, 75–76, 100; purity and, 62–64;

law (*continued*)

    Sandford v. Scott and, 22, 52–54, 76–87, 98, 108, 187n27, 188n30–31; slavery and, 71–76; temporality of, 95–98; terror and, 75–76, 97–98, 106–9; violence and, 75–76, 155–56. *See also* antiblackness; contract law; outlawing; police practices; Taney, Roger

Lectures on the Philosophy and Practice of Slavery (Smith), 120

Lee, Maurice S., 17

leprosy, 119–22

Lester, Julius, 173n2

Levinas, Emmanuel, 74, 197n29

liberalism, 88–89. *See also* humanism; metaphysics

Liberator, 54–55

"Life in Philadelphia Series" (Clay), 151

"Limitation of Being, The" (Heidegger), 66

"Literary Debate in the Darktown Club, A" (Worth), 155*f*, 155–56

Long Emancipation, The (Berlin), 178n25

Lott, Tommy, 156

Luhmann, Niklas, 95

Lukács, Georg, 189n45

Madness and Civilization (Foucault), 138

Maine, 131–32, 135

malapropism, 154

Maldonado-Torres, Nelson, 156–57, 197n29

manumission, 96–97

Marriott, David, 13, 113–14, 140, 146, 168, 181n21

Martin, Trayvon, 16

masochism, 198n38

materiality. *See* reification

mathematics, 116–18, 129–39, 191n15. *See also* calculation; statistics

Mbembe, Achille, 148

McBride, Renisha, 16

McKittrick, Katherine, 116–17

medicine. *See* diseases; scientific thinking

Meillassoux, Quentin, 183n37

Melick, Charles Wesley, 191n20

mental alienation, 112–18

metaphysical holocaust, 13–23, 25, 42–44, 62–64, 109, 116, 124, 130, 139–45, 158–59

metaphysics: antiblackness and, 5–6, 20–21, 26–48, 64–67; colonialism and, 12; free black as paradigmatic problem for, 6, 50–59; Heidegger and, 7–10, 12–13, 20, 28–37, 40, 173n3, 181n12, 187n23, 190n1, 191n10; infrastructure of, 1–2, 7–9, 49–54, 60; the law and, 64–67; nothing and, 5–6, 27–48, 50, 52–53, 58–59, 143–50; ontology and, 2, 4, 7–9, 49–50, 124; *Sandford v. Scott* and, 22, 52–54, 76–87, 98, 108, 187n27, 188nn30–31; scientific thinking and, 5, 10–11, 21–23, 37, 46–47, 60, 110–22, 139–42, 159, 191n10; violence and, 9–12, 16, 21, 39, 53–54, 57, 62–64, 75–76, 101–9, 118, 128–30, 143–50, 158–59, 174n6. *See also* humanism; law; ontology; postmetaphysics

Metzl, Jonathan, 129

Michigan, 131–32

Miller, Monica L., 198n43

Mills, Charles, 74

Morrison, Toni, 195n10

Moss, Henry, 121, 192n25

Moten, Fred, 27, 43, 59

Mullarkey, John, 175n15

Murphy, Henry C., 185n55

Musser, Amber Jamilla, 198n38

Myers, Amrita Chakrabarti, 178n26

Nadel, Alan, 93

Nancy, Jean-Luc, 8, 20, 38–40, 63–71,

Picture Freedom (Cobb), 199n44

placelessness, 43, 52–58, 65–76, 81, 86–93, 112–18

Plague of Fantasies, The (Žižek), 197n34

plaintiffs in error, 78–81

Plato, 4, 31, 66, 179n3

play, 147–50, 160–61

pleasure, 160–61, 198n38

pleonasm, 154

police practices, 2–4, 18, 23, 169–72

politics, 48–59, 88–90, 153, 179n3, 181n16, 182n25, 199n47

pornotroping, 29–30, 180n10

Possenti, Vittorio, 17

postmetaphysics: definitions of, 4–5; epistemology and, 35–36; free black paradigm and, 4; the law and, 63–64, 72–74; ontological terror and, 170; outlawing and, 108–9; relationality and, 181n16; strikethrough and, 32–33, 118. See also metaphysics; ontology; and specific theorists

power (Foucauldian), 123

presence, 10, 29–30, 68–70, 93–96

primitivism, 174n12, 180n7

projection, 6, 9–10, 15, 23, 147, 149, 159

proper metaphysical question, 22–36, 43, 48–52, 60, 119–22, 148–58, 166, 181n12

property. See contract law; self, the; slavery

protest psychosis, 129

punishment, 159–60

purity, 49–50, 62–64

Purvis, Robert, 53–54, 185n49

quantification, 116–18, 129–39. See also calculation; scientific thinking

Question Concerning Technology, The (Heidegger), 22, 173n3

race, 33–34

Race, Law, and Resistance (Tuitt), 71

Rae, Gavin, 182n27

recognition, 3, 6, 41–43, 83–84, 90, 97, 101, 108, 121, 149–55, 164

Red, White, and Black (Wilderson), 89–90

reification, 6–11, 16–30, 88–89, 99–108, 115–18, 140, 147–53, 188n39, 189n45

relationality, 5, 15–16, 41–43, 62–73, 78–84, 94, 99, 101, 162, 181n16, 186n1

Remains of Being, The (Zabala), 180n7

"Remarkable Case of Mental Alienation" (Wragg), 112–18

representations, 143–68, 180n10, 194n1

Republic (Plato), 66

Richmond Enquirer, 93

rights, 84–87, 91, 97–98. See also citizenship; humanism; law

rubbing, 121–22, 141–42

Rush, Benjamin, 23, 119–22, 192n25

Sandford v. Scott, 22, 49, 52, 54, 76–87, 98, 108, 187n27, 188nn30–31

Sartre, Jean-Paul, 74, 183n33

saturation, 59, 61, 76–77, 81–83, 149

Scarry, Elaine, 127

Scenes of Subjection (Hartman), 88–89, 91

schematization, 37, 115–17, 122–23, 159

scientific thinking, 5, 10–11, 21–23, 37, 46–47, 60, 110–42, 159, 191n10

"Scope and Context of Plato's Meditation on the Relationship of Art and Truth, The" (Heidegger), 66

Scott, Darieck, 198n38

Scott, Dred, 22, 78–79, 108, 187n27

Scott, Rebecca, 101–2

self, the, 99–106, 108, 123–24, 132–33, 164

semiotics, 148–49, 195n7

Sensational Flesh (Musser), 198n38

Seshadri-Crooks, Kalpana, 81, 133

Sexton, Jared, 54

Sharp, Douglas, 194n6
Signature of All Things, The (Agamben), 19
signatures, 105
signs. *See* catachresis; representations; statistics; visibility
Sim, J. Marion, 141–42
simultaneity, 95
singularity, 19–20
slavery, 3–4, 9; abolitionism and, 53, 191n19; "contrabands" and, 157–58; emancipation and, 10–11, 18, 22–23, 86–87, 96–100, 106–8, 117–18, 131–39, 152–53, 178n25, 185n55; equipment in human form and, 81–87, 94–95; free black and, 52, 100–106; the law and, 71–76, 85–87; metaphysical holocaust and, 44–45. *See also* antiblackness; emancipation; free black; freedom
Slavery and Social Death (Patterson), 91
Smith, Andrew, 120
Smith, James McCune, 193n34
Smith, Mark, 122
social death, 91, 139–41, 188n33. *See also* death
Some Phases of the Negro Question (Melick), 191n20
sovereignty, 93, 153
spatiality, 131–39. *See also* placelessness
speaking, 104, 148, 152–54
Specters of Democracy (Wilson), 199n47
Spillers, Hortense, 14, 22, 26–31, 37–48, 58, 75–76, 99, 109, 115, 143–49, 180n10
spirit, the, 171–72
Spivak, Gayatri Chakravorty, 132, 144, 193n43, 199n46
state of exception, 93
statistics, 23, 131–39

suffering, 11–12, 36–37
surveillance, 18
suspension, 94–98, 108–9
Szasz, Thomas, 129–30

Taney, Roger, 52, 56, 76–87, 89, 98, 108, 144, 153, 187n27, 188n30
temporality, 23–24, 63–64, 108–9, 129–30, 150
Tennessee, 189n40
terror, 24, 97–98; definitions of, 65, 88, 118, 159, 173n2; formlessness and, 5–6, 24, 32–37, 175n16; humor and, 162–63; insanity and, 112–18, 129–42, 192n31; the law and, 75–76, 97–98, 106–9; Negro as embodiment of, 32–35, 37–60; pain and, 127–29; police tactics and, 169–70; reification and, 100–106
thanatology, 40–41
Thinking about Law (Ben-Dor), 66
Thirteenth Amendment (to the Constitution), 3–4
Thompson, William Fletcher, Jr., 196n20
Three-Fifths Compromise, 3, 117
Tomblin, Barbara, 157
Toward a Global Idea of Race (da Silva), 123
Tuitt, Patricia, 71–73
Tuskegee Study, 141–42
"Two Conceptions of Freedom" (Berlin), 177n18

Vallandigham, Clement Laird, 166
value, 157–59, 170–71
Vattimo, Gianni, 8, 10–12, 36, 174n9
Verwundung, 4, 7, 11, 32, 118, 132, 173n3
violence, 21, 39, 51–64, 75–76, 101–6, 118, 128–30, 143–50, 155–59, 171–72
visibility, 70, 75–76, 80–81, 84–85, 99–100, 113, 143–51, 194n1, 195n19
vitiligo, 121

Wagner, Bryan, 39, 73
Walcott, Rinaldo, 148, 171
Walker, David, 154
Walker, Grant, 120
wandering, 55–56
war, 156–61, 197n29
Washington, Harriet, 121
Weheliye, Alexander, 20, 180n10
West, Cornel, 175n15
"What Is Metaphysics?" (Heidegger), 181n12, 190n1, 191n10
whiteness, 104–5
Wilderson, Frank, 16, 41–42, 61, 74, 89–90, 133
Williams, Patricia, 71, 73
will to power, 6, 11, 160
Wilson, Carol, 107
Wilson, Ivy, 199n47

withdrawal, 7, 15, 27, 64–73, 86, 102, 146, 183n37
Woodard, Vincent, 25
Worth, Thomas, 155f
Wragg, W. T., 112–18
Wright, Michelle, 174n7
Wynter, Sylvia, 14, 30, 35, 58, 60, 146, 184n41

X: The Problem of the Negro as a Problem for Thought (Chandler), 49

Yancy, George, 118
Yarema, Allen, 192n21

Zabala, Santiago, 7, 30–31, 180n7
Žižek, Slavoj, 149–50, 160, 197n34
zones of indistinction, 93, 97, 103, 153–54